RUNNING THE GAUNTLET

The *Queen Elizabeth*, loaded with 15,000 troops and bristling with anti-aircraft guns, sails from New York. (Courtesy U.S. National Archives)

Running the Gauntlet

How Three Giant Liners
Carried a Million Men to War,
1942-1945

Alister Satchell

CHATHAM PUBLISHING
LONDON

Dedication

To my grandson Michael

Copyright © Alister Satchell 2001

First published privately in Australia by the author in 1998 under the title
The Great Gamble

This edition published in Great Britain in 2001 by Chatham Publishing,
61 Frith Street, London W1V 5TA

Chatham Publishing is an imprint of Gerald Duckworth & Co Ltd

British Library Cataloguing in Publication Data
A catalogue record for this book is available from the
British Library

ISBN 1 86176 164 3

Typeset by Dorwyn Ltd, Rowlands Castle, Hants

Printed and bound in Great Britain by Bookcraft (Bath) Ltd

Contents

Acknowledgements

I direct my initial thanks to a gentleman unknown to me, a Mr Paul Reynolds, literary agent of New York. By chance I came across his publication, *How to Write a Non Fiction Book*, and this brought to mind my wartime diaries, deteriorating in an old box in the garage. Hence this book.

Valuable assistance has been provided by wartime colleagues and friends. These include Captain Edwin Seim, Commander of the US Army section of the *Aquitania*'s gun crew, of Beaufort, South Carolina. Alwyn Jay RAAF of Federal, NSW, a member of a Liberator Squadron flying out of Iceland, provided details of procedures and his experiences whilst sweeping ahead of independently-routed troopships. Brian Walker of Hampton Hill researched valuable information at the Public Records Office at Kew, whilst my brother, Tony, a genealogist, assisted in several areas. I am also indebted to David Bonsall of Moorabbin

My wife Jean contributed ably in the gathering of material and in research, and gave encouragement and support. I am grateful to Annette James, whose word processing skills and grasp of manuscript requirements and indexing preparation were vital to the completion of the work. Finally, I am indebted to the organisations and individuals who gave permission for the reproduction of photographs. In some instances where fees were applicable on account of copyright protection, the entitlement was waived. Amongst those who extended multiple courtesies and to whom I express my gratitude were the Imperial War Museum of London, the New York Times, and private collector Mr Frank O Braynard of Long Island, New York. I am also grateful for the assistance given by the National Maritime Museum, Greenwich, London.

Introduction

The most rapid and highly organised transportation of troops in history was underway by the latter months of 1942 following the entry of the United States into the Second World War in December 1941. Britain, from where the principal invasion of Europe would be launched, became the destination for the greatest number of soldiers, airmen and women of the auxiliary services, and the central theme of this book is the carriage by sea of United States and British Empire troops from North America to the Clyde Estuary in Scotland.

The author, a lieutenant in the Royal Australian Navy Volunteer Reserve, was one of the two cipher officers in the 46,000-ton Cunard White Star liner *Aquitania* between March 1943 and July 1945. He sailed in all the ship's fifty-three Atlantic crossings between New York, Halifax or Boston, and Scotland, spending 395 days at sea. Shipboard knowledge of the daily strategic situation was confined to the captain, cipher officers, gunnery and bridge officers. Cipher officers attended pre-sailing conferences. The author, technically in breach of 'King's Regulations and Admiralty Instructions', kept personal diaries, locked in the safe with the ciphers, and these records proved to be invaluable in guiding this work.

In addition to the *Aquitania*, Cunard owned and operated the *Queen Mary* and the *Queen Elizabeth*. Sailing independently, as distinct from in convoy, these three ships formed the nucleus of an 'Atlantic shuttle service'. President Truman, in a 'Message to Congress' on 2 June 1945, referred to them as 'Britain's three proudest liners', and British Prime Minister Sir Winston Churchill estimated the contribution of the Cunarders to the movement of troops shortened the war in Europe by twelve months. Between mid-1942 and May 1945, some 4½ million United States personnel set out to cross the Atlantic from the ports of New York, Boston, Hampton Roads and Charleston, with New York contributing 75 per cent of the total. Canadian, Australian and New Zealand forces embarking also from Canadian and U.S. ports, raised the overall number to well in excess of 5 million.

These Cunarders sailed without surface escort until the final months of the war when pairs of British destroyers were provided to patrol ahead for the last few hundred miles of the 3500-mile zigzag route to Britain.

The Atlantic Ocean.

Aquitania. (Courtesy New York Times)

Allied planes gave intermittent cover during daylight depending on the availability of aircraft, the level of known U-boat activity and the distance of the particular ship from Allied airfields. The *Queen Mary* and the *Queen Elizabeth*, steaming at close to 30 knots, each carried up to 16,000 troops, whilst the slower *Aquitania*, making about 22 knots, had a capacity for 8000 troops. The sinking of any one of these liners would have amounted to the greatest single disaster in the history of the war at sea.

During the 1943-45 period, the Germans introduced the acoustic torpedo, the schnorkel and radio-controlled aerial bomb. The Allies and the Germans both had varying degrees of success in cracking the other's codes and the Allied decrypting operation termed 'Ultra' is discussed. The book describes several running battles between U-boat wolf packs and convoy escorts waged concurrently with the passage of the *Aquitania*. A comparison of this troopship's movements with those of one particular U-boat captain, Herbert Werner, disclosed that between May 1943 and April 1945, the paths of the *Aquitania* and Werner could well have crossed or converged on no less than seven different occasions.

The narrative branches occasionally into other areas. The writer's initial sailing traversed the Indian Ocean from Australia to South Africa, the South Atlantic from Capetown to Rio de Janeiro, and then on to New York. When the ship passed through a relevant area, a short reference is made to a number of maritime disasters including the torpedoing of Cunard's *Lusitania* and the freak collision when the *Queen Mary* sank the cruiser HMS *Curaçoa*.

The author came to know well the five captains with whom he sailed and he recites a number of memorable anecdotes. The Cunard Line had dominated the Atlantic passenger trade for over a hundred years and the

Queen Mary. (Courtesy Australian War Memorial)

narrative touches upon the struggles for the Atlantic Blue Riband and the unconfined pleasures of the rich during peacetime travel.

Twenty-one visits to New York, adding up to about six months residing in the luxury section of a floating hotel on the fringe of Manhattan's nightclub, restaurant and theatre districts, combined with a wealth of hospitality, provided ample opportunity to experience the good times. An Australian's memories of the high life in wartime New York may be of interest to some of the millions who lived and worked there, and who saw the Great Liners come and go – and also to the millions of veterans who emptied their pockets during the frenzied days of the final furlough before their ship pulled out. On the other side of the Atlantic, the author visited London on four occasions and his adventures would have been shared by many visiting servicemen. Westbound voyages intermittently involved the carriage of thousands of German prisoners of war, and the final visit to New York, with a shipload of U.S. Normandy veterans, culminated in a 'Coming Home' welcome on a lavish scale.

Distinguished British author, Jan Morris, in her book *Manhattan '45*, describes the splendours of New York during the latter war years. She selected the June 1945 return of a Cunarder, loaded with victorious troops, as history's symbolic moment to highlight the pinnacle of the existence of her 'town of all towns'.

While this book is based on the author's experiences in the *Aquitania*, it is also essentially an account of the basic operations of the other two 'proud liners', the *Queen Elizabeth* and the *Queen Mary*, to which frequent reference is made.

Queen Elizabeth. (Courtesy Imperial War Museum, London)

These three ships had in common aspects of their operations which did not apply to any other troopships. They shared the same anchorages in the Clyde and adjoining docks in New York. Cunard officers and crew members were generally rotated between the three. Embarking and disembarking procedures were identical, as were messing, accommodations, recreations and safety procedures. The only major differences lay in the number of troops which could be accommodated and in their speed capabilities. The three crossed the Atlantic independently routed and not in company with other merchant ships or surface escorts.

It is a tribute to the British Merchant Navy, to the Allied Naval and Air Forces and to the Cunard Line that not a single life was lost amongst American, Canadian, Australian, British, New Zealand and other nationalities, both men and women, and numbering just over one million, who crossed the Atlantic to Europe in these three liners.

Prologue

Several hundred weary soldiers leaned against the railings of the giant troop transport shortly after first light on the morning of Monday, 10 May 1943. These early risers were part of a draft of about 8000 officers and men, the majority of whom had boarded the vessel between 11 p.m. and 3 a.m. that night. The ship lay docked at Pier 86, one of the termi nals of Britain's Cunard White Star Line on the West Side of midtown Manhattan, and thin streaks of vapour rising from all four funnels pub licised that the engineers were working up steam for an early departure.

A typical G.I., Private Joe Staaff, had his mind in a whirl as he languished against a stanchion on the boat deck while on policing duties. New York City was awakening from its brief sleep of two or three hours, and cars of early workers and delivery trucks sped intermittently along the West Side Elevated Highway, against which the ship's bow seemed almost to lean. At the adjacent dock, the French Line's Pier 88, the starboard side of the hulk of the capsized and burnt-out *Normandie* rose above the buildings as a grim warning to one of seafaring's greatest dangers.

Peering down over the starboard side railing to a gangplank below, Joe watched two stokers, somewhat the worse for wear, assisting each other aboard, followed at a discreet distance by two U.S. Navy shore patrolmen. Astern, the mighty Hudson River, close to a mile wide at this point of its journey from upstate New York, stretched across to the New Jersey shore, swiftly carrying the spring thaw from New England's snow-fields down to the Atlantic.

Six months earlier, Joe Staaff had a steady job as a freight handler, employed by the Rio Grande Railroad in their yards in Durango, Colorado. His parents had emigrated to America from Sweden and from the age of four onwards, Joe had lived in this beautiful town on the south western rises of the Rocky Mountain chain. His experience of city life was limited to a visit to a married sister in Denver, although he frequently accompanied his father, a brakeman with the same company, on one of the world's most spectacular railway journeys from Durango to Silverton.

The arrival in the mail of his draft call-up notice in October 1942 was accepted with a calm resignation. Joe was eighteen and several school-

The moment of truth has arrived for the 8000 troops below deck. The *Aquitania* at New York's Pier 86 has raised a full head of steam, the last gangway is about to be withdrawn, the crewmen at station ready to cast-off lines, whilst on the port side tugs will be taking up slack on their ropes. The starboard 3in forward gun is already manned ... For the troops the war is about to begin. (© Corbis Images)

mates had already enlisted. He hoped to be sent to the Pacific because somehow that theatre seemed closer to home. And if it became his lot to shoot someone, better it be a Jap than a German.

The four months Joe spent training as an infantryman passed quickly enough. The final leave period at home ended during the second week in April 1943, and three days later Joe's unit arrived at Camp Shanks, a staging camp for the Port of New York located in New Jersey. This fact, combined with the type of training and clothing issued, all added to a certainty that a sea voyage to Europe now lay ahead.

The morning parade of Saturday 8 May brought the announcement that all leave had been suspended and that letters for posting would not be accepted after midnight. This news, in a way, came as a relief. Joe had spent most of his money during two wondrous excursions into Manhattan, the camp was congested, and the sooner the job abroad was over and done with, the better. The following day the men stowed their belongings into barracks bags and boarded a relay of trains to Jersey City. A shuttle service of ferries chugged their way in darkness across the Hudson and about 3 a.m. Joe finally hauled his bags and equipment up a gangplank and then way down to 'F' deck where he lay exhausted on his allotted standee bunk.

The ship bore no insignia of identification, but a military policeman, shepherding the column of troops along the dock, disclosed in confidence that this was the *Aquitania,* the third largest liner afloat. The appearance of the ship with the four funnels, correctly suggested to Joe that it was the same vessel he had seen on the cover of *LIFE* magazine in the library at Camp Shanks. After a fitful sleep, Joe had climbed his way up to duty on the boatdeck from where he would gain a last glimpse of his homeland.

Joe's training as an infantryman gave him some measure of confidence that he and his buddies would somehow take care of themselves when they came to grips with the Germans after landing in Europe. The air force and armoured corps would have those Germans good and softened up beforehand. But Joe was not too sure about this boat ride across the ocean. For a start, he had read that the Atlantic could be real rough and certain to make you seasick. Secondly, he didn't even know how to swim, the Animus River back home being too cold, even in midsummer. Joe had seen on the newsreels ships torpedoed by U-boats and he wondered whether all those anti-aircraft guns could reach high level bombers.

Joe was not keen about having to sleep for a week or more in that hell hole down on 'F' deck. You could bet all the officers would be in cabins well above the water line where there was no risk of a torpedo exploding under your bunk. They would have a much better chance of shouldering their way into a lifeboat. Then what about that red flag flapping at the fore-mast. The soldier nearby said the ship was British, and although Joe supposed the Limeys were all right, he was not keen about trusting his life to them. Maybe the ship was just owned by the British and crewed by the U.S. although, come to think of it, he hadn't seen any gobs around. Anyway, at least there was the comfort, as Joe mistakenly assumed, that the ship would be travelling in convoy protected by battleships, cruisers and aircraft carriers manned by the good old U.S. Navy. And at the end of it all, there would be those girls in London he had been told about. Also, they spoke the American language.

Private Joe Staaff was still soliloquising on the boatdeck when at 8 a.m. the Cunard Cadillac drew up at a gangplank to collect Captain Battle, the chief navigating officer, the chief radio officer and the cipher officers to drive them downtown to the sailing conference at the Naval Control

Office at Battery Place off Lower Broadway. The briefing included the disclosure that on the previous Wednesday, 5 May, eleven merchant ships had been sunk when convoy ONS 5 bound from Britain to North American ports had been attacked by forty U-boats south of Halifax. This onslaught involved the largest concentration of U-boats ever assembled for an attack on any convoy throughout the war. This information was strictly limited to those who attended the conference.

Joe Staaff had been allocated to the fourth or last breakfast sitting and he returned to the boatdeck shortly before 10.30 a.m. Smoke was now billowing from the stacks, huge ventilator fans vibrated, longshoremen on the docks were hauling ropes and gangplanks, while on the port side, tugs were taking up lines and nosing their way into position.

Soon the great liner would be gathering way, sailing majestically down the Hudson towards the open Atlantic, and Captain Battle would address attentive troops over the speakers. Before long, the towers of Manhattan would drop out of sight into the haze, and a last view of America would stir great emotions in the hearts of the troops, feelings which would be shared during the two following years by over two hundred thousand soldiers who would sail from North America in the *Aquitania*. The lines were cast off and a slight movement was felt as the ship began backing out into the stream. A Cunard publicist once wrote: 'It is the city, not the ship, that moves – seeming to withdraw itself from us like a reluctant hand in a long and lingering farewell'.

CHAPTER 1

The 'Grand Hotels' of the North Atlantic

The Cunard Line played a far greater role in the transportation of troops in both World Wars than any other shipping line, and in the context of this book, the company's history is of some relevance. The navies of the Great Powers did not include major troop carriers in their fleets, relying upon commandeering passenger liners to meet their requirements, either for trooping or as armed merchant cruisers. Britain, followed by Germany, France and Italy, dominated passenger traffic in peacetime, particularly on the most travelled seaway, the North Atlantic Ocean. The United States played a smaller role having a limited seafaring tradition.

Many G.I.s were by no means unfamiliar with the history of the Great Liners and their owners. From the turn of the century onwards, these ships featured prominently in the public eye, from the pages of society magazines to cards in even the cheapest pack of cigarettes. The newspapers reported the arrivals and departures of prominent citizens, and the names of the vessels in which they travelled, whilst Hollywood romantic comedies of the 1930s frequently included a trans-Atlantic segment. A holiday in New York usually involved a ferry boat ride around Manhattan Island, a feature being close views of 'Steamship Row', the stretch along Twelfth Avenue between Forty Six and Fiftieth Streets where the Cunard, French and Italian liners docked. Thus some soldiers on boarding these independently-routed liners initially had the expectation of an experience which they never dreamed would come their way.

Throughout its history, the Cunard Line was involved in keen international competition, particularly with Germany. Not only did the participants struggle for the especially lucrative North Atlantic passenger business and mail contracts, but later were spurred by the prestige of gaining and holding the prized Atlantic 'Blue Riband' for the fastest crossing. The company was founded by Samuel Cunard, a Quaker merchant born in Halifax, Nova Scotia in 1787. Joined by three partners from Liverpool, he formed the Cunard Steamship Company which successfully tendered for a British Government contract to provide a

Cunard's paddle steamer *Hibernia* of 1422 tons inaugurated the first Liverpool to New York regular service in 1857.

two-weekly mail service between Liverpool, Halifax and Boston. Four wooden steamers inaugurated the service in July 1830 when the SS *Britannic*, at an average speed of about 9 knots, reached Boston in 14 days. The other ships were named *Arcadia*, *Caledonia* and *Columbia*, thus beginning a practice of naming Cunard vessels with words ending with the letters 'ia'. Later, three notable exceptions were the *Queen Mary*, *Queen Elizabeth 1* and *Queen Elizabeth 2*.

Operations were transferred to New York in 1889 and Cunard dominated the mail and passenger services by its ability to provide the fastest crossing, but intense competition from Germany was now developing with the launching of three fast liners between 1897 and 1907, all of the Norddeutscher Lloyd Line, and named after the Kaiser and two other members of his family.

Migrants to the United States from Europe hardly enjoyed the luxuries which were now becoming available to the better-off. Social observer Samuel Johnson came up with: 'A man in a jail has more room, better food and commonly better company', while Charles Dickens wrote: 'Nothing smaller for sleeping was ever made, except coffins'. In 1913 and 1914 Germany launched three ships all over 50,000 tons, the *Vaterland*, *Bismarck* and *Imperator*.

Cunard had begun major programmes in 1907 with the launching of the *Mauretania* and *Lusitania*. The former became the largest and fastest ship in the world and crossed the Atlantic in four days, eleven hours,

Passengers provided their own meals in the early emigrant ships.

averaging 26 knots, a record which would stand for 22 years. The launching of the *Aquitania* followed in 1914 and she was to serve the Company for 36 years, the longest period of all. Britain's White Star Line had also provided competition with its *Olympic, Britannic*, and for the first four days of her maiden voyage, with the *Titanic!* Cunard lost 22 vessels in the 1914-18 war, the majority being torpedoed by German U-boats. The losses included *Franconia, Alaunia, Andania, Aurania, Carpathia* (rescuer of *Titanic* survivors), *Ultonia, Ivernia, Lusitania, Lycia, Valeria, Laconia (1), Ascania, Flavia* and nine smaller passenger ships. The four surviving liners were *Aquitania, Mauretania, Coronia* and *Carmenia*.

At the Versailles Conference in 1919, the Great Powers split the remains of German passenger fleets. Cunard's portion of the spoils was the *Imperator* (52,000 tons) which was renamed *Berengaria* after the wife of King Richard the Lion-Hearted. The United States grabbed the biggest, the *Vaterland* (60,000 tons) which she operated as the *Leviathan*, whilst the British countered by bagging the *Bismarck*, later called the *Majestic*, for the White Star Line. Few prizes remained although Canadian Pacific collected three smaller vessels averaging about 20,000 tons. Nothing worthwhile came Australia's way.

Germany again entered the Atlantic passenger competition in the late 1920s with the construction of the 50,000-ton liners *Bremen* and *Europa*, each of which gained the Blue Riband. In 1930 the British Government began to finance construction of the *Queen Mary*, an 81,000-ton liner capable of reaching 32 knots. The Great Depression suspended all work between 1931 and 1934, but she set out on her maiden voyage between Southampton and New York in May 1936, recapturing the Blue Riband for Cunard – a year earlier, the French Line's *Normandie* had wrested the prize from the Germans on her maiden voyage. The interior design of the

The Grand Dining Room of Cunard's *Lucania*. Her sister-ship *Campania* gained the Atlantic Blue Riband in 1892, crossing in 5 days 17 hours.

Queen Mary was a disappointment to some lovers of the maritime arts with detractors claiming her garish shapes and decorations resembled those of an Odeon Cinema. On the other hand, the *Normandie* was regarded as the ultimate in elegance, unlikely to be surpassed.

Liners were built and scrapped in the 1930s according to commercial considerations alone, with apparently no thought being given to possible troop carrying requirements of the military. A new, smaller and slower *Mauretania* was built by Cunard along with several liners renamed after First World War casualties. The year 1935 witnessed the demise of the original 'Atlantic Greyhounds', *Mauretania* and *Berengaria*, whilst the *Olympic* and the United States' *Leviathan* were withdrawn and scrapped in 1938. The following year, Britain's *Majestic* burned to the waterline whilst being converted to a training ship. However, the travelling public, as confirmed by bookings, never turned away from the *Aquitania*.

The construction of the *Queen Elizabeth* had begun in July 1936. Slightly larger than the *Queen Mary*, her maiden voyage consisted of a secret dash in an unfinished condition across the Atlantic in March 1940 to New York to join the *Queen Mary* prior to the conversions to troop carriers. Of novel interest during the 1930s was a short-lived threat to shipping companies by the appearance of the German dirigibles, *Graf Zeppelin* and *Hindenburg*. Scheduled flights to Rio and New York in 1936 came to an abrupt end the following May, when the *Hindenburg* caught fire and exploded on being tethered at Lakehurst,

New Jersey. Cunard and White Star, under pressure from the Government, had completed a merger in 1934 and operated as Cunard-White Star Ltd.

The Cunard Line Ltd continues strongly to the present day although this account does not extend beyond the end of the Second World War. In 1950, the Company changed its name from Cunard-White Star Ltd to Cunard Ltd. The advent of jet aircraft flying the Atlantic in 1959 dealt all shipping companies a staggering blow, but some have survived, largely with a reliance on cruising. Cunard's flagship, the *Queen Elizabeth 2*, still dominates the Atlantic outside the cruising season when she joins other ships of the line. Thus the Cunard emblem, a golden lion, wearing an imperial crown and holding aloft a globe of the world, still adorns the House Flag and the caps of their officers, just as it had when the company began operations in 1840.

The servicemen who sailed in the independently-routed Cunard liners hardly expected to enjoy any of the luxurious aura successfully promoted by peacetime publicists. The enlisted men, confined to the lower decks, would not even catch a glimpse of what remained of the peacetime surroundings and furnishings. Extensive areas of cabins and public rooms of all classes had been ripped out to make way for standee bunks and messing halls. The first class lounges and dining rooms of the *Queen Mary* and *Aquitania* remained untouched, but progressively showed signs of wear. Occasionally a soldier, briefly stationed during lifeboat drill on 'A' deck outside a stateroom, might nudge the man beside him to look at the luxury within. The fitting of the *Queen Elizabeth* for the trade had been postponed until war's end, and apart from a limited number of cabins, conditions were somewhat spartan for all.

A brief description of the circumstances and lifestyles of those who travelled in the 1920s and which existed in the 1930s should help complete the background before some millions of servicemen experienced their introduction to war. The luxury of which they knew, but would never experience, would be so near, yet so far. Cunard attracted the cream of the North Atlantic passenger business after the First World War. The society magazines and gossip columns reported on the triumphs of the international set, and the public was kept well informed as to the names of the ships in which travelled the people who mattered. New York bankers, Wall Street brokers, Pittsburgh steel men, railroad magnates, senators, film stars, opera singers, British aristocracy and Russian princes of dubious origin with fancy titles all received a mention. The ships served only good booze and this circumstance attracted dry-throated Americans during those trying years of the twenties. Lord Dewar, when about to sail from New York in the *Aquitania,* was asked by the press about his thoughts on Prohibition, replied: 'I found it better than having nothing to drink'.

'Floating Palaces' was a term favoured by the publicity experts. Sailings from New York were scheduled for midnight to enable the farewell parties to be wound down in time for the visitors to descend the gangplanks, whilst retaining sufficient strength and sobriety to hurl their streamers. Horse-drawn coaches, Pierce Arrows, Packards and Stutz Bearcats transferred the visitors to their hotels, Fifth Avenue Townhouses and Upper East Side apartments. Lingering visitors were frequently off-loaded into the pilot's boat at the Ambrose Lightship.

Cunard adopted the practice of disclosing on the passenger lists a traveller's honours or degrees, however obscure they might be, in order to position the person accurately in the caste system, a matter of some importance in table, cabin and deck chair placement. The Cunard slogan 'Getting there is half the fun' was changed in the 1930s to 'Ships have been boring long enough'. The advertising man must have been a genius!

The *Aquitania* was regarded as 'the most fashionable liner' of the twenties. Her 'long gallery' was termed 'The Atlantic Rue de la Paix', offering gowns which would ensure that one's wife or companion would be abreast with the leaders of fashion when she stepped ashore at Cherbourg and made for Paris. The Grand Tour was seen as a crash course in sophistication.

Cunard ponderously advertised that 'half the pleasure of doing a thing really well consists of letting the other people – the ones who are not doing the thing at all, but would like to if they could – know that one is enjoying the very best there is to be had'. What else hasn't changed? 'How you travelled was who you were' was another slogan. One of the shipping companies put it delicately when breathlessly describing an Atlantic sunset as an hour of 'speculative detachment ... only the soft mild rush of the wind is heard swirling against the impervious ship – and the faint stray cadence of a violin, a tinkling wisp of furtive laughter'. Another gem: 'Hundreds of multi-coloured lamps shed their soft radiance on the forms of beautiful women gloriously gowned and handsome men in immaculate evening dress who dance the hours away to the music of a jolly orchestra'. Tell that to the G.I.s!

There were other reasons for 'doing Europe' between the wars. The London 'season' was important, but its accessibility raised problems. However, entrée was not too difficult if there were some money around, and provided it was not too 'new'. A marriage to a chap with even a minor title such as an 'Honourable' for eighteen year-old Rosalie would be a prize, but not without the problem of getting the fellow to do any work back in the store at Grand Rapids.

An intrepid photographer snaps a boiling Atlantic from the deck of Germany's 50,000-ton liner *Europa*.

The fashion shows in Paris were useful, if only to get mother and daughter out of the way while father slipped off to sample the delights of Montmartre. Moving on, the spas at Baden Baden and Marienbad were guaranteed to enhance one's health, even though the gambling tables may require a further remittance to be despatched by the accountant back home. In those days, one had to leave home without the American Express Gold Card. As a final gesture, Cunard thoughtfully assisted passengers in the conservation of their funds when despatching cables home, by offering a choice of cut price coded expressions to meet most contingencies. Some examples were: BACK – Baggage gone astray – FADE – Am out of funds – HOOF – Seriously ill, no hope of recovery.

Cunard did not lose sight of the fact that a proportion of the troops, particularly those amongst the officer classes, were likely to be fare-paying passengers of the future. Deck officers, pursers, stewards and crew members were always well turned out, maintaining a politeness under trying circumstances. The quality of the food served in the officers' dining rooms, the china and cutlery, was excellent considering the circumstances. The officers' library was well stocked with publications, fully illustrated, depicting the grandeur of peacetime travel.

The story of the unescorted Cunarders would be incomplete without an initial reference to the principal battle arena itself, the North Atlantic

The 'Old' *France* rolls in a quartering sea in the North Atlantic.

Ocean. Throughout the history of seafaring, the world's most tempestuous seaway has claimed its own victims without the assistance of torpedoes, depth charges, mines, shells and bombs. The cold, gales and towering seas were major factors in battles between convoys, escorts and U-boats. Ships were slowed, scattered and left behind to fend for themselves. The conditions frequently prevented land-based air cover either from taking off or locating a convoy. Escort carriers were unable to launch aircraft, whilst refuelling and rescue operations were frequently impeded. Thus the ocean itself was the second enemy.

The most direct route between New York and the Clyde is about 3000 miles but in wartime, allowing for extensions of route to avoid U-boat concentrations, and also for zigzagging, the distance stretched to an average of about 3750 miles with the journey from Halifax about 3000 miles. Modern liners now cover the distance in less than five days in comparison with the days of sail when three weeks was good going for an eastbound crossing compared with up to forty days returning into the prevailing westerly winds.

In 1913, eastbound and westbound routes were designated by international agreement to reduce the dangers of collision. Fog is a constant hazard, particularly where the warm waters of the Gulf Stream encounter the cold Labrador current. Originating in the Gulf of Mexico, the Gulf Stream is initially narrow and deep with temperatures up to 20 degrees warmer than the waters of the stretch separating it from the eastern seaboard of the United States. Opposite Cape Hatteras, it spreads out to the north-east with declining intensity, but its influence nevertheless keeps many European ports ice-free. When sailing due east from New York, its impact about four hours later is remarkable. Seafaring buffs say that if a shipboard attachment were sought, this was when the girls became the most susceptible.

The iceberg menace begins in April and persists until August when the bergs melt on reaching the Gulf Stream. After the *Titanic* catastrophe in 1912, the International Ice Patrol was established to broadcast warnings which include the rate and direction of drifts. The combination of fog and icebergs becomes a nightmare for a captain. Precautions include watching for birds which might be based on an iceberg, searching for 'growlers' – the small pieces of ice which break away from large bergs and which drift to leeward, the sounding of the ship's siren to precipitate an echo, and above all to be constantly checking for a sudden reduction in temperature. The 'Frantic Atlantic' is the ocean with the world's most tempestuous weather, where the shipping lanes are in high latitudes, and where gales occur regularly for at least six months of the year. In winter, daylight can last for less than six hours A later chapter describes a westbound crossing of the *Aquitania* in January 1944 when a full gale, the maximum force 12, was encountered, extending the crossing by four days and reducing the reserves of oil and water to dangerous levels. The intensity reached a degree beyond the experience of any of my colleagues.

In the introduction to his 1951 publication *The Cruel Sea*, a story of the corvette HMS *Compass Rose* – a North Atlantic convoy escort – the author Nicholas Monserrat wrote 'But the men are the stars of this story. The only heroines are the ships: and the only villain the cruel sea itself.'

CHAPTER 2

The Giant Cunarders Before the Shuttle Begins

The *Aquitania* was the only liner to have served as a troop transport in both World Wars and it is appropriate that she should play the central role in this narrative. The ship also has the distinction of having remained in passenger service longer than any other grand liner, a lasting tribute to her comfort, style and engineering. Accordingly, her history is now recorded here in detail additional to comments made in the previous chapter.

Walter Lord, in a forward to the 1981 book *Majesty at Sea*, described 'The Golden Age of Travel' as the period between 1897 and 1 December 1949: 'The era of those great majestic four-funnelled liners that drew attention wherever they went'. Beginning with the maiden voyage of Germany's *Kaiser Wilhelm Der Grosse*, he concluded: 'Some 52 years later, the Cunard Liner *Aquitania* arrived at Southampton from Halifax on 1 December 1949. When the bridge signalled "finished with engines", the last four-funnelled liner was gone'. Lord added, 'The thought of an *Olympic* or an *Aquitania* with three funnels causes one to shudder at the marring of the most symmetrically beautiful creations of shipbuilding art'. The dust jacket of that publication illustrated the famed painting of the *Aquitania* sailing up the Hudson against the Gothic Towers of the Woolworth Building.

The *Aquitania* had her keel laid down in 1911. She was built and engined by John Brown and Co. at Clydebank, Scotland, and was launched by the Countess of Derby in the presence of 600,000 spectators on 21 April 1913. The name translates as 'Land of the Waters', and was taken from the richest of the three divisions of Roman Gaul. On 30 May 1914 she set out on her maiden voyage to New York, joining the original *Mauretania* and *Lusitania* to enable Cunard to provide a luxury sailing to New York every Saturday of the year.

The *Aquitania*, which became and remained Cunard's flagship until the *Queen Mary* entered service in 1936, was built to provide accommodation for about 3100 passengers with a crew of 980. She was of 45,646

John Brown's Shipyard at
Clydebank 1910. The *Aquitania*
is shown in the first stage of her
construction.

The *Aquitania* shortly before
launching. (Courtesy
National Maritime Museum,
Greenwich, London)

The rudder and port side screws of the *Aquitania*.

gross tonnage and propelled by four screws each of four blades. Her length was 902 feet, beam 97 feet, and with a maximum speed of 23 knots, she was capable of sustaining 22 knots. Like the *Mauretania* and *Lusitania*, she had four large funnels, technically unnecessary, but a symbol of prestige. (The *Normandie's* third funnel was used as a dog kennel.) The hull had a double skin, and sixteen bulkheads extended athwartships from port to starboard. The Parsons turbines weighed 9000 tons and occupied 84 feet of the ship's length, the propulsion 'equalling the heave of 5 million galley slaves'. The nine decks began with the 'Boat' and then the 'Promenade' or 'A' deck and continued down through 'B', 'C', etc. to the 'Lower Orlop' deck. The promenade deck, which the author's cabin overlooked, extended 650 feet along each side.

The first class lounges, staterooms, smoking room and library were on 'A' and 'B' decks with first class cabins extending down to 'E' deck. The first class dining room on 'D' deck could be reached by two elevators or a grand stairway also known as a companionway deluxe. Public rooms were panelled with a variety of woodwork handsomely carved by Italian craftsmen and the staterooms lined with tapestries of ornate silk. A Frenchman, Charles Mews, the architect for the international chain of Ritz hotels, with his British partner Charles Davis, were the interior designers. The Palladian Lounge and Carolean Smoking Room have been described as 'faultless as anything that has ever appeared on the Atlantic'. In the latter, a full length portrait of King James II imperiously surveyed the smokers. An Elizabethan grill room, a Louis XIV dining room, and a Pompeiian swimming bath, flanked with fluted columns, all

The *Aquitania*. A truly beautiful portrait of the 'ship beautiful'. (Courtesy The Mariners Museum, Newport News)

added to the splendour, which was described as 'an Anthology of European culture'. Other features included a gymnasium, theatre, veranda gardens, main and branch libraries, hospital, cinema, nursery, kennels, police force and fire brigade. The Long Gallery or High Street was a shopping mall which included chocolate, jewellery, fancy goods, tobacconist, clothing, book and hairdresser's shops on one side and an open cafe on the other. When you had exhausted your cash, there was always the branch of the Midland Bank.

The staff encouraged the playing of the various deck games by day, the amenities even including a putting green. At night the veranda gardens were partly cleared, and it was here that the fancy dress and masked balls were held. Some horrible shocks were undoubtedly experienced on the latter occasions. Concerts in the lounge would frequently include a performance by an entire theatrical company rehearsing before an opening at Covent Garden or on Broadway. Otherwise, an opera singer or theatrical star could always be found amongst the passenger lists. Actress Bea Lillie was heard to have asked 'When does this place get to New York?'

A typical dinner menu in the Grande Salle-à-Manger listed eighty items of food spread over eight courses, with the finest selection of French wines available to wash it all down. Sir James Charles, Cunard's senior captain in the 1920s, was a gourmet of some distinction, and he took a

Aquitania's Grill Room fitted out in early Jacobean Style.

personal interest in the *Aquitania*'s catering supervised by an array of *chefs de cuisine*. A Cunard hand-out described the experience of being invited to dine at the Captain's table: 'Sir James Charles' tastes were vaguely those of Emil Jannings playing Henry VIII. Stewards rolled in carcasses of whole roast oxen one night, and the next evening herds of grilled antelope surrounded by a hilltop of Strasbourg foie gras, surrounded by a hilltop of peacock fans. The Americans loved it, the English took it in their stride.' Those passengers carefully singled out to share his table were expected to follow his practice of partaking in every course. Items on the list of provisions for a single trip included 10,000 oysters, 1200 lobsters, 3000 chickens, 500 ducklings, 280 turkeys, 450 brace of grouse, 450 brace of pheasant, 1200 Bordeaux pigeons, 1000 quail and 4 turtles.

The designer Davis is said to have been asked why he fashioned the interior to resemble another of his Ritz hotels rather than a ship. He replied that many passengers were rich American widows prone to sea-sickness, who may prefer to imagine they were residing in a hotel. The architects were among the first to prevent smells from bilges and engines

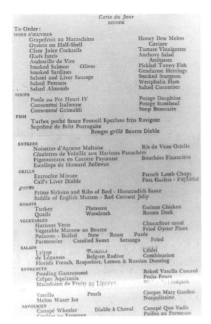

Above left: Specimen *Aquitania* menu for the tables over which Sir James Charles presided.
Above right: Section of *Aquitania*'s Palladian Lounge in Georgian style.

from reaching passenger areas, and the ship was said to have a fragrance of flowers and soap. An attraction was the total absence of vibration.

After taking over the renamed *Leviathan* from the Germans in 1919, the Americans spent a fortune to upgrade that vessel in an attempt to lure a larger portion of the Atlantic business from Cunard. The task was hopeless – Prohibition followed the ship across the ocean thus thwarting a principal reason for going abroad in those days. Subsequently, one of the owners of the *Leviathan* said: '*Aquitania* is the most popular ship in the world and it cost us nine million dollars to find out'.

The *Aquitania* had completed only three Atlantic voyages when the First World War broke out. The ship was requisitioned by the British Government in May 1915 after lying docked in New York and then converted to an 'armed merchant cruiser' at the Mersey Dock at Liverpool. Over a period of four days, 4000 men are said to have carted off 2000 truckloads of furniture, furnishings and fixtures. The hull and superstructure were painted grey, eight 6in guns were mounted, and a Captain of the Royal Navy was appointed as commanding officer. Then the White Ensign was hoisted, the siren sounded, and off she went in search of the enemy. At this point, the thought was beginning to strike home that her conversion to a fighting ship was absurd on account of her size as a target compared with her limited firepower, the thinness of her hull, and her comparative lack of manoeuvrability.

Aquitania as a troopship in the First World War. If the paintwork camouflage failed to conceal the ship at least it probably terrified the enemy.

Assisted by four tugs, the *Aquitania* enters Southampton Water in 1916 in her hospital livery of white combined with a green band, red crosses and buff funnels. (Courtesy Imperial War Museum, London)

What can now be regarded as a fortuitous circumstance occurred on the very first day of her foray on 8 August 1915, when she was involved in a minor collision with the Leyland liner *Canadian* of 9000 tons. The *Aquitania* immediately steamed back to Liverpool for repairs, by which time the merchant cruiser idea had been abandoned. The shipwrights were again called in and the vessel was converted to a troop transport, dazzle-painted in black, white and grey diamond patterns. Later in 1915 she transported British troops to Lemnos to take part in the disastrous Gallipoli campaign, carrying over 30,000 in a 3-month period. In order to bring these troops home at the end of the fighting, the *Aquitania* had to be converted into a hospital ship and was described as looking 'truly magnificent' in its livery of a white hull with a green band and buff funnels.

The *Aquitania* was laid up in Liverpool at the beginning of 1917 on account of the U-boat menace, but following the entrance of the United

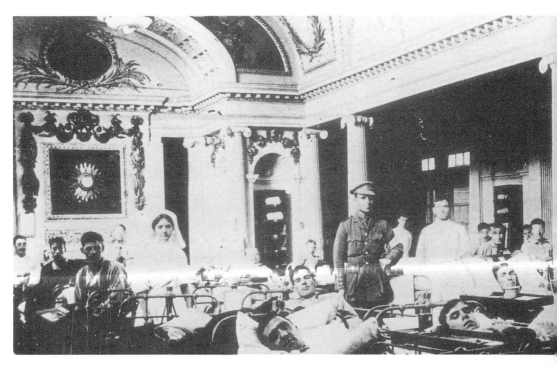

A section of *Aquitania*'s Palladian Lounge converted to accommodate wounded British troops returning from the ill-fated Dardanelles campaign during the First World War. (Courtesy University of Liverpool Archives)

States into the war in that year, she was painted once more and began trooping across the North Atlantic. On 9 October 1918, eastbound west of Ireland and carrying 8000 troops, she was joined by an escort consisting of five U.S. destroyers. All ships were zigzagging when the steering gear of USS *Shaw* jammed, and cutting across the track of *Aquitania*, she was cut cleanly in half in a sheet of flame. The watertight compartments of the destroyer held and only 12 sailors were lost: *Aquitania*, only slightly damaged, continued to Liverpool.

Following the Armistice, the *Aquitania* and *Mauretania* between them returned 130,000 Americans and Canadians to their homelands. Following a brief refit, the *Aquitania* returned to passenger service in June 1919, but four months later was returned to the yards for an extensive program of renovations. During the 1920s, she engaged in a number of Caribbean and Mediterranean cruises in winter months, and remained Cunard's flagship until the *Queen Mary* entered service in 1936. The *Aquitania* was not designed to capture the Blue Riband, which explained her longevity, absence of vibration and her superiority as a seaboat.

Between the outbreak of war and the Japanese attack on Pearl Harbor in December 1941, the transportation of troops across the Atlantic was

Following the outbreak of the Second World War, the U.S.A. despatched three liners to return American tourists from the U.K. No mistaking the neutrality of USS *Manhattan*. (Courtesy U.S. Archives)

comfortably handled by smaller Allied liners, generally in convoy. The servicemen consisted of Australians, New Zealanders and Canadians and it was not until mid-1942 that the build-up of U.S. troops developed to the level that the larger Allied liners scheduled to be independently routed, were progressively converted to maximise accommodation and brought into service. The *Aquitania* and the *Queen Mary*, and for a shorter period the *Queen Elizabeth*, had been engaged in trooping Australians and New Zealanders in the Indian Ocean, with the occasional return to Britain for crew exchange.

The *Aquitania* had been on passage between New York and Southampton when war was declared on 3 September 1939. The voyage was completed with the ship zigzagging and blacked-out, and the return sailing to New York was confirmed. Shortly beforehand, the U.S. passengers were addressed by a member of U.S. Ambassador Joseph Kennedy's staff, who warned that the Germans may torpedo a ship of a 'belligerent nation' without warning. They were informed that a contingent of U.S. ships including the *Washington*, *President Roosevelt* and *Manhattan*, would shortly be on their way with American flags painted on both sides. All

In New York's 'Steamship Row' 1940 – From top; *Rex, Aquitania, Queen Mary, Normandie*, and *Île de France*.

this was sufficient to persuade a significant number of Americans to withdraw their business. A segment of the British first-class passengers attended dinner nightly in formal dress, and purposely displayed an air of hilarity and bravado to impress the British spirit upon the remaining Americans. Cunard honoured the forward bookings of Americans who could not gain passage otherwise, and the *Aquitania* continued on the Atlantic service until late December when she joined the *Queen Mary*, which had remained in Cunard's New York docks since September.

On 10 December the *Aquitania* sailed from Halifax in a troop convoy consisting of five liners carrying the First Canadian Division of 7400 troops. The escorts included the British battlecruiser *Repulse*, the battleship *Resolution*, and the fleet carrier *Furious*. On about the same date, Cunard's *Samaria* of about 20,000 tons had sailed from Liverpool carrying civilian passengers. The top secret route of the convoy was unknown to the Liverpool authorities, and apparently the vessels were routed on almost identical opposite courses. Radar installation had not yet begun, and in mid-Atlantic the darkened ships met. The *Furious* had

The *Queen Elizabeth*, with skeleton crew, making a secret dash on her maiden voyage to New York. (Courtesy Frank O. Braynard Collection)

her radio mast torn away and the *Samaria* next struck the *Aquitania* a glancing blow on the port side followed by two near-misses with other ships. This embarrassing event was recorded in the log of the navigating officer of *Furious*, Lt Cdr C A Jenkins, but remained largely unknown, although I had heard it mentioned after joining the *Aquitania*.

The British Ministry of War Transport had taken over the direction of all British liners after the outbreak of war, although supervision and crewing remained with the company. The *Aquitania, Queen Mary* and the *Mauretania* were subjected to limited conversion for troop carrying, and sailed from New York for Sydney on 23 March 1940. Australia had immediately followed Britain in declaring war against Germany and divisions of volunteers were becoming available for transport to Britain, and subsequently to the Middle East. On 5 May 1940 the three Cunarders, in company with four other transports, each in excess of 30,000 tons, sailed for the Middle East. Whilst on passage, the threat of the German invasion of Britain developed, and the convoy was diverted to the U.K.

The *Aquitania* docked at Wooloomooloo, Sydney, about to load Australian troops for the Middle East in 1941.

via Cape Town. The Australian Government had always insisted that its troops be provided with naval escorts, and by the time the convoy reached the North Atlantic, the senior escort, the battlecruiser *Hood*, was supported by two fleet carriers, two cruisers and eight destroyers, with Sunderland aircraft providing additional protection.

The newly constructed *Queen Elizabeth*, with an escort of four destroyers for the first 200 miles, had arrived in New York on 20 March 1940. She remained there until the following November when she sailed to Singapore for conversion into a troopship. She joined the other two of Cunard's triumvirate in Sydney in February 1941. These vessels then engaged in carrying Australian and N.Z. troops to the Middle East, journeys which were marred by the effects of extreme heat in crowded ships without air conditioning. On several occasions troops were on the point of rioting, and deaths from heat occurred early in the voyage amongst prisoners of war when subsequently on passage to New York.

The *Queens* began the transportation of U.S. and Canadian troops to Europe in 1942 while the *Aquitania* had engaged in a variety of duties in addition to the Middle East run. In November 1941 she had transported troops to Port Moresby and also to Indonesia for onward passage to Singapore. Returning from Indonesia on 24 November 1941, the

Survivors from the German raider *Kormoran* about to be rescued from their lifeboat by
crew members of the *Aquitania* on 24 November 1941.

Aquitania rescued 24 German sailors from a raft. They proved to be survivors from an engagement involving HMAS *Sydney*, which had
encountered the armed German raider *Kormoran* five days earlier.
Attempting to establish identification, *Sydney* approached within the
extraordinarily close distance of about one mile, with the ships abeam.
Exchanging its bogus Dutch colours for the Nazi flag, the *Kormoran*
launched torpedoes and opened fire with its 6in guns. The *Sydney*, with its
radio out of action, its aircraft destroyed along with the two forward gun
turrets, torpedoes having struck beneath the bridge, and with no signal
having been sent, drifted away burning fiercely, and nothing further has
ever been heard of her. The *Kormoran*, also heavily damaged and burning,
sank following the explosion of her mines, having been abandoned by her
crew. All information regarding the encounter came from the surviving
German crew members. The loss of *Sydney*'s entire ship's company of 42
officers and 603 ratings remains Australia's greatest naval disaster.

During the next four months the *Aquitania* ferried women and children
from Hawaii to San Francisco, returning with servicemen. August 1942
found her bound for the U.K. for crew leave and replacement and she
then crossed to New York where a permanent U.S. gun crew was attached
to supplement and reinforce the British gunners. From there she sailed to
Cape Town, Suez and Wellington, returning to Suez on 5 January 1943.

The danger of a collision with a troop transport should be remote, but
a disaster on 2 October 1942 demonstrated that, like the sinking of the

The *Queen Mary* and *Queen Elizabeth* greet each other for the first time off Sydney Heads whilst exchanging berths between Jervis Bay and Athol Bay on 9 April 1941. (Courtesy National Library of Australia).

Aerial photo of *Queen Elizabeth* outward bound from Sydney Harbour.

Titanic, the impossible could happen. The *Queen Mary*, under the command of Captain Illingworth, was steaming towards the Clyde loaded with U.S. troops, and the master had been advised he should rendezvous north west of Ireland with the British anti-aircraft cruiser, *Curaçoa* – 450 feet long with a displacement of 4,200 tons. In these earlier days, this protection was provided. The cruiser's maximum speed of 25 knots was insufficient for her to remain in company with the *Queen Mary* unless she forewent conforming with the zigzag pattern, and it was the intention of her commander, Captain John Birdwood D.S.O., R.N., to fall back gradually, with the *Queen Mary* overtaking along the cruiser's port side, and then take up a position slightly astern of the liner.

A crew member of the battleship HMS *Nelson* photographs the *Aquitania* sailing in convoy from the U.K. to the Middle East, via Capetown in 1942. (F. Bamber)

The *Curaçoa* was in company with six R.N. destroyers, and the latter proceeded to carry out anti-submarine sweeps about four miles ahead. Both the *Mary* and *Curaçoa* had sailed in close formation on three previous occasions, and the subsequent evidence of Captain Illingworth together with other evidence, pointed to the officers of the cruiser being aware that the *Queen Mary* always followed a zigzag pattern in accordance with the instructions to all independently-routed troop transports.

First Officer Stanley Wright of the *Queen Mary* had been relieved by Senior First Officer Noel Robinson a few minutes before the collision occurred. Robinson and his junior officer Hewitt simultaneously realised the danger as the vessels appeared to yaw together. Robinson gave the order hard to port, but the next moment the bow of the *Queen Mary* struck the *Curaçoa* on the port side about 10 feet ahead of the stern, propelling her around 90 degrees and then striking her again. The stern section, representing about one third of the cruiser, sank within five minutes. The remaining forward and midships sections temporarily recovered to an upright position, but then followed suit. A number of troops aboard the *Queen Mary* responded by hurling their life jackets overboard, but the liner continued on her way, although at the reduced speed of 14 knots. Two of the six escorting destroyers turned about and

An artist's reconstruction of the *Queen Mary* slicing through the anti-aircraft cruiser HMS *Curaçao*, following a collision in the Western Approaches. (Courtesy University of Liverpool Archives)

sped to the rescue, picking up alive the captain, one officer and 99 ratings, while 338 officers and men perished.

The author subsequently sailed under Captain Illingworth, and also with First Officer Wright. A security cover blanketed the disaster, and the loss of the *Curaçoa* was not officially announced until after the war ended. It had not been possible to hush it up altogether, the *Queen Mary* having limped into Gourock at half speed with her bow obviously damaged. Temporary repairs were improvised, and the vessel returned to New York where a section of the bow was replaced. The facts of the collision inevitably became known within the company.

In February 1949, the House of Lords upheld on appeal an earlier decision of the Court of Appeal that the officers of the *Queen Mary* were one-third responsible for the collision and the Navy two-thirds. Statutory protection enjoyed by the Admiralty did not extend to Cunard whose one-third responsibility effectively made the company responsible for all claims. That was how things worked.

The *Queen Elizabeth* was sighted on 9 November 1942 by a U-boat. This was revealed in a 1999 publication entitled *Hitler's U-Boat War* by an American author, Clay Blair. References will be made subsequently to

The *Queen Mary* in the Boston Navy Yard for repairs following her collision with
HMS *Curaçao*. (Courtesy Frank O. Braynard Collection)

two sightings of the *Aquitania* and one of the *Queen Mary* by U-boats
revealed in his book.

> On November 9, 1942, *U-704*, commanded by Horst Kessler, divert-
> ed to chase the giant ocean liner *Queen Elizabeth*, westbound at high
> speed. Kessler got close enough to fire four torpedoes at the liner but
> soon after he reported he was forced to abort to France owing to severe
> illness of a crewman. Kessler claimed one hit on the *Queen Elizabeth*,
> but failed to specify it was the ocean liner, not the battleship of the
> same name, thereby causing considerable confusion at U-boat head-
> quarters. The hit could not be confirmed.

Whilst the sighting can be accepted as authentic, any high-speed chase
and the firing of four torpedoes may be discounted, and certainly the
'hit'. The battleship *Queen Elizabeth* was not in fact at sea at that time.

A section of a convoy transporting the Australian 9th Division from the Middle East to Sydney, off south coast of Australia in February 1943. From the left; *Queen Mary*, *Île de France* and *Aquitania*.

The British cruiser HMS *Gambia* escorted several convoys, including the Cunarders carrying Australian and New Zealand troops to and from the Middle East. (Courtesy RAAF Museum, Point Cook, Australia)

U-704 was listed as having been scuttled by the Germans at a northern port in May 1945. Somehow it survived the war since 1942, but hardly in the North Atlantic.

In late 1942, the Australian Government, ignoring strong objections from Winston Churchill which were based on a policy of 'beat Hitler first', had insisted that the Australian Ninth Division, which was engaged in the African desert, be withdrawn to combat the Japanese threat to our shores. In order to provide the necessary transport, the *Queen Mary* was temporarily withdrawn from the Atlantic Shuttle Service which was getting under way and she joined the *Île de France*, *Nieuw Amsterdam* and the *Aquitania* to form a convoy to be escorted to Australia by the cruisers *Devonshire* and *Gambia*. The ships reached Sydney on 27 February 1943 and here the author joined the *Aquitania* four weeks later.

CHAPTER 3

The Atlantic Battle – The Early Years

The Battle of the Atlantic commenced within hours of the formal declaration of war on 3 September 1939 when the British passenger liner *Athenia* was torpedoed shortly before dark 200 miles west of the coast of Scotland. The 14,000-ton vessel carried 1200 passengers and crew and 115 were drowned. Hitler denied any involvement, claiming the British had engineered a stunt in the hope of embroiling the United States. He was mindful that the sinking of the *Lusitania* in May 1915 was a factor which eventually propelled the U.S. into the First World War. On 23 November the P&O liner *Rawalpindi* sank within an hour after encountering the German heavy cruisers *Scharnhorst* and *Gneisenau*. All except 11 crewmen perished.

The convoy system was introduced soon after the outbreak of war. Destroyers and corvettes escorted groups of westbound merchant ships to a point about 200 miles west of Ireland, where the merchantmen would head off independently at maximum speed to their respective destinations. The escorts then awaited the arrival of eastbound vessels to form convoys for the final stages of the homeward voyage. At the beginning of 1940, U-boats operated generally within the Western Approaches, and few patrolled west of 20 degrees west.

In March 1940, the tempo of the Battle of the Atlantic slowed as many U-boats were withdrawn to their bases in preparation for the invasion of Norway. The German success in that campaign was followed by the overrunning of the Low Countries and France, and the Nazis rapidly swept down the Atlantic coast to the Biscay ports of Brest, La Rochelle, St. Nazaire, Lorient and Bordeaux. By the end of 1940 these Atlantic ports had become the hub of submarine operations, the U-boats being housed in pens protected by concrete approaching 20 feet thick, and providing complete protection from the repeated R.A.F. bombing attacks.

Cunard suffered the loss of three liners during June 1940. The greatest number of casualties in the history of the company occurred on 17 June off the coast of the French Atlantic port of St. Nazaire when an estimated 6000 troops, members of the British Expeditionary Force,

The *Athenia* sinking by the stern 200 miles west of Ireland on 3 September 1939. The explosion of the first torpedo fired in the Second World War echoed around the world. (Courtesy Popperfoto)

On 17 September 1939 the British fleet carrier HMS *Courageous* sank within 15 minutes in the Western Approaches with the loss of 518 crew members, after being torpedoed by *U-29* which had penetrated the destroyer screen. (Courtesy Imperial War Museum, London).

crowded aboard the *Lancastria* in an attempt to escape the advancing German armies. Luftwaffe Stukas struck the vessel with three bombs, one descending cleanly down a funnel. Within 20 minutes the vessel had foundered and although details of those who had boarded the ship were never established, rough estimates put the death-roll around 4000. This disaster at sea was only exceeded in the Second World War by the loss of Germany's *Wilhelm Gustloff*, described in a later chapter. During the same month, the company's *Corinthia* was torpedoed west of Ireland, whilst another passenger liner, the *Andania*, met a similar fate south of Iceland. The sinking of the liner *City of Benares* in September 1940 was singled out for wide publicity in the United States. Proceeding west-bound unescorted and carrying hundreds of evacuee children for Canada, she was torpedoed and sunk by *U-48*. Amongst the children saved were a number who spent a week or more in lifeboats.

October 26 was to become the saddest day in the history of Canadian Pacific. Built in 1931, the 42,000-ton liner and flagship, the *Empress of Britain*, while on passage from Capetown to Liverpool with 643 passengers, was bombed and set on fire 70 miles west of Donegal by a German

The Cunard liner *Lancastria* was sunk by dive-bombers on 17 June 1940 during the evacuation of B.E.F. troops from St Nazaire. About 4000 men were believed to have drowned. (Courtesy University of Liverpool Archives)

aircraft patrolling in the Western Approaches. She was eventually taken in tow but two days later was struck by two torpedoes fired by *U-32*. It is of interest to note that this liner, of a tonnage only 4000 less than the *Aquitania* and built 17 years later, sank in four minutes. Two days later, *U-32* was depth-charged and brought to the surface by HMS *Highlander*, which rescued 29 of her 38 crew members. The loss of this liner was one of many to subsequently reduce the capacity of the Allies to move troops across the Atlantic.

On 5 November, one of the most gallant actions of the Battle occurred. HX 84, a convoy of 38 ships laden with food bound from Halifax to the U.K., was being escorted by the British armed merchant cruiser, *Jervis Bay*. She was under the command of Captain Fogarty Fegan, Royal Navy, and her crew were mostly merchant seamen serving with the Royal Naval Reserve. Her principal armament consisted of four 6in guns. Several days earlier, the German pocket battleship, *Admiral Scheer*, armed with 11in guns, had sailed from its base in Norway into the Atlantic unnoticed by British patrols. Late in the afternoon of 5 November when south of Iceland, her Captain Krancke detected smoke

Action-packed photo of civilian passengers and crew members desperately attempting to escape from a passenger liner sinking by the head in the Western Approaches.

on the horizon, and shortly after convoy HX 84 was sighted. The *Jervis Bay* sailed directly towards the German requesting identification and at the same time ordering the merchantmen to scatter. The *Scheer* opened up with its 11in guns, but the *Jervis Bay* pressed straight on to bring the German within range of her own fire. Within less than a half hour the unequal contest was over, and the merchant cruiser went down with heavy loss of life. Captain Fegan, by engaging the enemy in this direct fashion, enabled the merchantmen to disperse to such an extent that the *Scheer* succeeded in sinking only five ships from the convoy. Captain Fegan was posthumously awarded the Victoria Cross. The sailings of North Atlantic convoys were suspended for two weeks, until it was established the *Admiral Scheer* had continued her foray into the South Atlantic.

It was inappropriate to concede a German could be a hero, but many admired the courage of some U-boat commanders, and in particular that of Prien, Kretschmer and Schepke. Lorient on the French coast became known as the 'Port of the Aces', and Admiral Doenitz had his headquarters in nearby Kerneval. When in harbour, these commanders and their crews were provided with everything heroes are supposed to need and to deserve. Plush hotels, vintage champagne and girls, beauties brought in

U-Boat survivors hopefully awaiting rescue. (Courtesy Imperial War Museum, London)

from Berlin and Paris, were amongst the rewards. On 14 October 1939 Gunther Prien, in command of *U-47*, had penetrated the defences of Britain's principal naval base at Scapa Flow. He torpedoed and sank the battleship *Royal Oak* at anchor within a mile of shore, the loss of life totalling 833 officers and men. In August 1940, following a voyage of two weeks in *U-99*, Otto Kretschmer was awarded the Knight's Cross by Admiral Raeder after sinking seven ships, and in October during further encounters, he torpedoed six merchantmen in the Western Approaches. One of Schepke's many exploits consisted of torpedoing five ships in three hours in April 1940.

In March 1941, Germany initiated her wolf pack tactics and the three aces all ended their careers in the same month. On 8 March Prien's U-boat was sunk by HMS *Wolverine* without a survivor. Schepke's submarine was depth charged and rammed by the destroyer HMS *Vanoc*, the German captain being crushed by the bow against his conning tower. Kretschmer in *U-99*, following an ASDIC contact by HMS *Walker*, was depth-charged to the surface and raked with gunfire. The crew leaped into the water and was rescued by the attacker, whose captain, Donald MacIntyre D.S.O. D.S.C., confiscated Kretschmer's binoculars. In a handsome gesture, he returned this treasured souvenir after the war.

On 27 May 1941 the 52,000-ton German battleship *Bismarck* was sunk south-east of the Azores by combined units of the Home and Mediterranean Fleets. Earlier in her foray from Norway out into the

This lone temporary survivor photographed by crew of *U-124*. German Regulations and accommodation problems prevented his rescue. (Courtesy German Federal Archives, Koblenz)

Atlantic, she had sunk the ageing British battlecruiser *Hood*, which was struck in the magazine by a shell. Only three survived from a crew of about 1500. The greatest chase in naval history then developed and continued until a torpedo, launched from a Swordfish aircraft, put the German's steering mechanism out of action. The battleships *King George V* and *Rodney*, the latter with enormous forward firepower of three 16in triple turrets, closed in and silenced the *Bismarck*. She finally sank after having been struck by ten torpedoes and several dozen 14in and 16in shells. Only about 100 of the crew of over 2000 men were saved. This last day in the life of Admiral Lütjens also happened to be his birthday.

The Japanese attack on Pearl Harbor on 7 December 1941 triggered the full conversion of the Allied liners into troop ships. Rapid transportation was essential, there being no point in holding fast ships back to match the speed of the slowest vessel in an escorted convoy. The added knots was seen as a justification for accepting the risk of enormous casualties which would result should one of the *Queens*, carrying 16,000 troops, be torpedoed, with the nearest rescue vessel being perhaps a hundred or more miles away. The increasing availability of long-range Liberator aircraft was another factor in the decision.

The formal declaration of war by Hitler on the United States four days after Pearl Harbor had ended the American domestic polarisation regarding her entry into the European war. Churchill visited Washington later the same month and discussed the transportation of troops with the U.S. Chief of Staff, General George Marshall. Churchill subsequently wrote: 'He had agreed to send nearly 30,000 American soldiers to Northern Ireland. We had of course placed the two *Queens,* the only two 80,000 ton ships in the world, at his disposal for this purpose. General Marshall asked me how many men we ought to put on board, observing that boats, rafts, and other means of flotation could only be provided for about 8,000. If this were disregarded, they could carry about 16,000. I gave the following answer: "I can only tell you what we should do. You must judge for yourselves the risks you will run. If I were a direct part of an actual operation we should put all on board they could carry. If it were only a question of moving troops in a reasonable time we should not go beyond the limits of the lifeboats, rafts, etc. It is for you to decide." ' Marshall decided to load the ships to the maximum capacity, but it was not until the latter part of 1942 that sufficient troops had been trained for the planning for these and other large, fast liners to become fully operable. However, as an initial gesture to confirm America's intentions, the first contingent of U.S. troops arrived in Belfast on 26 January 1942.

In the meantime, U-boat warfare continued against merchant shipping proceeding in convoys with losses reaching alarming proportions. The Americans suffered the destruction of tankers along the eastern seaboard due to a failure to organise any convoy system, and these continued until March 1942. The previous month the British experienced a stinging embarrassment when a German battle group of *Scharnhorst, Gneisenau, Prinz Eugen* and several destroyers, sailed virtually unmolested through the narrow English Channel on passage from Brest to Norway.

In September 1942 Cunard lost two unescorted liners in the South Atlantic, both carrying Italian prisoners of war from the Middle East. The *Scythia* was torpedoed and sunk with many casualties, while the loss of the *Laconia* had more serious consequences in that it resulted in Hitler forbidding any future attempts to rescue Allied seamen. On 12 September, sailing from Cape Town to Freetown with 1800 prisoners and civilians, *Laconia* was torpedoed and sunk by *U-156* 500 miles from her destination. U-boat Commander Hartenstein surfaced and finding the warm waters alive with Italians, signalled for instructions. Doenitz despatched three U-boats operating in the area to assist in a rescue in a plain language signal, and offering immunity from submarine attack to any Allied ships joining in. Three days after the attack, a U.S. Army Liberator, apparently unaware of the situation, bombed the U-boats but succeeded only in capsizing the lifeboats. Subsequently Vichy French ships from Dakar saved many of the survivors but Hitler now had an excuse to ban all rescue operations.

As 1942 progressed, the Allies improved their defences against convoy attacks. V.L.R. (very long range) Liberators were becoming available in slowly increasing numbers, having a capacity to reach out from their bases in Newfoundland, Iceland and Ireland for up to 1000 miles and to provide cover for a few hours in daylight. Six grain ships and six tankers were outfitted with flight decks enabling old, lumbering Swordfish air-craft to take off and patrol ahead of convoys. Casualties were heavy amongst the flyers of the Fleet Air Arm. These Merchant Aircraft Carriers were known as M.A.C. Ships. In larger convoys a merchantman occasionally carried a catapult from which a Hurricane fighter could be launched to tackle a marauding German Focke Wulf Condor. If beyond reach of land, the pilot would attempt to ditch alongside a rescue vessel and hope for the best.

The introduction of 'Escort Groups' further enhanced convoy protec-tion. These flotillas of up to ten frigates, sloops and corvettes hunted in the areas of greatest U-boat activity and would hasten to support the escort of a convoy under attack. In July 1942, the U.S. had begun despatching troop convoys to Britain, heavily escorted by Task Forces 37 and 38. T.F. 37 included the battleship *New York*, the cruiser *Philadelphia* and twelve destroyers, whilst T.F. 38 was made up of the battleship *Arkansas*, the cruiser *Brooklyn* and eleven destroyers. An average of twelve troopships sailed in each convoy. The U.S. simply did not have the large, fast liners which the Allies would be able to provide, in limited numbers, to transfer their troops to Europe with an acceptable degree of safety.

The landing of Allied forces under General Eisenhower in French Morocco and Western Algeria occurred on 8 November 1942. Surprise was complete and Casablanca and Oran fell quickly. The Moroccan landings were achieved by forces of 34,000 U.S. troops convoyed by U.S. Navy ships from the continental U.S.A., and by 32,000 British and U.S. troops from Britain, with units of Admiral Tovey's Home Fleet providing the escort. The Germans had assembled about 35 U-boats south of the invasion areas in the belief that the landings were to be made at Dakar. This miscalculation was a major failure of German Intelligence, and sev-eral days passed after the initial landings before six Allied ships were torpedoed. Additional ships were torpedoed whilst returning to Britain, including the troopships *Warwick Castle*, *Ettrick*, *Viceroy of India* and *Strathallan*, thus further depleting the resources for moving G.I.s to Europe and placing additional reliance on Cunard's future contribution.

The depletion of the escort forces for 'Operation Torch' added to the losses in the northern sector of the Atlantic, and, in November 1942, 117 merchant ships were sunk in the North America – U.K. shipping lanes.

German U-boat production had reached a new peak of about 25 per month and almost 100 U-boats were in operation, with about 50 prowling the North Atlantic. Foul weather and the limited daylight in December 1942 and January 1943 caused the usual seasonal reduction in activity, with both sides concentrating on their own survival against the mountainous waters whipped up by continuous gales. The *Queen Elizabeth* had recruited many Australian crew members during the period she was trooping in the Indian Ocean and some had returned in her to Britain. After a prolonged absence from home many applied for discharge and set out for Australia in early December 1942 in the liner ss *Ceramic*. Shortly after clearing the Western Approaches and heading south off the Azores, the unescorted vessel was torpedoed on 6 December. Only one of these ex-crew members escaped drowning.

In February 1943 fighting in the Atlantic intensified, with both sides suffering heavy losses. During the first three months of the year, approximately 200 merchant ships were sunk, the March figures being the worst for any month since the war began. This was the state of the Atlantic war when the author first arrived in New York on 4 May 1943 in the *Aquitania*, to begin the first of 53 consecutive crossings of the North Atlantic.

CHAPTER 4

An Introduction to Seafaring

On 14 March 1943, while serving in Naval Headquarters Melbourne, I accepted an offer of a shore appointment at a small naval base at Oro Bay on the north coast of New Guinea. A news item three days later, reporting that 25 Japanese bombers had raided the base, was hardly an encouragement, but it was not before time that I should actively participate in the war. On 19 March, the day before I was due to take pre-embarkation leave, a signal arrived from the Admiralty asking the authorities to appoint two cipher officers to both the *Aquitania* and *Queen Mary* which were about to depart unescorted from Sydney for Britain.

An offer to exchange my Oro Bay appointment for the *Aquitania* was irresistible, and the fact that I had only two days before leaving for Sydney was no problem. I was aged 23, without dependants, and the affairs of a university student took little getting in order. The offer of this appointment possibly had some connection with my association with a Lieutenant Cowen at Naval HQ. He had a phenomenal memory for the numbers of the basic cipher book which was replaced every three months. For my part, I had a knack of being able to write the subtraction of the numbers he would call, many from memory, from the basic cipher, directly to the transmission pad whilst looking at the deciphering tables. These time-saving factors involved led to our being allocated signals of urgency and of consequent interest. Cowen's talents took him far. Beginning with a Rhodes Scholarship, the many achievements of Sir Zelman Cowen in law finally led him to Australia's highest office, that of the Commonwealth's nineteenth Governor General.

I arrived in Sydney from Melbourne on the morning of Monday 22 March 1943 to board the *Aquitania*, which lay docked near the Sydney Harbour Bridge in an area with the distinctly Australian name of Wooloomooloo. Four large funnels could be seen towering above adjoining buildings. The *Queen Mary* rode at anchor out in the harbour with steam up, obviously on the point of sailing. I reported to the purser's office from where I was escorted to stateroom A10, on the port side of 'A' deck. As events turned out, I was to share this cabin with my fellow cipher

The author stepping out in Elizabeth Street, Melbourne, April 1941.

officer, Lieutenant Alex Milne R.A.N.R., for the next twelve months, and thereafter, following Milne's subsequent illness and departure, to occupy it alone until after the European war ended. Milne was not replaced and I remained the only cipher officer. I had not previously been aboard a luxury liner and was greatly impressed by this stateroom, untouched by the war. The bulkheads were lined with royal blue and gold silken tapestries patterned to resemble peacock feathers, and the cabin easily accommodated two full size single beds as distinct from bunks, with ample space remaining for the Queen Anne furniture. Three windows looked out across the promenade deck, about forty feet above the water-line. The glass had been painted black but they could be opened by day, and at night the use of a box device allowed fresh air to enter. Naturally a private bathroom and toilet came with this sort of comfort. The bath was supplied with salt water only, but our steward James thoughtfully provided a small hose to enable fresh water to be run from the adjoining hand basin. Two large wardrobes and dressing tables provided ample space for our gear. Alex Milne came aboard about midday and we were welcomed by Captain William C. Battle, a most impressive figure, and his decorations told of his First World War naval service. Cunard had always attracted officers of the highest quality, and all captains had extra master's tickets, with the majority also being commissioned officers in the Royal Naval Reserve.

The *Aquitania* had not previously carried naval cipher officers, and the Captain needed to rely on naval escorts for whatever signals of the more highly classified type the warships saw fit to pass on. The codes carried by the troopships were of low grades and some captains felt deprived of information. Thus if a diversion of route and/or a change of destination occurred, a minimum of detail would be passed by signal lamp but without explanation. Our arrival opened channels of information previously unavailable to these captains. The cipher room was at the boat deck level opposite the entrance to the Captain's cabin and adjoining a companionway leading directly to the navigation bridge. The senior Royal Navy officer aboard, as distinct from Merchant Navy officers, was Lieutenant Commander Alan O'Neil, an Englishman attached to the Royal Naval Volunteer Reserve, and he was in charge of the British section of the gun crew. Milne and I were under the jurisdiction

Lieutenant Alex Milne.

of Captain Battle, and our relationship with the gunnery officer remained largely social and indeed most pleasant. At the Purser's Office we signed the Ship's Articles as a 'Supernumerary Deck Officer', thus formalising our position under the Captain. We could claim we were concurrently officers in both services, and this proved to be the better of both worlds.

In the afternoon Milne and I visited the naval depot ship, HMAS *Kuttabul*, to collect the current ciphers and reciphering tables, and we returned to the ship for 'tea', as the British call it. In the wardroom, we met the majority of the ship's deck officers who at first seemed to accept the advent of two Australian naval officers with a measure of resignation. Our position had not been made easier by the fact that the *Aquitania*'s return voyage from the Middle East had been particularly trying. After loading, the convoy had been delayed in the East African tropical port of Massawa, and following a further period of waiting in the blistering Gulf of Aden where additional ships joined, the convoy set out for Australia at a speed considerably reduced by stragglers. Troop discipline suffered accordingly, inevitably accentuated by the fact that the Australian soldiers, who had been in combat in North Africa, would be returning to their homes, even though for a brief period, before being sent off again to tackle the Japanese. If our welcome were somewhat restrained, any

A profile of the *Aquitania* as a First World War hospital ship. The windows of the author's cabin are immediately below the lifeboat, athwart the forward stack. The enclosed bridge is located on the deck above.

prejudices were quickly forgotten, and within a few days we were on excellent terms with our Merchant Navy colleagues.

The following morning, Tuesday 23 March 1943, at 9.30 a.m., the *Aquitania* sailed for Britain via Fremantle, Cape Town and Freetown. Sightseers crowded the North and South Heads of Sydney's magnificent harbour, and numerous small craft followed the ship out. The heights surrounding Sydney's harbour, now partly covered by the mansions of the rich, provide shelter from the winds. Indeed, they do so to such an extent that during the 2000 Sydney Olympics still conditions forced the postponement of yacht racing on several occasions. Escort was provided by the Free French destroyer, *Le Triomphant,* and three Royal Australian Air Force planes swept our track as we headed south down the east coast of New South Wales. *Le Triomphant* had been assigned the nickname of 'The Reluctant Dragon' by naval wits in Sydney, founded on an alleged reluctance to go to sea. The French sailors, with their colourful caps adorned with red pompons, were said to be winners with the Sydney girls, and could see little point in braving the deep as an alternative. Others claimed these men had lost their enthusiasm for the cause after the British had blasted their battleship *Richelieu* at Dakar, and Force H had immobilised their battleships *Bretagne, Provence* and *Dunkerque* at Oran in July 1940. Whatever the position, the 'Dragon' performed well in rising seas until the time came for her to turn about. She then fell away into the dusk, and headed back to the delights of Sydney.

On the afternoon of 28 March, we made a rendezvous with the Dutch destroyer *Van Galen,* and the following morning, also protected by an R.A.A.F. aircraft, we arrived at the port of Fremantle on the south west corner of the continent. The ship remained at anchor at Gage Roads off the North Mole for 36 hours, and although leave was not granted to the crew, Milne and I considered ourselves obliged to visit naval headquarters, providing an excuse to spend an agreeable day ashore in Perth.

The *Aquitania* sailed the following evening, 30 March, for Cape Town with all tanks trimmed to the tops, a voyage of ten days and approaching the vessel's maximum range. Fortunately the ship was travelling light, the *Queen Mary* proceeding two days ahead, having taken all civilians who had been granted passage. On account of the Japanese war in the Pacific, Australian and New Zealand troops were no longer heading for Britain.

Our voyage to Cape Town through the 'Roaring Forties' was without incident, the only sighting being a distant merchant ship. Huge black and white albatrosses, with ten-foot wing spans and with their motionless gliding flights, followed the ship for days. We had been warned at Fremantle that radio transmissions indicated a U-boat was operating east of the Cape of Good Hope, but we did not receive any diversion signals, and business was slow in the cipher department. On 8 April a signal advised that the destroyer HMS *Quail* would rendezvous at 3 p.m. the next day, and the meeting was made punctually. We arrived at Cape Town at 9 a.m. the following morning where the depth of water was sufficient to enable the ship to dock rather than having to anchor in the roadstead. As we approached, the haze covering Table Mountain and Lion's Head suddenly lifted, unveiling a magnificent first view of South Africa.

Milne and I went ashore with the two U.S. Army gunnery officers, Captain Edwin Seim and Captain Frank Rollins. We were greeted by representatives of a committee for entertaining visiting servicemen, and were invited to a private house at the foot of Table Mountain with extensive views over the Bay. Later that night we went to the Stardust Club where my partner and I both celebrated our twenty-fourth birthdays. We remained in Cape Town for three days, made all the more pleasant by the ship's company being given introductions to city and sporting clubs, invitations to homes, and offers of tours into the countryside. The cable car trip to the top of Table Mountain is the first priority for visitors and a clear day afforded magnificent views in all directions. We also made the serpentine drive to Cape Point where the surf beaches rivalled our own.

The *Aquitania* sailed for Freetown, Sierra Leone, on the western bulge of Africa at 9 a.m. on Tuesday 13 April. The *Queen Mary* had left Fremantle six hours after our arrival and subsequently departed Cape Town the day prior to our appearance, with Britain, via Freetown, also her destination. We had been warned at the sailing conference of the presence of U-boats patrolling the waters at both the southern and northern approaches to Freetown. This former slave port, the 'White Man's Grave Yard', was the major fuelling station on the Britain to Cape Town route. An Admiralty report subsequently disclosed that during April alone, twelve U-boats operating off Freetown had torpedoed six ships.

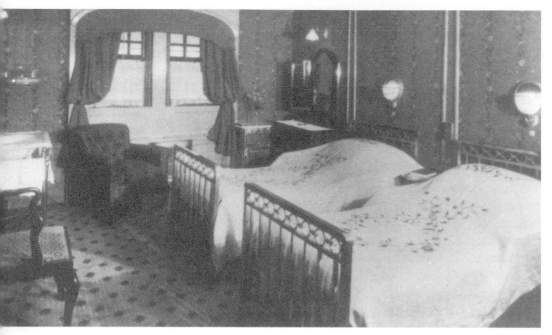

A twin-bedded stateroom in the *Aquitania* provided appropriate accommodation for the cipher officers.

The *Aquitania* was escorted out of Cape Town for 36 hours by the destroyer HMS *Queensborough*, after having embarked approximately 2000 civilians, including children. At 3 a.m. on 15 April, shortly before *Queensborough* was due to break off, we deciphered a signal diverting us to Rio de Janeiro. Later we learned that the *Queen Mary* had narrowly avoided an encounter with a U-boat off Freetown, and that Admiralty had decided against risking the slower *Aquitania*. The diversion, as it turned out, had the effect of prolonging the voyage by three weeks. The vessel did not have the range to travel direct from Rio to the U.K. and we finished up proceeding via New York, where a delay occurred for the installation of increased troop accommodation and radar.

The following days passed as pleasantly as one could wish. Unlike the Roaring Forties, the twenty-fourth parallel provides balmy weather in April. Sunbathing and deck sports were the order of the day, with the sea only slightly rippled by the trade winds. Flying fish fluttered down the sides of the vessel as the bows parted the shimmering waters. St. Helena, with Napoleon's canopied cot said to be prepared for Hitler, lay to the north.

The *Aquitania* anchored in Guanabara Bay, the harbour at Rio, at 10 a.m. on Wednesday, 21 April, eight days after leaving Cape Town. The weather had remained perfect throughout and the voyage was as expected, free of incident, the irregular route having the effect of diverting us from the normal South Atlantic shipping lanes. A Martin Mariner aircraft swept ahead during the afternoon prior to our arrival, and a similar aircraft patrolled the following morning.

Pundits say that if passage is available, the only way to arrive at Rio is by sea, coming in from the east. The sky was clear as the sun began to rise astern, and the foredecks had been crowded since dawn for the initial glimpse of the world's most spectacular natural skyline, gradually climbing the horizon ahead. First, the ridge of the Gavea surfaced off the port bow, followed a few minutes later by the vertex of the massive statue of Christ the Redeemer. Gradually other peaks and ranges rose into view, including the Sugar Loaf and Pico de Papagaio (Parrots Beak) at the west and east entrances respectively to Guanabara Bay. Before passing through into the harbour, we sailed within easy viewing of Copacabana Beach, the five-mile crescent of pale sand, and Avenida Atlantica, the boulevard with handsome apartment buildings bordering the length of this swimmers' paradise. The Rio airport thrusts out into the Bay and the movement of aircraft added to the spectacle. Our passage was free and we were being paid for good measure.

Rio did not have a dock with sufficient depth to allow the *Aquitania* to tie up, and we lay at anchor out in the bay. The ship was to sail within twenty-four hours and a ban was placed on going ashore. Milne and I advised Captain Battle that we would be expected to attend at the office of the British Naval Attaché to collect any signals with deferred priority, so he agreed we could go. Following a visit to the Attaché's office, we engaged a taxi and drove along the Avenida Atlantica, risked the basket car ride up Sugarloaf, and visited the famed tropical botanical gardens. Returning to the ship, we found the U.S. transport *West Point* had docked. Her name had been changed from US. *America* to avoid the national ignominy in the event of her being sunk by the enemy, an alteration perhaps hardly pleasing to the Military Academy.

The *Aquitania* sailed for New York at 5 p.m. on Friday 23 April, loaded down with fuel and water for the estimated voyage of eleven days. There would be little to spare, but at least we could divert to the Bahamas or call at Bermuda if necessary. The ship was now receiving the daily U-boat report from the Admiralty, which placed several submarines operating to the east of St. Paul's Rocks. Captain Battle took the somewhat irregular step of breaking radio silence by sending a signal seeking permission to divert west of the Rocks. Neither air cover nor surface escort was being provided, the ship being far from Allied bases. In January, a convoy had lost four ships out of twelve off the coast of Brazil, and during the following July, fifteen U-boats were reported to be operating between Brazil and the Caribbean.

U-175 sinking by the stern after being depth charged by U.S. Coast Guard Cutter *Spencer* on 17 April 1943. US crew members are seen rowing away after having briefly boarded the doomed submarine. (Courtesy U.S. Coast Guard)

A survivor from *U-175* about to be rescued by a lifeboat from U.S. Coast Guard Cutter *Spencer*. (Courtesy U.S. Coast Guard)

Approaching the Windward Islands zigzagging began and lookouts were strengthened. Here we were crossing the convoy routes followed by tankers sailing from Trinidad and the Caribbean to supply the Allied operations in North Africa and in the Mediterranean. A few weeks earlier, a convoy of nine tankers escorted by only one destroyer and three corvettes was intercepted to the north-east of Trinidad and shadowed. A pack of U-boats was directed to the convoy and seven of the nine tankers were torpedoed. One tanker, on bursting into flames, illuminated four U-boats between the convoy and escorts.

On 2 May we passed within about thirty miles of Bermuda from where a U.S. Navy Catalina patrolled ahead for several hours. The *West Point* left Rio about twelve hours after ourselves, but having a faster turn of speed, had overtaken us off Bermuda. She remained in sight for two or three hours and we exchanged messages of goodwill by lamp. We were due to arrive in New York on the morning of 4 May and one could sense the gathering excitement amongst the passengers. Apart from having had surface escorts for brief periods out of Australia and in and out of South Africa, the journey to New York could be described as one of an independently-routed passenger ship. That role was about to continue with the *Aquitania* becoming part of the North Atlantic unescorted shuttle service.

The morning was cool and misty when I went up to the bridge at 6 a.m. on 4 May 1943. A U.S. Navy blimp carrying out an anti-submarine patrol swept our track – surely a dream target for the gunners of a surfaced U-boat. Passengers had unpacked their cloth caps and tweed overcoats for the occasion, and the women sported their scarves to combat the chill many had not experienced for years. A repeat of the Rio landfall was anticipated when the pinnacles of Manhattan's towers would gradually climb above the horizon ahead. The mist, or was it smog?, was delaying their appearance, but the presence of seagulls, the discoloration of the water, the smells of a great city, the distant hooting of tugs and ferries and the faint roar of traffic proved the navigation was true.

Engine revolutions were cut back and our fog horn sounded regularly. Slow, dead slow, then the outline of the Ambrose channel lightship emerged directly ahead. Reversing engines churned the water astern, bringing the 45,000 tons close to a stop. The pilot, customs, health and immigration officials scrambled up a Jacob's ladder, and soon we were again underway at quarter speed as the Manhattan skyline, in all its grandeur, broke out of the fog.

Having done some preparation in the ship's library, I was able to identify a number of skyscrapers including the Woolworth Tower, the Chrysler, Empire State and Singer buildings. The Woolworth building, constructed in 1913, was once included in the 'Seven Wonders of the World' listings. The Art Deco Chrysler building, further uptown, with its magnificent tower, and still regarded by many as America's most beautiful skyscraper, was completed in 1930, and for a short period was the world's tallest. The Empire State next gained that distinction, and in spite of the building of the even taller World Trade Centre, the Chrysler remains to many New Yorkers their talisman. Brooklyn Bridge, the architectural triumph of its age, was instantly recognisable as we passed the entrance to the East River, and it was reassuring to see it had not collapsed into the water as publisher William Randolph Hearst had predicted with certainty in 1898. Poets, artists and composers of music have been inspired by its beauty – quite an achievement for a bridge which has now survived its hundredth year.

Continuing up the Hudson with the illusion of passing almost underneath the Midtown skyscrapers, the ship approached two tugs idling in mid-stream opposite Pier 86. This 1400-foot dock is a continuation of 46th Street, a ten-minute walk from Times Square or three minutes in a cross town bus. With engines stopped, we drifted slowly to the tugs which took up the lines. Then fussily sounding their hooters, they pulled the bow around and nudged the vessel slowly alongside. The largest Atlantic liners usually docked between Piers 80 and 90 inclusive. This stretch of the Hudson known as 'Steamship Row' extends from 40th to 50th Street on Manhattan's West Side. The Cunard company operated out of Piers 86 and 90, and during our subsequent twenty visits to New York, as distinct from Boston and Halifax, the *Aquitania* docked at Pier 86, while the *Queen Mary* and *Queen Elizabeth* used Pier 90, docking on opposite sides during the rare occasions when in New York together. The French Line had operated from the intervening Pier 88. Piers 86 and 90 were now guarded by a contingent of 750 military police, and hoardings provided some protection from public viewing, apart from the office blocks.

Many crew members retained landing permits from previous visits. The immigration people described me as an 'Alien Seaman', and after being photographed and fingerprinted, I was eventually issued with a permit to which was attached additional vital information including height, weight, eye colour and scars. The above classification made me feel something like a stoker on a Panamanian freighter, but I cheered up a little a year later when described as a 'Mariner' in addition to an 'Alien Seaman'. The ship had been absent from New York for 226 days and had not been fumigated during that period. The U.S. Army gunnery Captain, Ed Seim, complained in his report that his crew members had not received any mail during that period and that vermin including rats was present in their quarters.

In the evening, I went ashore with the Senior Third Navigating Officer, John Woods. He had been to New York several times previously and knew his way around. We stepped out the pier gates into 12th Avenue and walked north to a point opposite the far side of Pier 88, the scene of a tragedy. Fifteen months earlier on 9 February 1942, the French liner *Normandie* had caught fire. This vessel of 82,000 tons, 1029 feet long with a beam of 117 feet and designed by Russian Admiralty émigré B. Yourkevitch, had held the Atlantic Blue Riband, returning from her maiden voyage to New York in 1935 at an average speed of 30.31 knots.

The burnt-out hulk of the *Normandie* lies on the iced-over Hudson, at Pier 88, helpless as a stranded whale. (Courtesy U.S. Archives)

She was described as the 'largest object yet built and set in motion by man'. Her dining room exceeded in length the Great Hall of Mirrors in the Palace of Versailles. Following the fall of France in 1940, the Vichy Government decided to lay up the liner in New York for the duration. However, when Germany declared war on the United States in December 1941, the U.S. Government determined to seize the *Normandie* and to convert her into a troop ship. She was renamed *La Fayette*. The alterations had commenced only weeks before the fire, the cause of which was suspected to be sabotage. However, an enquiry ruled out this theory and the board concluded that a workman using a torch had inadvertently ignited a heap of life jackets. The fire spread quickly below, and every fire boat and many units from the N.Y. Fire Department attended. Huge quantities of water were poured into the ship, to such an extent that her moorings broke and she keeled over in the mud on to her port side. The vessel became a total loss and some concluded that the fire boat crews had been over-zealous. After a period of indecision, the wreck was finally refloated, and on 3 November 1943, the empty hulk was towed to Brooklyn's Erie Canal where in 1947 it was sold and cut up for scrap. That was how the pride of the French Line – perhaps the ultimate in floating elegance – met her end. The opportunity for the U.S. to operate a truly great liner had been cruelly snatched away. The disaster placed an additional strain on the other transports to meet the deadlines for the planned invasion of Europe in the summer of 1944.

After that depressing introduction we walked to Times Square where Broadway snakes through 7th Avenue over four city blocks, and surveyed the wealth of entertainment available in that area known as the 'Pulse of America'. New York provided facilities for servicemen which were unequalled elsewhere. The evening became something of a blur – a succession of bars, the Merchant Navy Club, girls, night clubs and taxi rides. During the following days, we did what most people do on their first visit to New York. The Empire State Building, Central Park, the Bronx Zoo and dinner at the Waldorf Astoria were all on the list. We saw movies at the Roxy and Paramount which were preceded by live shows featuring the 'Big Bands' – Benny Goodman in one instance and Jimmy Dorsey in the other. I also found myself being taken by a girl to a church service at St. Patrick's on Fifth Avenue, another architectural gem.

This brief visit had provided only a preliminary taste of what New York had to offer, but on our return we were to become properly organised, and better placed to enjoy to the full the metropolis which was to remain our base for the duration.

CHAPTER 5

The Logistics of the Eastward Crossing

The *Aquitania* was now due for a major refit. For many months urgent maintenance work had been accumulating, some of which could be done only in dry dock. Extensions of trooping accommodation, painting, electrical and other work had been possible in Sydney, but the limited workforce had to be shared with the *Queen Mary* and ships of the Royal Australian Navy and U.S. Pacific Fleet Against this, the unplanned diversion to Rio and New York had upset the arrangements of the 2000 passengers and particularly crew members who were well overdue for leave. Thus only six days were made available to begin the program which would be completed over a 29-day period when we would return to New York on 9 June. Docking facilities in the Clyde at Greenock were the preserve of the Royal Navy, and little worthwhile could be accomplished with the ship at anchor off Gourock. In any event, the risk of air attack required a fast turn-around.

Shipboard activity during these six days in New York was intense, around the clock. One of America's largest corporations, Bethlehem Steel, had been appointed as the major contractor for Cunard's maintenance, repairs and conversions and had vast workshops and storage facilities in the buildings extending down the lengths of Piers 86 and 90. The efficiencies of their workforce were obvious. The most vital item of all was the installation of a radar set on 'Monkey Island' above the bridge. The electrical systems of the then 30 year-old ship were about to be subjected to enormous strains, and even the considerable work done in this area did not prevent the outbreak of fire from time to time. Alarm systems were extended and together with an efficient fire brigade, this hazard, as it turned out, was always successfully contained.

The installation of Swedish Bofors guns strengthened our anti-aircraft defences. Stretches of standee bunks, four tiers in height, replaced wooden bunks and hammocks in areas where Australian and New Zealand troops had slept. The overall planning of the trooping operations of the three Cunarders was now being shared by the British Ministry of War Transport, the Admiralty, the American Army Transport Authority in

Standee bunk accommodation in the *Queen Elizabeth*'s subsequent Cabin Class Gymnasium accommodated eighty GIs in each twin row. (Courtesy Frank O. Brayard)

conjunction with the Cunard Line. These arrangements now led to a large staff of U.S. officers and enlisted men being appointed to the *Aquitania*, in line with what had taken place earlier with the *Queens*. These administrators worked closely with Cunard's staff captain and with the British O.C. Troops, Colonel Heppenstall. The Colonel had joined the *Aquitania* the previous year and following a rather memorable day I had in his company in Perth, mostly spent at the Weld Club, he 'appointed' me a regular chess opponent, a role I rather enjoyed. The Colonel worked in close co-operation with the U.S. O.C. Troops and with every apparent success.

The Port of New York, which embarked over three and a quarter million troops between 1942 and 1945, moved almost double the numbers handled by the second busiest port, San Francisco. The Army established holding camps known as 'Port Staging Areas' near the major ports of embarkation, and New York was served principally by Camp Shanks in the state of New Jersey and Camp Kilmer in New York State. Each of these staging areas had a holding capacity of between 25,000 and 30,000 men, and from mid-1943 until 1945, they operated at or close to these limits. On receiving the call from the Port Commander, the troops were despatched by train from the Home Stations, and those scheduled to sail from New York spent an average period of two weeks at Camp Shanks or Camp Kilmer. The G.I.s were expected to be adequately trained before arrival at these camps, but full facilities were available to rectify any omissions or deficiencies in training or equipment. Here the men were briefed on shipboard routines and disciplines, and also on techniques in the evasion of capture, in escaping, and resisting interrogation.

Troops were not held incommunicado from the outside world, any security risks being accepted by the authorities. The men remained unaware until the last moment as to when they would be shipping out, and were left with the not very difficult task of guessing the country of destination. The camps maintained pools of trained men who could be slotted into a unit in the event of last-minute replacements being required on account of contingencies such as sickness, or the occasional absence without leave or desertion. In May 1943, approximately 250,000 troops were banked up, both in the nearby staging camps and in other centres, ready for transportation. Prior to the invasion the average waiting period had been reduced to eight days.

Loading procedures and accommodation arrangements were similar for all the large Cunarders although in the *Queen Elizabeth* and the *Queen Mary* the numbers were greater and varied between summer and winter. In the warmer months the *Queens* carried in excess of 15,000 troops with the bunks accommodating two rotating shifts. Thus loaded, the ships barely cleared the Hudson Tunnel. The *Aquitania* conveyed about 8000 men in both summer and winter, with the crew and staff bringing the total to above 9000. Stability became a serious problem, particularly for the *Queens* when at maximum load for crossings outside the winter months. Additional troops and water, combined with the effects of armaments, ammunition, life-saving equipment, and magnetic mine repelling degaussing cables, caused top-heaviness, particularly towards the end of a crossing when the tanks below the waterline approached depletion. The taking aboard of seawater to combat these effects caused unacceptable cleaning problems. The *Queens* could roll alarmingly to 25 degrees or more under these circumstances and the zigzag, occasionally abandoned, accentuated the roll. The *Queen Elizabeth* was reported to have recorded a list of 37 degrees on her inclinometer when struck by a massive wave off Ireland in 1944. A watchkeeper recalled viewing only the sky to port and the sea to starboard on a quick twist of his head. The *Aquitania* with lesser loadings, combined with being a superior seaboat, did not experience these difficulties to the same degree.

An advance party of troops numbering up to 2000, and consisting of loading, guard, defence, medical and mess details, boarded two days prior to sailing in order to become familiar with their duties. These men were allotted duties for the voyage including those of provosts, anti-aircraft gunners, lookouts, mess hall and passage cleaners, store carriers, vegetable peelers and numerous other duties. A man did the same job

Chow line passing through the *Queen Mary*'s First Class Restaurant. (Courtesy Imperial War Museum, London)

throughout the voyage while others escaped all duties, fairness not being allowed to interfere with efficiency. About twelve hours before departure, the main body of troops travelled by train to Jersey City and, after darkness, crossed the Hudson to the river end of Cunard's Pier 86 or 90. The operation was carried out in silence. Each soldier had hung on him his weapon, gas mask and pack, and wore his helmet on which was chalked the number which appeared against his name on the passenger list. On his name being called, each soldier stepped up to a desk where he was identified by his unit commander and allocated his compartment number. The company grade officers moved with their men to the allotted bunks where all remained until embarkation had been completed. The efficiency of the system enabled 15,000 troops to be loaded on either of the *Queens* within five hours and the embarkation was usually complete by 2 a.m. or 3 a.m. The loading of the *Aquitania* averaged about three hours. Within a further six or seven hours, the ship would normally be under way.

Troopships had three loading capacities officially described as Normal load, Overload and Maximum load. Maximum load involved two men sharing a bunk on a rota system and could be employed in the Atlantic where the voyages were short compared with the Pacific, and the weather cooler. U.S. transport regulations required that 'the total numbers be kept within the capacity of life saving equipment'. Presumably a life jacket met the definition for the Cunarders, it being obvious that the lifeboat and raft accommodation was inadequate.

The ship's captain had ultimate control over all personnel on board when at sea. However, the British and U.S. O.C. Troops joined forces to deal with high-ranking travelling officers such as generals, who did not always take kindly to shipboard routines imposed upon them by comparative juniors. I recall an incident at sea when a general, in transit to Halifax, had delivered to the cipher office a signal to be transmitted by breaking radio silence, requiring personal passage by air from Halifax to Washington. I decided it would be politic for the ship's captain himself to deal with the general.

The ships were divided into three sections, the forward being designated Red, midships White and the stern section Blue. Every soldier was provided with a coloured disc to be displayed at all times along with his identification tag. The principal duties of the military police were to ensure that the colour system was not breached, and that life jackets were carried at all times. A man caught without his jacket was ordered to fetch it from his sleeping quarters, and in the meantime the policeman confiscated his boots or shoes. Stories were told of senior generals pussyfooting along corridors in their socks in search of their (or anyone else's) lifejacket. To reduce traffic jams, one-way systems operated in the crowded sections. Nevertheless over ten minutes would elapse before all troops could reach their so-called 'Boat-Stations'.

Troops were quartered in cleared sections, the majority being formed by the removal of the bulkheads separating the original cabins. The standee bunks were crammed into these areas, mostly in tiers of four, depending on the height of the deckhead. Constructed of metal frames into which canvas was laced, they would be hinged by day to an upright position. These so-called bunks were hygienic, easily installed in cabins or public areas, and were no more uncomfortable than one would expect. Many first class cabins accommodated twelve times their number of peacetime passengers.

Catering, a mammoth exercise, was under the control of the Purser and Chief Steward, assisted by their numerous clerks. The permanent staffs rostered troops to work in shifts under cooks, chefs, butchers, bakers, pantrymen, storekeepers, waiters and stewards. Something like 300,000lbs of provisions were loaded for a typical Atlantic round-trip. It was important to make provision for crossings lengthened by gales and/or diversions on account of U-boat activity. The disembarkation and subsequent embarkation in Scotland added a further three or four days,

Standee bunks accommodate participants in a floating crap game. (Courtesy Imperial War Museum, London)

so it was necessary to provide food for about a three-week period – provisions rarely being loaded in Britain on account of food shortages. Canteens or 'sales commissaries' sold cigarettes, chocolates, soft drinks and toilet articles. Although litter bins were widely distributed, sweeping parties continuously gathered up wrappers and packets. Mercifully, the sale of chewing gum was banned, it having been a great opportunity for the British to strike a blow against a habit they claim to have always deplored. This disapproval was unknown to their children at home, whose catchphrase on spotting a G.I. was 'any gum chum?'.

The Red Cross and padres did their best to provide recreation, and to entice the troops away from gambling, which was on the forbidden list – but the shooting of dice was hardly unknown. Enterprising crew members, skilled in gambling, occasionally talked their way into a clandestine poker or blackjack school, taking the precaution of wearing a pair of left-behind G.I. dungarees. Concerts, movies and church services were held daily, and gramophones, records, books, draughts and chess sets were available. Bans were placed on clothes washing, electrical appliances, flashlights, cameras and alcohol. Looking back, the discipline was extraordinarily good, both in the manner in which it was administered and observed.

Troops attending a concert in a mess hall in the *Queen Elizabeth*. After the war this room was decorated to become the First Class Dining Room. (Courtesy University of Liverpool Archives)

The ocean crossing was an ordeal for the majority of the enlisted men. They endured cramped conditions where the ventilation could hardly cope with the odour from masses of bodies, aggravated by limited bathing and the absence of laundry facilities. Some troops had never sailed in a ship, nor for that matter, seen the sea. Seasickness affected many, particularly during the first day or two, together with homesickness and perhaps a distorted idea of the dangers from U-boats and enemy aircraft.

Many would scan the seas and the horizon, looking for a torpedo track, a periscope or conning tower to break the surface. They were at the ready to shout towards the nearest gun position. Americans had a history of avoiding European wars, their ancestors having made the journey across the Atlantic to get away from it all. Unlike all Australians, New Zealanders and Canadians who took passage, the Americans were generally conscripts, often believing they were there only because of the attack on Pearl Harbor, which, now generally forgotten, had obliged Hitler to declare war upon America. The evidence is nevertheless clear that such attitudes did not affect the fighting performances of U.S. forces when they stepped onto enemy soil, flew over its airspace, or hunted its

Signs posted throughout the Cunarders interpreted signals from sirens, klaxons and bells.

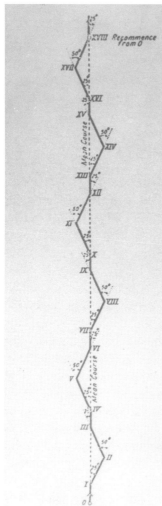

A typical two-hour zigzag pattern.

U-boats. Some would probably look back on their Atlantic crossing as their most dangerous war experience, military logistics requiring the numbers of fighting men actually engaged in combat to be far less than those engaged in such matters as supplying, servicing, planning and administration.

Life saving drills were scheduled to take place daily. All open deck space became crowded when finally all troops had reached their allotted stations after the initial sounding of the alarm bells. Passageways became jammed, and at the first drills, troops could end up anywhere. Not only the authorities but the troops themselves were aware that life saving equipment was totally inadequate, and that thousands would have to rely on their 'Mae West' jackets alone. All would not be hopeless for those fortunate enough to gain a place in a lifeboat. The four crewmen allocated to each of *Aquitania*'s 80 lifeboats with a capacity for some 4500 passengers, were certificated. Storage was provided for biscuits, drinking water, buoyancy tanks, four oars, a sail, sea anchor, compass, flares and matches. The chances of a perfect launching of 80 boats in the frantic North Atlantic amidst panic and from a steeply listing ship would be remote but the presence of these lifeboats was a morale-booster. The ratio in the *Queens* was much worse than in the *Aquitania*.

The sailing schedules for the *Queens* were planned to avoid these ships being anchored in the Clyde and passing both inward and outward bound through the Western Approaches during the period of the full moon. This policy involved these vessels remaining in New York for eleven days, about six more than otherwise necessary, in order to comply with the 28-day lunar cycle. With the accumulation of troops awaiting passage in 1943, the policy was abandoned. Later that year, the round trip was reduced generally to a three-weekly period. The *Aquitania*, carrying fewer troops and approaching the end of her career, was never subjected to moonlight restrictions. Although our time at sea exceeded that of the *Queens*, the carriage of fewer troops allowed a faster turn-around. Our sailing time for each cycle averaged about 15 days, with three days in the Clyde and four in New York, or a total of 22 days, about the same as the *Queens'* amended schedule. At one stage in 1944, we were almost in tandem with the *Queen Elizabeth* for several round trips in succession, although these became interrupted by voyages to Halifax and short delays for maintenance. Exact coincidence was avoided in the Clyde on account of servicing difficulties out in the stream.

All independently-routed troop transports were armed against surface and air attack. The *Aquitania* had two 3in guns forward and two 6in guns aft, but these weapons would hardly have been able to cope with an enemy warship, particularly when our size as a target and the thinness of our hull were considered. Our protection against air attack, generally to be expected in the Western Approaches or in the Clyde, was formidable. Apart from the above-mentioned heavier guns, the armaments consisted of Swedish 20mm Oerlikon cannon, Bofors, British Vickers and U.S. Browning 0.5in machine guns. The Vickers and Brownings were progressively replaced by Oerlikons. A rather quaint anti-aircraft device came in the form of rockets to which cables were attached. The trick was to fire them just ahead of low-flying aircraft which were supposed to become entangled in the cables and crash into the sea. The anti-aircraft defences were capable of shooting down a reconnaissance aircraft attempting an attack but the likelihood of a troopship surviving an onslaught by a number of bombers would have been slim, with gutting by fire being the likely outcome.

Our guns were manned by permanent members of the British and U.S. Army Artillery Crews. Army Captain Edwin Seim and First Lieutenant Frank DiCashio were in charge of about 50 men. The British

The British segment of *Aquitania*'s gun crew consisted of volunteers from the Royal Navy and Royal Marines. (Courtesy Lt Cdr Maurice Hobday)

Royal Marines manning one of *Aquitania*'s anti-aircraft batteries. (Courtesy Lt Cdr Maurice Hobday)

gun crew was made up of about the same number of Royal Navy and Royal Naval Reserve Ratings and British Army gunners, all under Lieutenant Commander Hobday. The ratings were known as D.E.M.S. gunners, from the designation Defensively Equipped Merchant Ships and all were volunteers. The definition of a volunteer – 'the fellow who is left standing when all the others have taken a pace back' – did not apply to them. The army gunners came from the Maritime Regiment of the Royal Artillery. On eastbound crossings additional gunners and look-outs were enlisted from the troops to reinforce the permanent crews. Westbound, these reinforcements were frequently unavailable, but fewer lives were then at risk. Captain Seim often complained in his

One of *Aquitania*'s two 6in guns. (Courtesy Lt Cdr Maurice Hobday)

Aquitania's cipher and signalling staff in August 1944 following the departure of Alex Milne. C.P.O. Robertson is second from left, next to author. Apologies to the remainder whose names, but certainly not faces, have become lost from memory after 50 years. (Courtesy Lt Cdr Maurice Hobday)

reports to his U.S. base of insufficient practice shoots and faulty 3in ammunition.

The *Aquitania*'s radar proved to be invaluable during darkness and periods of poor visibility. Although rain squalls and high seas interfered with the efficiency of these early model sets, radar could generally be relied upon to fix a surfaced submarine, and even a conning tower under favourable conditions. A radar contact immediately resulted in the senior watch officer ordering the quartermaster to turn hard away causing the ship to flinch and to take on a steep list. These sudden changes of course, differing markedly from the more gentle zigzag lean-over, induced

Aircraft from North Atlantic bases provided intermittent daylight protection. Here an airman snaps the *Aquitania*, putting in her best effort as always, in a calm sea.

anxiety amongst crew members who surmised the reason. The tension continued until the speed of the ship had put the contact astern and the experience, not infrequent at night, found me attending at the cipher office and the bridge, 'just in case'. The radar operator could determine whether the ship was being followed, and the radio officers might pick up transmissions on the U-boat frequencies should a submarine commander report his lost opportunity to headquarters. Shore monitoring of enemy radio traffic left no doubt we would have been reported several times, as were the *Queens*.

During daylight hours when eastbound, Cunarders were well served by an abundance of look-outs. The bridge personnel consisting of two officers of the watch, a quartermaster, naval signalman and gunnery officer, scanned the seas for the track of a streaking torpedo, and in the Western Approaches the sky received equal attention. The Captain spent many hours each day on the bridge and in the chart room. The look-out in the crowsnest, doing a two-hour watch with binoculars, was selected not only on account of his eyesight, but also for possessing an immunity from seasickness. He was the best placed to make the first sighting in competition with the radar, but with the vessel rolling in a quartering sea, this man would describe parabolic arcs of perhaps 50 or 60 feet once or twice each minute. He was at least spared having to climb up and down an external ladder, the mast being of sufficient diameter to provide internal access. He would race up the 80 steps, a few at a time, as the ship plunged in rough weather.

Additional look-outs with powerful binoculars were posted on each side of the bridge. These men, drawn from the travelling troops, were relieved at short intervals to avoid eye damage. In the Western Approaches, and also when running the mid-Atlantic gap, the gunners were frequently placed 'watch on watch'. Instead of using the rotating 'dog watch' system which involved 8 hours duty every 24 hours, they were rostered 4 hours on and 4 off. German prisoners of war on westbound crossings gave the impression that they would have made the best look-outs of all. When given an airing in the barbed-wire enclosure on deck, their attention rarely strayed from the water. Their patriotism would have hardly extended to welcoming the sight of a torpedo track.

Zigzagging was always observed with the course being altered every few minutes – a special clock automatically buzzing as a reminder to the quartermaster. The Admiralty issued books giving a selection of patterns to be followed hourly, day and night. The extent of each change of course would vary from turn to turn to a maximum of 50 degrees. Practical limitations to the number of combinations of turns made repetition of previously-used patterns inevitable. The zigzag had the effect of increasing the overall distance travelled by an average of 10 per cent.

Other precautions included keeping to a minimum the amount of smoke billowing from our four funnels, and also the degree of its blackness. Complaints from the bridge to the engineers were frequent, but it was usually a case of where there is speed there is smoke. Rubbish, accumulated daily by the ton, was dumped shortly after sunset as a precaution against the passage of a large vessel being detected by a floating trail. At night, total blackout was strictly observed, and troops were kept clear of the open decks as a precaution against a cigarette being lit through forgetfulness. The banning of radio receiving sets was a safeguard against the enemy using a directional device to obtain a bearing. For the same reason, the use of electric razors was prohibited.

The crewing of the *Aquitania*, *Queen Mary* and *Queen Elizabeth* followed the same patterns. Similar round-trip durations together with docking or anchoring together on both sides of the Atlantic facilitated the same arrangements for the interchange of crews between the ships. Leave was granted to crew members after six round-trips, which, after allowing for maintenance periods in New York, worked out at about every six months. A seaman could expect to spend close to three weeks at home and still rejoin his friends in the same ship. Captains and deck officers, being under greater stress, were granted longer periods of leave which could result in an interchange between vessels. During my service in the *Aquitania*, the ship was commanded by Captains Battle, Ford, Fall, Illingworth and briefly by Sorrell and Cove. The majority had also been masters of one or both of the *Queens*.

The Captain alone carried the ultimate responsibility for the safety of the ship and spent many hours, both day and night, on the bridge. His cabin was only a few steps away down a companionway, and at sea he never left these two areas. The Staff Captain was second in command but in practice he engaged in internal administration, and not in navigation. The Chief Officer and the Junior Second Officer were allocated the 4-8 watches in the mornings and afternoons, while the 8-12 watches were the responsibility of the Junior First Officer and the Senior Third Officer. The Senior First Officer and the Intermediate Third Officer were in charge of the 12-4 watches. The Senior Second Officer was known as the Troop Officer, his duties being administrative and supervisory and as assistant to the Staff Captain. Two quartermasters, the steerers of the ship, shared each watch, and also on bridge duty was an R.N. signalman, a bridge messenger, and two binocular look-outs. A gunnery officer, either British or American, also stood watch having direct communication with every gun position. The cipher officer delivered signals relating to route alterations direct to the Captain whether he was on the bridge or in his cabin. The cipher officer was free to visit the bridge at any time, and every afternoon would plot the daily U-boat distribution report from Admiralty on a map in the Chartroom following its inspection by the Captain. The radar shack on 'Monkey Island' was strictly out-of-bounds to all. Two technicians were continuously on duty under John Hartly, a Cunard radio officer who had been specially trained.

The location of cabins for the crew was determined by the nature of the duties combined with their rank. The cabins of the watch officers were on the same deck as the Captain's cabin with the cipher office, slightly aft of this area, as was the wardroom. The communication ratings occupied a former stateroom on the starboard side of 'A' deck, converted to house six wooden bunks. The position was the equivalent to that of the cipher officers' stateroom on the port side. The deck, gunnery and communication officers used the first class dining room on 'D' deck. This handsome room extended across the entire width of the *Aquitania*. The engineer officers had their own mess. These arrangements, with some variations, prevailed in the *Queens*. Accommodation for other crew members was spread all over the ship with cabin sizes ranging upwards from two berth. However, segregation from the troops' accommodation was maintained. Crewmen had a bar known as the 'Pig and Whistle' where the weak British beer was rationed. Cunard officers did not have a bar, being expected to drink their own limited rations of beer and/or spirits in their own cabins. Americans attached to the ships' staff were also provided with this privilege, strictly forbidden in all U.S. ships.

British Customs officers were kept busy in their attempts to control smuggling. Liquor was no problem, U.S. officials being alert to prevent any being taken aboard in New York, and ship's officers having little to spare from their meagre ration. Two hundred cigarettes were permitted but nylon stockings and watches were more prized. I would take ashore expired reciphering tables and superseded publications in a locked bag marked 'confidential', and was never stopped. The ramifications of being caught ruled out any thought by ship's officers of engaging in that line of business.

I was approached on a few occasions by U.S. officers in transit to post letters they had written on the way over to relatives back home, on the ship's return to New York, thus considerably expediting their delivery. I had no doubt their contents were quite innocent but mindful of censorship regulations, I explained I had no idea as to the ship's next destination, which was hardly true but a way of avoiding offence. I had no wish to lecture our Allies.

The intensity of the activity aboard the *Aquitania* during the above six day period in New York, increasing the trooping accommodation by some 3000, the installation of new armaments, kitchens, storages etc. must rank with the efforts of Henry Kaiser in building Liberty ships. Twelfth Avenue was periodically blocked by transports queuing at the entrance to Pier 86 to keep the materials moving in. The twelve-hour work shifts never allowed for a pause in the bedlam which made sleep almost impossible for the crew members of the ship's company who were not involved, and amongst whom I could count myself. Although a drydocking and further maintenance work remained, 'Running the Gauntlet' for the *Aquitania* was about to begin.

CHAPTER 6

May 1943 – Not a Merry Month

The sailing of the *Aquitania* from New York on 10 May 1943 marked her first crossing as a member of the 'independently routed shuttle service'. The participation of the *Queen Mary* and *Queen Elizabeth* up to this stage has been recorded. The remaining major liners already involved, or shortly to join, were Cunard's *Mauretania* (35,000 tons), the *Andes* (26,000 tons) of Britain's Royal Mail Line, the *Empress of Scotland* (26,000 tons) of Canadian Pacific, the *Nieuw Amsterdam* (36,000 tons) of the Holland-American Line and the *Île de France* (43,000 tons) of the French Line. (With the assistance of the U.S., the British managed to keep the latter two vessels out of the hands of the German and Vichy governments, along with the ill-fated *Normandie*.) Mussolini had timed his entry into the war to avoid his two largest liners, the *Rex* (50,000 tons) and *Conte de Savoia*, being intercepted by Britain or being held in New York. The U.S. Naval Transportation Service operated amongst others the *Wakefield* (24,000 tons), the *West Point* (26,000 tons), the *Mount Vernon* (24,000 tons) and *Monticello* (23,000 tons). These U.S. ships trooped mostly in the Pacific but were intermittently brought into the Atlantic during 1944 and 1945. Concurrently with the operations of the shuttle service, slower and smaller troop ships crossed the Atlantic in large convoys with surface escort, bound for the U.K. and the Mediterranean.

At 8 a.m. on Monday 10 May 1943 the Cunard chauffeured Cadillac arrived at Pier 86 to take Captain Battle, Senior First Officer Leslie Goodier, the Senior Radio Operator George Parsons, Alex Milne and myself to the sailing conference at the Naval Control Office at Combined Operations Headquarters on Lower Broadway. The *Mauretania* was scheduled to sail the same morning and her briefing ended shortly after we arrived.

These conferences took place either on the morning of the day of departure or late on the afternoon before. The principal objects were to furnish and to explain a provisional route for the voyage, and to provide briefing on the tactical situation in the Atlantic. A U.S. Navy Captain presided in

Queen Mary running the gauntlet. The troops wearing life jackets at Boat Station drill would have been well aware of the inadequacy of life saving equipment. (Courtesy Imperial War Museum, London).

New York and a R.N. Commander at Greenock in the Clyde. The route, prepared by Admiralty, usually consisted of six or seven legs, involving a change in direction at the completion of each segment. In practice, the track was altered at least twice by signals during the course of each voyage, both for security purposes in the event of a possible leak of information or enemy decrypting of signals, and also for the purpose of positioning the ship as favourably as possible, as the U-boat situation ahead changed from day to day. Other diversions of route were of an emergency nature, such as when cross bearings on a U-boat's radio transmission indicated the ship had been sighted by the enemy, a nearby convoy came under attack, or U-boats had been sighted by aircraft on the track ahead.

The conference provided details of any convoys or independent ships we were likely to encounter in the first two or three days of the voyage; additional information on these matters was provided by signal as the crossing progressed. A map showed the estimated U-boat dispositions in the North Atlantic and we noted on this occasion that about eighty submarines were operating, with many located in the 'gap' – outside the range of air patrol. The weather forecast for the first two days was provided together with the location of any known icebergs likely to be encountered. Routine checking included ensuring we had the current reciphering tables and drum settings, the changeover time from Washington Radio to Whitehall Radio, and our expected time of arrival at the Clyde based on the provisional route.

The briefing included a reference to a heavy U-boat attack which occurred the previous Wednesday, 5 May, when eleven merchant ships were sunk from a convoy sailing from Britain for Halifax. Details were not disclosed at the conference, but this proved to be convoy ONS 5, consisting of forty-three ships, which had set out from the Clyde on 22 April, escorted by two destroyers, one frigate, four 'Flower' class corvettes with two trawlers as rescue vessels. Lieutenant Commander Peter Gretton Royal Navy in the destroyer HMS *Duncan* was the senior officer in charge. On the night of 28 April, it was concluded from the monitoring of nearby radio transmissions that the convoy was being shadowed by four U-boats, and the following morning a merchantman, SS *McKeesport*, was torpedoed and sunk. During the next four days gales raged, and only intermittent air cover could be dispatched from Iceland and Newfoundland. The convoy became badly scattered and the main body was reduced to thirty ships by 3 May.

HMS *Duncan* was compelled to detach to St. John's Newfoundland on account of impending fuel exhaustion, but she was replaced by five escorts from that port. The weather had frustrated further U-boat attacks but while the convoy lay almost hove-to, eleven submarines took up position immediately ahead. Further to the west, an interception line of thirty U-boats lay spaced at intervals of 10 miles, east and south of Newfoundland. By nightfall, when the airwaves were alive with excited exchanges between the U-boat commanders, it was estimated that forty submarines had been homed in, the greatest number to menace a single convoy in the entire war.

Next day, 5 May, chaos reigned. As indicated above, eleven merchantmen were sunk in spite of forty attacks made on U-boats by the surface escorts, and by Canadian aircraft from Halifax and St. John's. The pressure was eased the same night by a decision of the U-boat Command in Germany to divert the main group of U-boats to intercept convoy SC 128 which had set out from Halifax for Britain. The concentration of enemy submarines had been to the degree that two were in collision when passing through a column of ships, and each succeeded in dispatching the other to the bottom. The *Aquitania* sailed four days after this action was broken off.

Troop transports invariably pulled out on time. A full head of steam had been raised and the tugs were ready with their lines attached when our contingent returned from the conference. All hands were to station for leaving harbour. After a series of hoots from tugs and moderated blasts from the ship's siren, combined with a flurry of activity on the dockside as the longshoremen removed the gangways, the lines were slipped, the turbines began to spin, and the reduction gears engaged.

Movement became discernible as the ship commenced sliding out into the stream with the water bubbling and boiling beneath her stern. Within fifteen minutes the tugs had pulled and nudged the ship clear of the dock leaving her facing south down the Hudson. The *Aquitania*, assisted by the current, was underway.

The *Mauretania* sailed in line ahead, having backed out from Cunard's Pier 54, about two miles further down the river. The two vessels gradually gathered momentum and one could imagine a spy or two glancing down from their office towers on the scene below. After the ship passed through the Narrows, Captain Battle's voice came over the public address system. Initially he reminded the troops of some matters about which they would already have been briefed by their officers. Above all there was the danger of fire at sea. He said that the risk of the ship being lost by fire could equal that from enemy action. Smoking was the principal hazard, with the chance of lighted butts thrown over the side being blown back through an open porthole or cabin window. He also warned against the tell-tale trail caused by the throwing of rubbish overboard, the showing of lights, and the use of radios and electric razors and other forbidden items. He emphasised the need for the conservation of fresh water, and the necessity to carry life jackets at all times. Reference was made to the alteration of clocks which were advanced one hour on each of four nights when travelling easterly. (In this respect, the westbound crossing was more popular with the ship's company as it provided an extra hour for recreation or sleeping according to one's inclinations.) The Captain made the position clear that in the event of a man going overboard, under no circumstances would the ship turn about to pick him up. He could have added it would be just as well to take something to read.

We reduced speed approaching the Ambrose Lightship to drop off the pilot. The day was clear and the skyscrapers shrank gradually down to the horizon, disappearing beneath the edge. A U.S. Navy blimp patrolled ahead, and at about 2 p.m. moved out several miles on our starboard beam and dropped depth charges but without signalling the reason or the outcome. The *Mauretania*, having a slight speed advantage, gradually pulled away and by dusk had disappeared ahead. Some passengers were always disconcerted by the absence of surface escort, but by way of minor compensation a Catalina flying boat relieved the blimp and patrolled until sunset. The influence of the Gulf Stream, with increasing temperature and humidity, was now noticeable and flying fish were being scattered by the bows.

The day following our New York departure, Catalinas again provided air cover from dawn until late afternoon, when the receipt of the daily U-boat report confirmed that the concentration of U-boats would not be

A Mariner aircraft of the U.S. 74 Squadron scores a direct hit on *U-128* on 17 May 1943, the day before *Aquitania* reached the Clyde. (Courtesy U.S. Navy)

reached until the third day. About 3 p.m. we had changed course slightly to avoid a waterspout swirling several hundred feet skywards. Viewed from a ship the size of the *Aquitania*, it was nothing more than an interesting natural phenomenon, but from a small, slow-moving craft, the approaching spiral must have been an object of terror.

During the early hours of 12 May, a signal advised that a R.C.A.F. B-17 Flying Fortress from Newfoundland would arrive at dawn and remain for about five hours, and the aircraft's engines were heard for about a half hour before first light. It stayed until 10 a.m., patrolling about four miles ahead from 60 degrees on the port to starboard bows. Another R.C.A.F. B-17 then arrived, continuing the sweep until early afternoon. The U-boat situation report showed that at midnight we would be entering a rectangular area in which twenty-five submarines were calculated to be on interception patrol, but a diversion signal at 7 p.m. routed us slightly towards the southern sector of this area. The ship would now be beyond the range of practicable air cover for the next three days.

Day Four, 13 May, was fine and the sea calm by North Atlantic standards with a breeze 'flicking up a million cats' paws'. Captain Battle informed the troops over the speakers that we would be passing through an area of some danger during the next three days and emphasised the importance of observing all regulations. Lookouts stood 'watch on watch' at defence stations during daylight hours, and the engineers attempted to coax an extra knot out of the 'Old Lady'. During the afternoon our Chief Petty Officer Telegraphist Robertson picked up transmissions on the U-boat frequency which, from the signal strength and the irregular hour, indicated our position was being reported by a

Life rafts dropped from the Mariner aircraft saved the lives of 51 crewmembers who were picked up by USS *Moffitt*. (Courtesy U.S. Navy)

Two bombs from an Avenger aircraft flown from USS *Bogue* about to strike and sink *U-569* on 22 May 1943. (Courtesy U.S. Navy).

submarine commander who had failed to gain position for a shot. The fifth day brought us within 500 miles of the Azores Islands, which were under the sovereignty of neutral Portugal, who denied the Allies the use of an air base.

During the afternoon, we passed several drifting smoke floats, rafts and an overturned lifeboat. Survivors were not to be seen, and at least we were spared the trauma of having to press on, leaving them to their fate. The afternoon U-boat report showed some movement of submarines towards the north, and this might have been the result of the passage of convoys out of Halifax. The following day, we would have to change route also to the north, and no longer could we postpone passing through a concentration of U-boats. It was already apparent that the voyage would extend beyond the expected seven and a half days.

Late in the afternoon, a second boat station drill for the day was ordered. The troops took up positions on the upper decks, on the successive promenade decks below, and on the fore and after decks. At times of crisis they were issued with a box of 'K-Rations' hopefully to sustain them in the event of the ship having to be abandoned, and these were ready for distribution.

I awoke on 15 May, the sixth day, to feel the ship pitching and rolling in by far the heaviest weather we had encountered since leaving Sydney. The wind kept whipping the crests off the rolling green hills and the quartermaster had difficulty in maintaining the course. The woodwork creaked and groaned in protest, but the ship kept ploughing ahead. The barometer descended below 29 inches and the gale was estimated at force 9. At times the vessel listed in excess of 20 degrees, and frequently the screws raced as they lifted above the heaving surface. Under normal circumstances, the Captain would have reduced speed to avoid the risk of damage, but the engineers remained under instructions to deliver maximum revolutions. We would take waves 'green' over the bow, which surged along the foredeck. Worse storms were subsequently experienced, particularly in January 1944, but this would do for my initial crossing. Many troops were seasick and the attendance of army officers in our dining room was down to about one third. This was just as well for the stewards – crockery and cutlery kept sliding around in spite of the damping down of tablecloths, and the raising of the fiddles. About 4 p.m. we received a signal from Admiralty advising a U-boat transmission in the immediate vicinity indicated our position and course had been again reported, but the accompanying reminder to proceed at maximum speed was greeted with something resembling a snort from Captain Battle. The U-boat report that afternoon showed thirty submarines in the area through which we were passing. Sailing alone, we were at least spared the problem of trying to keep station.

The storm subsided during the early hours of the seventh day. A signal advised that a Liberator would arrive at 6 a.m. from Gibraltar and that it would be relieved later by a Catalina from Plymouth. The occasions were rare when aircraft would fly to this area from as far distant as Gibraltar, but we were outside the range of available aircraft from Britain on account of the limited allocation of Liberators to R.A.F. Coastal Command. A heavy fog closed in and shrouded the ocean at dawn, and reduced visibility remained until late in the afternoon. The Liberator did not come into view at any stage, but from time to time its radio telephone transmissions and engines could be heard. On balance, the concealment provided by the fog was more likely to be of benefit than the aircraft having clear visibility. Author Alwyn Jay R.A.A.F., quoting from his records, advised me: 'On 16 May 1943, Flying Officer Cyril Burke R.A.A.F. was captain of a Liberator escorting the *Aquitania*. During the escort, he sighted three U-boats and attacked two, both inconclusively, but at least they were put down'.

At 2.30 p.m. a momentary sighting of an aircraft through a cloud gap was obtained. The glimpse was too brief to establish recognition, and the Captain sounded action stations for the gunners. We were within range of German Focke Wulf Condors operating out of the Merignac Base near Bordeaux, but a few minutes later another sighting together with the flashing of recognition signals confirmed the aircraft was the Catalina.

The afternoon U-boat report predicted we would emerge from the enemy-infested area about midnight, and it showed there had been a concentration of five U-boats in the position directly on our route at 10 a.m. – perhaps an indication of a planned attempt at our interception. About 4 p.m., a further signal asked us to keep a lookout for lifeboats with survivors, and to report their positions after darkness if anything were sighted. We had then reached the latitude of 50 degrees north, and the hours of daylight were lengthening.

A signal in the early hours of 17 May, the eighth day, advised that a Sunderland flying boat would patrol from first light to 3 p.m., when another would relieve. The page and line indicator groups in the signal were corrupt but after about 30 minutes of experimentation, we managed to break it. The priority rating was neither emergency nor immediate, a clear indication that a change of route was not involved. In the morning when James our steward removed the blackout screens from the windows on bringing the tea at 7.30 a.m., I could see the Sunderland patrolling as it reached the limit of its sweep on the port side. The ship was required to report its E.T.A. (expected time of arrival) about 24 hours before reaching its destination unless, because of the tactical situation, it was deemed unwise to transmit. We signalled at dusk that we expected to arrive at Gourock in the Clyde at 9 p.m. the following day.

The ninth and last day of the voyage, 18 May, was fine and the seas were smooth. The U-boat report of the previous afternoon showed the waters of the inner Western Approaches relatively clear of the enemy, except for a few submarines in transit to and from Norway, and air cover was not provided. The long hours of daylight, combined with increasing air patrols, were pushing the majority of U-boats west of 20 degrees West. In the morning we sighted on an opposite course an outward bound O.N.S. convoy of forty ships, well escorted, and soon after we

Sea Hurricane aircraft attached to the Auxiliary Carrier HMS *Biter* saved two convoys in May 1943 from heavier casualties. (Courtesy Imperial War Museum, London)

passed within about 50 miles of the north-west corner of Ireland. About 3 p.m., when approaching the Scottish coast, action stations was sounded. On reaching the bridge, I watched an aircraft, identified by the gunnery officers as a Junkers 88, begin to circle the ship, out of range of the guns. It made no attempt to flash recognition signals in reply to our demands, and we were about to call for fighter assistance when it headed off to the north-east towards the Luftwaffe base at Stavanger in Norway. Apparently it was returning from a convoy-spotting patrol and was either without bombs, or the air crew had no stomach to test our defences. In addition, it may have been stretching the limits of its fuel supply, as it did not attempt to shadow for any length of time. There is the story of a German Focke Wulf Condor distantly circling a convoy for hours, and the senior escort asking the Luftwaffe pilot by lamp to reverse direction as his gunners were becoming giddy. The signal was acknowledged and the German complied.

Landfall occurred at about 4 p.m. when the Mull of Kintyre rose into view on the port bow. Ailsa Craig appeared next on the starboard bow, followed by the Isle of Arran, Little Cumbrae then Cumbrae, all bathed in purple light. Years later, I was reminded of the scene by the lyrics of Alan J. Lerner in 'Brigadoon', especially as this happened to be the month of May:

> The mist of May is in the gloamin'
> And all the clouds are holdin' still
> So take my hand and let's go roamin'
> Through the heather on the hill.

Whilst passing Cumbrae, Spitfire fighters, the star performers in the Battle of Britain, made low runs along both sides of the ship, the pilots waggling their wings in welcome to the troops. We passed through the boom gate at Gourock at 8.30 p.m. and dropped anchor adjoining the fleet aircraft carrier HMS *Furious* and the battleship HMS *Warspite*. The telegraph rang through 'finished with engines' and that was it for crossing number one. Yes – 'getting there had been half the fun' as we were told by Cunard's peace-time slogan!

Few U-boat captains having a significant period of active service survived the war, but Kapitanleutnant Herbert A. Werner, the author of the 1969 publication *Iron Coffins*, was a notable exception. The book reveals the remarkable coincidences of U-boats commanded by Werner, and the *Aquitania*, being in the same areas in the North Atlantic at the same times on seven different occasions. References will be made progressively to these potential encounters, the first of which occurred on the above crossing. Werner had sailed from Brest in *U-230* on 24 April 1943 to join twenty-five U-boats on interception patrol centred around 45 degrees north and 25 degrees west. In his book, Werner describes being involved in furious combat through 12 May to 16 May with escorts of two separate convoys which would have been protecting the above-mentioned HX and SC sailings. I estimate we would have passed in the vicinity of Werner on 15 May, a day on which Admiralty advised our position had been reported. Six submarines were lost by the Germans in these battles, but Werner managed to reach Brest on 29 May with his boat damaged by depth charges.

I undertook the exercise of attempting to complete an expanded picture of the overall combat situation during this particular crossing, by gathering information of the events surrounding the passage of three large convoys which were at sea between 10 May and 18 May. All three travelled easterly from North America to Britain, two taking the 'southerly' route which had been followed by ourselves, and the other the 'northerly' route near Iceland.

The New York section of slow convoy HX 237 sailed on 1 May, and three days later the Halifax portion merged to make up a total of forty-six merchantmen. Ten escorts consisted of the merchant aircraft carrier HMS *Biter*, destroyers, frigates and corvettes with the senior officer aboard HMS *Broadway*. On 7 May, radio transmissions and sightings indicated that about five U-boats were shadowing, and on the tenth day three U-boats were located and attacked. This was the day the *Aquitania* sailed following a similar southern route. During the night of 11 May, a straggling merchantman, SS *Fort Concord*, was torpedoed and sunk. Next day, two more stragglers proceeding separately, the Norwegian freighters

SS *Sandanger* and SS *Brand,* were despatched in a similar fashion by *U-221* and *U-603.*

An aircraft from HMS *Biter* was flown off to investigate, and its failure to return suggested that it had been shot down by one of the U-boats. Numerous enemy sightings were reported by the escorts and covering aircraft, and a combined attack destroyed *U-89* about 700 miles south-west of Ireland. The final success came when a Sunderland from Coastal Command, co-operating with escorts HMS *Lagan* and HMCS *Drumheller,* sank *U-456* in the closing stages of the voyage of HX 237. Fifteen survivors from *Fort Concord* were picked up, and three lifeboats carrying additional crew members were sighted from the air, but could not be located again. These may well have been the survivors the *Aquitania* had been asked to look out for on 16 May. We overtook this convoy on a route slightly to the west on 17 May.

Convoy SC 129, consisting of twenty-six ships, sailed from Halifax on 2 May and on 5 May was joined by escort group B2 from Argentia in Newfoundland. The senior officer was Commander D.G. McIntyre in the destroyer HMS *Hesperus.* He had captured U-boat ace Otto Kretschmer in March 1941. Other British escorts included HMS *Whitehall, Clematis, Gentian, Heather* and *Sweetbriar.* This convoy was also routed to the south and astern of the above-mentioned HX 237.

On 11 May, the day after the *Aquitania* sailed from New York along a nearby route, the British freighter *Antigona* and the Norwegian ship *Grado* were torpedoed and sunk about 300 miles north-west of the Azores. The escorts had received no advance warning of the immediate presence of submarines – the convoy was outside the range of land-based air cover, and, unlike HX 237 about 400 miles ahead, was not accompanied by an escort carrier. German records revealed prior knowledge of the approach of the convoy, and they had established an interception line of eighteen U-boats. Escorts depth charged and damaged the attacker, but it made its way back to base.

The same evening Commander McIntyre sighted and attacked *U-223,* captained by Leutnant Wachter. The U-boat dived, was blasted to the surface, and then fired several torpedoes at its pursuer. Fortunately the acoustic torpedo was not then in operational use, and all missed the narrow target. The destroyer moved in with its 4in guns firing, and, closing at reduced speed rather than ramming hard, her bow rolled the submarine over. McIntyre had put the *Hesperus* out of action for several months the previous year after sinking a U-boat by ramming, and did not seek a full repetition of that performance. Believing the U-boat to be crippled by depth charging and gunfire, and anxious about the convoy, McIntyre rejoined the other escorts. However, as it turned out, Wachter managed to carry out temporary repairs, and eventually made his way back to St. Nazaire. One of his crew members had been thrown over the side by the impact with the destroyer, and was given up as lost. Having bobbed around in his life jacket for many hours, this chap was more than pleasantly surprised when *U-359* happened by chance to break surface fifty yards away. The youth was said to have flabbergasted his shipmates when he turned up at St. Nazaire several weeks later.

The following morning *Hesperus* and *Whitehall* destroyed *U-186*, and next day sightings by escorts and radio U-boat chatter indicated about twelve submarines were in contact. *Hesperus* reported the situation to Admiralty, and the Fifth Support Group consisting of four ships, and including the carrier *Biter*, were detached from the more heavily escorted HX 237 ahead, and ordered to join SC 129. By 13 May, the convoy had come within range of air cover from Britain, and the following day a Liberator commanded by Pilot Officer Gaston of the Royal Australian Air Force, after a six hour flight from Northern Ireland, sighted and sank *U-266* while patrolling ahead of the convoy which reached Liverpool on 20 May, two days after we had arrived at the Clyde. I estimate we overtook SC 129 also on 17 May.

The third eastbound convoy at sea during this crossing of the *Aquitania* was designated SC 130, and it sailed from Halifax on 11 May. Consisting of thirty-seven ships, it was protected by an escort of eight vessels under the command of Lieutenant Commander Peter Gretton in the destroyer *Duncan*. It will be recalled he had been the senior officer of the ill-fated ONS 5 which had lost eleven ships on 5 May. Gretton was subsequently promoted to become the youngest captain in the Royal Navy.

The first six days passed uneventfully with the convoy being covered during daylight by Flying Fortresses of the R.C.A.F. out of Newfoundland, but on the seventh day it became apparent from radio transmissions that four U-boats were shadowing. Shortly before first light on 18 May, Commander Gretton ordered a 90 degree emergency turn to the south, and sightings by a Liberator from Iceland indicated this move had thwarted U-boats prowling the waters immediately ahead.

The interception line was nevertheless widely spread, consisting of seventeen U-boats which had detached from the pack of forty earlier involved against ONS 5. Later the same morning, aircraft sighted five submarines lying in wait on the track and forced them to dive. In the afternoon, four more U-boats were detected on the surface and as darkness closed in, two Liberators from Iceland sighted another six still further ahead. During the next two days fourteen sightings were reported by aircraft, but by the tenth day of sailing, 20 May, the wolf pack had dropped out of contact. The destroyer *Duncan* in company with HMS *Snowflake* destroyed *U-381,* and the same day a Liberator of 120 Squadron R.A.F. sank *U-954.* All crew members of the latter U-boat perished, including the son of Grand Admiral Karl Doenitz, who lost a second son a year later in an E-boat encounter. At this stage many U-boats were returning to base for refuelling and for fresh supplies of torpedoes, and this may explain the apparent lack of zest to attack this heavily defended convoy. Stragglers and independently routed ships were the preferred victims, and statistics compiled at the end of the war revealed that 70 per cent of all sinkings came within that category. During the three months to the end of June 1943, seventy-three U-boats were sunk and sixty-nine were commissioned. Between 10 May and 17 May twelve U-boats were sunk in the North Atlantic by combinations of ships, carrier-based and shore-based aircraft. During the same month, U-boat operational headquarters was transferred from Paris to Berlin.

U-boat commanders were left in no doubt as to what was required of them. After an excellent record as a watch officer aboard *U-124,* Kapitanleutnant Heinz Hirsacker was appointed commander of *U-572* and within three months had sunk three Allied ships. He was ordered into the Mediterranean in early 1943, but apparently by this time things had become a bit much for him. He turned back at Gibraltar on the pretext his hydrophones were damaged, a claim denied by other officers. Found guilty on a charge of 'Cowardice', he appealed to Hitler! The execution by shooting, well publicised throughout the German Navy, took place on 23 April 1943.

Our arrival in Gourock was an occasion for celebration by the ship's company. The majority of members had been away from their homes for almost a year and were keenly anticipating leave, particularly when the rumour spread that the ship would remain in the Clyde for about two weeks. Never again would a Clyde turnaround exceed six days. Milne and I were looking forward to our first visit to London. The Empire ties were still strong and the British Capital was the first attraction for any Australian traveller or serviceman. The sound of the bugle was enough for many to sign up for the first ship – it did not always matter too much who was about to fight whom.

The disembarkation of troops began early next morning, commandeered pleasure steamers including *King George V* and *King Edward VII,* shuttling hundreds of troops at a time from the anchorage to docks at Gourock and Greenock. These operations usually extended over many hours, depending on the weather and the duration of daylight. In winter, the disembarkation could run into a second day. Two tenders, the *Romsey* and *Rowena,* were shared by troops and the crew whilst the *Ashton* was reserved for ship's officers. The G.I.s then entrained for their destinations, usually in England as distinct from Scotland or Wales. Air Force personnel proceeded to their bases mostly in the eastern and southern counties, while the remainder went to army camps, the majority also being located in similar areas and within reach of those ports eventually to be used for the invasion of Europe. The British railway network was efficient and widespread, and the majority of troops moved by fairly direct routes to their training camps. England had not been successfully invaded since William the Conqueror had defeated King Harold at Hastings, after which she had never again been the same. Now it was the Americans who were coming.

CHAPTER 7

London – Then Westward Bound

The *Aquitania* and the *Queens* always anchored in the Clyde Estuary at Gourock, the more convenient and extensive docking facilities at Greenock further up river being put to use by the Navy. The liners needed nearly a half mile of swinging length and a depth of 40 feet when at anchor. Gourock is a small resort 25 miles west of Glasgow. I found the two features of interest were the Bay Hotel, where one could await the lighters in comforting warmth, and a challenging golf course on the heights above the town.

The evening before we had arrived, Captain Battle had invited Milne and myself to join him for dinner. In wartime, he always had meals in his day cabin unless circumstances required him to eat in the chart room, and I was later told by Chief Officer Boston that the Captain had hardly left the bridge during the previous four days. His day cabin was beautifully furnished and sufficiently large to entertain travelling celebrities in peacetime. We were the only guests and were waited on by his 'tiger', the designation for the Captain's personal steward on British liners. The expression reverts to the days of the East India Company when the masters of that company's vessels employed young Asians as their personal stewards, and tried to outdo each other by dressing them in splendid oriental silks, generally striped. Stewards thus came to be known as 'tigers', but eventually the shipowners put a ban on the practice when the competition got out of hand.

Milne and I welcomed this opportunity to talk informally with the Captain. When we were appointed to the *Aquitania*, everything indicated we were going to Britain, but we had no idea what would then happen. However, it had become fairly clear in New York that the *Aquitania*, together with the *Queens*, would have to remain in the Atlantic indefinitely in order to deliver the G.I s across to Europe. If Milne and I were to be discharged from the *Aquitania*, there appeared to be three possibilities for us – appointment to a shore establishment in Britain or the Mediterranean, appointment to a warship as distinct from a transport operating out of Britain, or to return to Australia. We both wished to

Lady cleaners known as 'Mrs Mops' go down on hands and knees to scrub decks during the turnarounds at Gourock. (Courtesy Frank O. Braynard)

remain at sea, but the only sea-going appointment from Britain would hardly be to anything smaller than a destroyer. Specialist cipher officers were not generally appointed to small ships, the medical officer or a watchkeeping officer performing the limited duties required; in most instances, ciphering would be done by the staff of the ship carrying the senior officer of the group or squadron.

The idea of living in the wardroom of a capital ship swinging around a buoy at Scapa Flow or at Rosyth in the Firth of Forth hardly appealed. The protocols seemed a greater threat than the enemy. Humorists in those days claimed that in better British families, the eldest son was brought up to inherit the Country Seat and the Estates in order to keep things together, while the remainder had to make do with the Church, the Royal Navy, or a remittance in Australia if the family wanted to get the chap out of the way. An exaggeration no doubt, but we had no hesitation in deciding that to remain in the *Aquitania* was the 'safest' for us. There was no point in spoiling what promised to be at least a comfortable war. It would be idle to deny that the prospect of being based in New York was another factor which influenced our attitude.

Captain Battle was going home on leave but said he hoped to return to the *Aquitania* after 'a trip off', as it was known. Milne and I had made every effort to establish an excellent rapport with him, and had developed the utmost respect for this merchant service officer. He told us he would inform the representatives of the Ministry of War Transport, who would board the vessel in Gourock, that he would prefer our appointments to be continued. The Ministry took an interest in the delicate balances which existed in these transports involving the Navy, Merchant Navy, the British Army and the Americans. The ships' captains had critical roles to play and the authorities would not want a captain upset by having imposed on him staff outside any expressed choice. These were our hopes, anyway.

Milne and I planned to go ashore first thing in the morning following our arrival to visit the Naval shore establishment at Greenock, known as HMS *Orlando*, two miles upstream from Gourock, and where we expected to learn whatever fate the authorities might have chosen for us. Before we went below for breakfast, two British naval lieutenants had boarded, and as it happened, they had not had breakfast either. One egg a week, a rasher of bacon a fortnight, and a scarcity of butter, sugar, tea and coffee was a good enough reason to turn out early to wolf down the unlimited fare in these ships. Our dining room steward, a man with the delightfully apt name of Springitt, looked after them well. They told us to report to Greenock, then went to have a look around.

At Greenock we were told that a signal would be sent to the Admiralty seeking instructions, and that we should enquire again the next day. The news that the two Australian cipher officers in the *Queen Mary* had been replaced was not encouraging. She had arrived almost four weeks ahead of us. The following day brought no news from the Admiralty, but the Commander at Greenock agreed we could proceed to London on the condition that we reported to Admiralty, and in the absence of other directions, to return to Gourock by 28 May. We needed no further bidding.

The British Government had introduced double summer time and ample daylight remained after we arrived at the Euston Terminal at 9.00 p.m. We had arranged for a room in a small hotel in Chelsea overlooking the Thames, and asked the taxi driver, a very chirpy fellow, to point out some of the Mayfair landmarks. Later we made our initial acquaintance with an English pub. About 2 a.m. we were awakened by a siren which we correctly assumed could only be the alert for an impending air raid. Distant anti-aircraft gunfire and bomb explosions were heard, and next evening the newspapers reported about six aircraft had dropped bombs on the East End with a number of civilians being killed. At that stage the attacks on London were spasmodic, and most residents remained in bed. During the train journey to London, I had struck up an acquaintance with a second officer W.R.N.S. (Women's Royal Naval Service) named

Helen. She was being transferred from Greenock to Gibraltar and was commencing two weeks' leave. Her parents lived about six miles from central London at Golders Green and I readily accepted her offer to show me the sights.

Wartime visitors suffered a disadvantage, with lights dimmed, art centres closed, food scarce and unpalatable, and transport and hotels difficult. Gutted buildings and drably dressed civilians hardly improved the scene. On the other hand, the variety of uniforms of all ranks of the British Commonwealth and Allied forces added colour, and the overall charm of London came through sufficiently to lure me back over the years. Dr. Johnson said it well:

No Sir, when a man is tired of London, he is tired of life; for there is in London all that life can afford.

The weekend is the most convenient time for circulating around Westminster and the city, and on the Saturday we explored the West End. On the Sunday, a friend's parents took Milne and myself motoring up the Thames Valley visiting Richmond, Hampton Court, Windsor, Eton, Maidenhead, Marlow, Stoke Poges, Burnham Beeches and Eton College. At Kew Gardens, an R.A.F. plane flew just above tree level causing confusion before its markings could be identified. People threw themselves down on the grass and then rather sheepishly pulled themselves to their feet. The incident pointed to the terrors of the Luftwaffe attacks on civilians.

The administrative section of the Admiralty was fully operative on Monday morning, and Milne and I made our way there by a roundabout route. Initially we crossed the Thames at Lambeth Bridge to see bombed areas on the other side of the river, and then recrossed at Westminster Bridge. I suppose if one had the pleasant task of introducing a visitor to London, here would be the place to begin. Standing halfway across the Thames facing west, you have on the left the great buildings of the Houses of Parliament with the waters lapping at the foundations. Directly ahead, the huge clocktower housing 'Big Ben' is silhouetted against the outline of Westminster Abbey whilst nearby, for good measure, the formidable warrior, Boadicea, sits astride her War Chariot. That's value for your money whilst standing on the one spot.

We walked along Whitehall to Admiralty Arch, and then into the Admiralty itself. Eventually we managed to see a Commander Banks, a charming man whom I suppose had been brought out of retirement to deal with people like ourselves. He said he had fond memories of Australians in the Battle of Jutland. The Commander could not discover

The Admiralty Tracking Room Team led by Commander Roger Winn. They played a major role in the compilation of the daily U-boat Disposition Report and in re-routing convoys. (Courtesy Imperial War Museum, London).

any record of our existence, but he assumed that the Australian Naval Board would agree with whatever fate the Admiralty should decide for us. He said it sounded as if we were content with our present appointments and should that be the case, then just lie low – advice as good as one could get.

Beneath this building, protected by heavy layers of concrete, the Admiralty 'War Room', also known as the 'U-boat Tracking Room', was housed. On a series of large charts attached to the walls of these bunkers, the locations of all British warships and convoys were plotted. The staff, consisting of naval officers and civilians, continuously adjusted the plots which also showed the estimated positions and courses of U-boats. Signals to ships such as the *Aquitania* ordering emergency changes of route emanated from the constant monitoring of the Atlantic chart, and these independently-routed troop ships received here absolutely number one priority, all in co-ordination with the Western Approaches Command at Liverpool.

Leaving the Admiralty, we returned along Whitehall to Westminster Abbey, probably the greatest single tourist attraction of them all. In the afternoon we toured the City from Temple Bar to the Tower, and ventured briefly beyond into Stepney and Whitechapel. The bomb damage in these slums was appalling, and it was evident that Hitler's National Socialism had no particular sympathy for the poor. Fifteen churches designed by Christopher Wren had been destroyed in the city, although property developers can claim a further nineteen, demolished over the centuries.

Earlier we had visited Australia House in the Strand on the way to the East End to call at the Naval Liaison Office where two Australians, 'Blanco' White and Dick Mims, did so much for the blokes passing through. (After the war, they arranged an annual dinner in Melbourne where naval officers who served out of the U.K. still gather – now ably organised by Clive Tayler and Keith Nicol. A lunch was arranged at Melbourne's Naval and Military Club on 10 May 1995 to commemorate the 50th anniversary of V.E. Day and to which widows and wives were invited for the first time.) A receptionist had intercepted us in an attempt to enlist two Australians to balance the numbers for a dinner being laid on at the Savoy Hotel that night in celebration of Empire Day. The hostess was a Madame De Romero, a former Sydney socialite, who became the wife of the Spanish Ambassador to London. We were not the types to let down our country on Empire Day, especially when the function was held at the Savoy, and we readily accepted the invitation.

The guest list included a number of airmen who had taken part in the raid by Lancaster bombers on the Mohne and Eder Dams a few days earlier, causing, *inter alia*, Dortmund to be flooded and the Krupp rolling mill 50 miles downstream to be put out of action through lack of power for a short period. Wing Commander Guy Gibson, later awarded the Victoria Cross, was amongst those present. The quality of the girls, clearly selected with considerable circumspection, matched the occasion, and Carol Gibbons and his Savoy Hotel Orpheans, the resident orchestra over many years, belted it out in fine style. We were grateful to have had the opportunity to meet these brave airmen. How ironical that the Fascist Caudillo General Franco had done something for the Allies, assuming it was he, and not Madame Ambassador, who ended up with the bill.

The next day, 25 May, was our last in London for this first visit. Milne and I roamed around Mayfair, visiting a number of the famed squares. I bought a new uniform at Geeves in Regent Street and also civilian clothing for wearing ashore in New York on suitable occasions. Books at Hatchards in Piccadilly completed my shopping. We saw the show at the Palladium featuring Tommy Trinder, followed by dinner in Soho. Finally at King's Cross Station we boarded the train for Edinburgh.

We arrived at the North British Hotel at the right moment to fluke a cancellation. Two and a half days here, combined with fine weather and long hours of daylight, allowed plenty of sightseeing. This included a visit to the Firth of Forth where the famous bridge, with twin spans 1700 feet in length, provides the principal road and rail link between the south and the major naval base at Rosyth, and north-eastern cities and onwards to the connections with Scapa Flow. The failure of the Luftwaffe to sever this link, which had taken eight years to build, is another of those mysteries of the Second World War. Capital ships of the Home Fleet lay in view along the north shore of the Firth at Rosyth, poised to intercept any break out by the *Tirpitz* and/or *Scharnhorst* from their Norwegian fjords.

We were expected back at the ship on 28 May and that morning caught the train to Glasgow. The hour there, pending a connection to Gourock, was sufficient to visit the principal shopping and commercial areas of Scotland's largest city. On boarding the ship, no signal from Admiralty awaited us. Greenock had no information, but we were told to assume our appointments remained. The next two days were spent sightseeing in the Clyde area. The river is just over 100 miles in length, rather exceptional in a country where no location is more than about 45 miles from the sea. The 'Tail o' the Bank', opposite Greenock, is the point where the river is regarded as ending, and the Firth of Clyde beginning. From here to Ailsa Craig, where the Firth becomes open sea, the distance is another 60 miles. Eight miles downstream from Glasgow on the right bank, stood the headquarters of the John Brown shipyards where the *Aquitania*, *Queen Mary* and *Queen Elizabeths 1* and *2* were all built.

On 13 and 14 March 1941, this district was subjected to massive air attacks when it was estimated that 12,000 houses were damaged or destroyed, and over 45,000 people made homeless. Employees of shipyards were reported to have turned up for work the next day, after having slept in the fields. Further heavy attacks occurred the following month. Downstream, Clydeside becomes something of a resort area. Opposite Gourock, Dunoon offers a number of comfortable hotels, whilst on the west coast of Ayrshire, where the Firth enters the North Channel, the famous golf courses of Troon, Turnberry and Prestwick humble the addicts of the sport.

German attacks from the air were an ever-present threat. Anti-aircraft batteries were entrenched on high ground on both sides of the anchorage, and gunners remained on the warships to make a significant contribution to the defence. In late 1939, the Home Fleet was transferred to this anchorage for a short period following air raids, and the torpedoing of the battleship *Royal Oak* at Scapa Flow. The occasions were rare when we would lay at anchor without one or more major battle units riding nearby. The British had a talent for selecting heroic and inspiring names for fighting ships as exemplified by some of the aircraft carriers.

A British Convoy Conference attended by ships' masters and navigating officers.

Indomitable, Indefatigable, Illustrious, Glorious, Courageous, Victorious and *Furious* were all inspiring choices.

The sailing conference for our first return crossing to New York took place on the afternoon of Monday 1 June in the convoy conference room of the Naval Control Office at Greenock. The area was designed to accommodate masters of dozens of merchant ships preparing to form large convoys, and also the captains of the naval escorts. However our newly appointed Captain Ford, together with his *Aquitania* contingent, occupied only a small corner of the room. Also present for the first and only time was the ship's newly appointed gunnery officer, Lieutenant Commander Maurice Hobday, R.N.V.R. We were then briefed by an R.N. Commander with a Lieutenant standing by. The conference procedures were similar to those described in New York. We were advised that Liberator cover would be provided on the first two days, that alterations to the route should be expected, and that the weather should improve by the third day. This route showed the provisional track closer to the great circle than on our previous crossing, on account of the reduction of U-boat activity following the German disasters of May, together with the return to bases by many others. Full scale enemy operations were expected to be resumed by August.

Captain Charles Ford (in uniform) was master of both the *Queens* and of the *Aquitania* (twice). Here he is in company with Sir James Bisset, Commodore of the Line and frequently wartime Captain of the *Queen Mary*.

The conference was completed in less than an hour. The Navy was well aware that Captain Ford, with his previous experience in the *Queens*, was not in need of any lecturing. However, that did not prove to be the case for the only three naval officers aboard, namely Hobday, Milne and myself. We had been told to wait behind and were then directed into a smaller room by the Commander. He proved to be an officer of considerable Atlantic experience, and had spent the earlier months of 1943 on the staff of Admiral Sir Max Horton, the legendary Commander-in-Chief of the key Western Approaches Command at Liverpool.

Alex Milne, a member of the peacetime naval reserve, had some seagoing experience, which was more than I could claim. The Commander realised that we needed extensive briefing on the vital importance of our duties and he did not spare himself. Initially he pointed to the importance of secrecy regarding the matters about which he would speak. He knew we must be aware that the large Cunarders and a number of other fast liners were crossing the Atlantic without surface escort, and with only limited air cover. He pointed out that the life saving facilities were inadequate, and that the sinking of one of these liners, particularly one of the *Queens*, would result in enormous casualties, dwarfing any previous disaster at sea. One torpedo would slow the ship at least sufficiently to permit further strikes and perhaps the gathering of other U-boats. The history of torpedoed liners showed a low rescue percentage, particularly as these vessels sank with a steep list towards the side of the strike.

The Commander went on to discuss other aspects of the dangers such as the comparatively flimsy construction of liners compared with warships, their propensity to burn following an air attack, and the cold and tempestuous weather of the North Atlantic. Perhaps by way of atonement, he assured us that our duty to be one of the last to leave the ship would not be to our disadvantage – with the chaos which would prevail in the water, last off would have the best chance. Further, his experience at the Liverpool Command convinced him that these independent troop ships were being protected by every Intelligence resource available on both sides of the Atlantic, and that their movements were continuously monitored against all incoming data. After buying us a drink, he sent us on our way with plenty to think about.

The *Aquitania* weighed anchor and sailed for New York at 10 p.m. on Monday 1 June 1943. Oil and water tanks had been topped and the supply vessels had drawn clear. The mail had been delivered and the army of women cleaners had departed. Captain Battle, as already indicated, had been replaced by Captain Charles Ford who had earned decorations for his service with the Royal Naval Reserve (R.N.R.) in the First World War. An impressive figure, standing about 6 feet 6 inches, he was to become Commodore of Cunard after the war on taking permanent command of the *Queen Elizabeth* – he had had intermittent command of her during the war. The British gunnery officer, Lt. Commander Alan O'Neil, was replaced by Maurice Hobday who now ranked as the senior naval officer aboard. Hobday, Milne, the two American gunnery officers, Ed Seim and Frank Di Cashio, and I shared a table in the dining room tended by Springitt. A sense of humour was common to all, and this was just as well, because many meals were enlivened by injections of international baiting. One of our favourite jibes, when hard pressed, was the conveniently forgotten fact that Hitler had declared war on the United States rather than the reverse. It was all good fun.

Milne and I explained to Hobday the working arrangement we had established with Captain Ford. This was fine with Hobday who had no wish to interfere with our routine at sea, being well occupied with his own men. The British and U.S. gun crews were of about equal strength. Hobday, who out-ranked U.S. Army Captain Ed Seim, was, I expect, nominally in overall command. I cannot recall an instance of any serious friction between them.

This voyage was our only Atlantic crossing when the ship did not carry passengers, either service personnel or civilians. For this reason, Cunard stewards were required to supplement the gun crews. Many defects still remained and required attention after a long absence from a naval dry dock, including plumbing and electrical work, and for these reasons we were about to be laid up in New York for just over four weeks. When westbound the ship would normally carry 2000 to 3000 passengers including diplomats, journalists, politicians, businessmen, repatriated servicemen, returning entertainment groups, and in particular naval and air force contingents, the latter being despatched to man newly constructed ships and aircraft. On several occasions, particularly after the invasion of Normandy, we carried 2000 or more German prisoners of war. Toward the end, U.S. flyers who had completed 30 missions or more were included in the passenger lists, whilst the *Queens* were equipped and staffed to carry American and Canadian wounded. The *Queen Mary*, with the most luxurious accommodation and additional speed, was allocated those passengers who mattered the most.

Reference has been made to the U-boat situation report which was broadcast daily to all British and U.S. Navy ships at sea at about 4 p.m. Greenwich Mean Time. It provided details of the latest estimates of the positions of U-boats in the North Atlantic, based on all scraps of information which could be gathered from Allied sources. This data included actual sightings, direction-finding bearings from radio transmissions, projections of earlier known movements, and intelligent guesses of the highly experienced experts at Admiralty. They would place themselves in the position of their adversaries at the U-boat command in Berlin, and second and third guess their intentions. Information was also supplied by cryptologists who at times were able to decipher German coded transmissions. This operation bore the code name 'Ultra' and is described later.

U-boats broadcasted routine ciphered reports during darkness as often as several times per week, and the transmissions were intercepted by monitoring stations in Britain, Washington, Halifax, Iceland, the Shetlands, North Africa and Gibraltar, and in the latter part of the war at the Azores. Many U-boat captains were careless in conversing with each other on low-power transmitters which could give nearby Allied escorts a bearing. Each listener swung a sensitive directional antenna until the signal volume reached its highest pitch, with two bearings being sufficient for a fix, while additional bearings increased the accuracy. A daylight transmission by a U-boat would normally be made only if the commander had a sighting of an Allied ship or convoy to report.

The daily U-boat report by the Admiralty specified individual U-boat locations where the dispositions were scattered, but in the areas of concentration such as in the 'Gap', only rectangular blocks of twenty or more U-boats might be shown over an area of perhaps 200 miles by 400 miles. Difficulties in making estimates arose from the fact that whereas some U-boats might remain in the same position, others would patrol back and forth along a line, whilst still others might be in transit covering up to 300 miles in a day. The Admiralty did not permit a troopship captain to make any decision regarding a deviation unless the ship had an actual sighting or radar contact. In the event of the report showing a U-boat on our track, we pressed on with the knowledge that we were being monitored ashore 24 hours a day, and that the particular U-boat was in transit or expected to move. We plotted the positions of the enemy on a large map in the chart room and brought it up to date daily.

The preparation of the report began at 7.30 a.m. in the Admiralty Tracking Room in Whitehall, when a group of experts under Commander Roger Winn started sifting through all the intelligence reports received during the previous 24 hours. The code-breakers at Bletchley Park and in New York would report any successes. At 9 a.m., a scrambled four-way telephone conversation between Winn at Admiralty, Admiral Sir Max Horton at the Western Approaches Command at Liverpool, Coastal Command H.Q. and Admiralty Trade Division Convoy Authority took place. All this led to the compilation of the A I G 331 signal, whatever route changes might be necessary for troopships and convoys, and air cover programs for the following day.

Our chief radio officer, George Parsons, was given the time and date based on our estimated crossing of the 45 degree west meridian, when the responsibility for broadcasting signals to the ship would be switched from Whitehall W/T to Washington Radio, or vice versa, depending on the direction of our crossing. Radio reception equipment was inferior in those days, and beyond 1500 – 2000 miles, signals could become indistinct under unfavourable conditions. Signals altering our route, i.e. a diversion, would be given a priority designation of 'emergency' or 'immediate'. An emergency signal received instant precedence at the transmitting station over all other traffic, and would be repeated again within fifteen minutes. The signal would also be broadcast by Whitehall, Washington and Halifax radios regardless of the ship's position. These messages were usually very brief and limited to the immediate action required, with further instructions being signalled later. A signal of 'immediate' priority, as distinct from 'emergency', could be expected to be broadcast within a few minutes if not instantly, depending on the competing traffic.

An error in ciphering rarely occurred in signals of high priority because of checking procedures. If the transmitting operator made a mistake, this was immediately corrected by the originator monitoring the transmission. A major problem occurred when the transmissions were indistinct on account of unfavourable atmospheric conditions, or when individual numerals were incorrectly read or missed altogether by the ship's operator. The ship's call sign always preceded the message text, and a second operator on duty would be alerted to duplicate the taking down of the signal to reduce the likelihood of error. The re-broadcast would also be taken down, and another operator would monitor an alternate transmitting station. I can recall only three of four instances where the deciphering of a signal involving an emergency change of route could not be commenced on account of garbled starting point indicator groups. With one exception, they were cracked within a short time, and before the Captain had decided to break radio silence. A signal of emergency priority was always assumed to involve a route change. These were occasions when you felt you had earned your pay.

Other signals received by troopships at varying times of the day included expected convoy sightings, generally rare, gale and iceberg warnings, and, after August 1944, details of any rendezvous with a pair of destroyers, usually positioned a few hours sailing west of Ireland. Any nearby transmissions in German code picked up by our radio operators were immediately reported to the bridge, but we did not break W/T silence. They should have been fixed also by shore monitors anyway. Our own transmissions were strictly limited and generally confined to the ship's expected time of arrival signal despatched after dark about 24 hours before we were due to reach port. Any enemy sightings, aircraft or U-boat, were to be reported.

U-boat activity had been scaled down during this initial visit to the Clyde. The enemy had sustained heavy losses during the first three weeks of May and in addition, a proportion of the U-boat fleet in the Atlantic was ordered to return to base for crew leave and replenishments. Daylight was now extending up to twenty hours giving submarines only limited opportunities to replace air, and to recharge batteries in comparative safety. Coastal Command reported a total of 213 U-boat sightings during the month.

The Atlantic was not altogether quiet on the day we sailed. Not far from our route through the Western Approaches, one of Britain's foremost sailors, Captain Frederick Walker, in command of the Second Escort Group, was hunting for U-boats. His command ship was HMS *Starling*, and the accompanying *Black Swan* class sloops were *Cygnet*, *Woodpecker*, *Wren*, *Wild Goose* and *Kite*. *Starling* made ASDIC contact with what proved to be *U-202* under Kapitanleutnant Poser, and the 500-ton U-boat, damaged by initial depth charge attacks, descended to 800 feet, a depth believed by the Allies at that time to be beyond the capacity of a submarine to survive. As a consequence, depth charges were not then being manufactured which could be set to explode beneath 500 feet.

After 14 hours, the U-boat's supply of air gave out and Poser was forced to surface. Cannon and machine gun fire, together with depth charges set at a shallow pattern, forced the Germans to abandon ship, and shortly after scuttling charges exploded. *Starling* and *Wild Goose* rescued thirty-one crew members, including Poser. Captain Walker had introduced for the first time the new method of positioning a directing sloop at a distance of about 1500 yards from where the contact could be maintained, and an attacking vessel slowly guided in, only this time to be initially thwarted by the limitations of the depth charges.

We arrived in New York on 9 June after receiving an emergency diversion during the previous night. During this crossing five U-boats were sunk in the North Atlantic, including *U-308* on 4 June by HM Submarine *Truculent*.

CHAPTER 8

New York, New York was a Wonderful Town

In 1987 a book was published by British author Jan Morris with the title, *Manhattan '45*. She portrayed Manhattan during the war years and the years immediately following as perhaps the greatest place to have lived, either before or since. She wrote:

> Ask almost anyone who remembers Manhattan then, and they recall it with proud nostalgia, even if they were poor or lonely; and if their memories have been heightened or bowdlerised by the passage of time, much of the delight they remember was real – a Gallup poll taken at the time found that 90% of New Yorkers considered themselves happy . . . Never again, perhaps, would it possess that particular mixture of innocence and sophistication, romance and formality, generosity and self-amazement, which seems to have characterised it in those moments of triumph.

Only a month had passed since the previous six-day visit to New York but that now seemed long ago and far away. On this second call, I was in a more settled frame of mind and ready to give attention to the multitude of attractions Manhattan had to offer. New York, was then indeed a 'Wonderful Town'. Always acclaimed as the most exciting, vibrant city in the United States, the war had propelled it far ahead of its competitors in that country or anywhere else. The soaring increase in shipping activity out of America's major port, combined with the influx of servicemen on pre-embarkation leave, multiplied its importance. Many leaders of the art world had fled Europe in the middle and late 1930s, and the majority seemed to have ended up in the environs of New York City, turning Manhattan into the world centre of culture – a position, I suppose, it has never lost. 'A filling station for the mind' described it well.

Jobs were available for all, and in spite of some nominal rationing, the shops were crammed with food and merchandise, with only gasoline and the new cars being scarce. Streets were free of crime, and we could walk back to the ship from Times Square down 46th Street at any hour without fear of molestation. Taxi drivers belied their reputations and were pleasant enough, frequently refusing tips from servicemen. The nearest to pornography was published by Esquire Magazine – a pin-up 'Varga Girl' in a one-piece swimsuit. The Hookers were Unhappy, and the Moral Majority would have been hard pressed to rustle up any business.

Every Broadway and off-Broadway theatre was packed nightly, and seats were prized for the Metropolitan Opera and Carnegie Hall concerts in season. The movie theatres consumed as many films as Hollywood could churn out – with hindsight a rather poor collection and often saturated with wartime propaganda. The larger movie theatres featured a live show before the interval built around one of the 'Big Bands', and offering the choice of, say, Benny Goodman, Duke Ellington, Count Basie or Louis Armstrong. I don't know how New Orleans, Memphis or Chicago made out with all the jazz stars in Manhattan. When Frank Sinatra crooned at the Roxy or Paramount, the queues of bobby soxers circled the block.

The popularity of night clubs peaked with the influx of servicemen. Converging from all parts of the country, these young men – the majority of whom had never visited New York before, and who perhaps privately feared they may never again have the opportunity – made a special last-minute effort to enrich their experiences. No purpose would be served in saving money at this stage of their lives – thus it was all stops out, and hang the expense. Taking a girl to a nightclub was an essential part of the final furlough exercise, and couples would queue up for admission behind the red silk ropes in the foyer. The Stork Club, El Morocco, the Rainbow Room, Copacabana, Cafe Society Uptown, the Latin Quarter, the 21 Club, were amongst the places to go.

The social columnists of the two mass-circulation morning papers, the *Daily News* and *Daily Mirror*, were Ed Sullivan and Walter Winchell. Each day they gushed the names of the celebrities spotted the previous night at these and at other favoured establishments, together with the identities of companions, and also details of any conversational pearls which may have been dropped. The impression was given that each columnist had personally done the rounds of all these places. The leading hotels featured entertainment and dancing, with the dinner show beginning at 8 p.m. and being repeated for the supper show about midnight. Amongst the hotels where you could not go wrong were the Waldorf Astoria, Astor, Plaza, St. Regis, Pierre, Sherry Netherland and the Biltmore.

Apart from the night clubs and hotels, high-class restaurants provided the delicacies of every country in the world. Migrants from Europe and the East had brought along their recipes and cooking skills, and the climatic and soil ranges in the U.S. enabled practically all types of exotic foods to be served. The transportation network ensured fresh delivery to

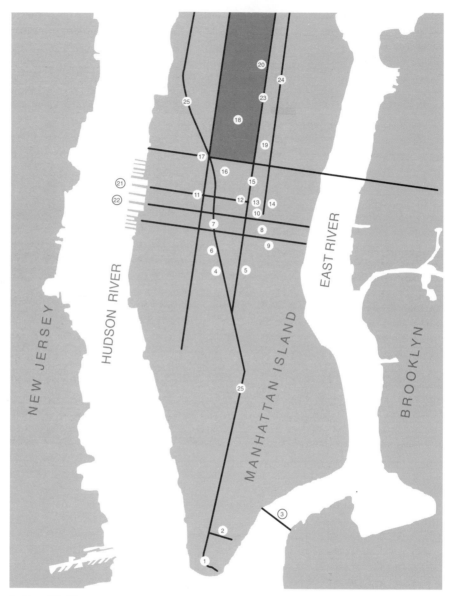

1. Cunard Building
   where sailing
   conferences held
2. Wall Street
3. Brooklyn Bridge
4. Pennsylvania Station
5. Empire State
   Building
6. Metropolitan Opera
   House
7. Times Square
8. Grand Central Station
9. Chrysler Building
10. Harvard Club of
    New York City
11. Madison Square
    Garden
12. Rockefeller Centre
13. St Patrick's
    Cathedral
14. Waldorf Astoria
    Hotel
15. Stork Club
16. Carnegie Hall
17. Columbus Circle
18. Central Park

Locations relate to WWII period

19. Delmonico's Hotel
20. Metropolitan
    Museum of Art
21. Cunard's Pier 90
    (Queen Mary and
    Queen Elizabeth)
22. Cunard's Pier 86
    (Aquitania)
23. Fifth Avenue
24. Park Avenue
25. Broadway
26. 59th Street
27. 50th Street
28. 46th Street
29. 42nd Street

Fifth Avenue, where New York's leading outfitters congregate. (Courtesy Andreas Feininger).

New York produce markets daily. The Chamboard and the Colony were generally rated as Manhattan's best restaurants. All prices in the United States were then subjected to controls supervised by the Office of Price Administration established in 1941, and the O.P.A. imposed ceiling prices on most commodities and services. Accordingly, the above-mentioned establishments were within the financial reach of many servicemen, who should have felt indebted to the administrator, the brilliant economist John Kenneth Galbraith.

Theatre tickets were available at a United Services Organisation office in the Hotel Commodore adjoining Grand Central Station. Theatres allotted a daily quota at about half price, while providing by no means the worst seats in the house. An officers' club thrived at Delmonico's Hotel at 502 Park Avenue. This hotel was conducted in the grand manner, having a history of catering for Manhattan Society over many decades. If somewhat in the shade following the construction of the Waldorf Astoria

Opposite: Manhattan in the 1940s.

A wartime postcard of Times Square. The enclosed roof of the Astor Hotel (upper left) frequently featured the bands of Benny Goodman and Harry James.

further down the Avenue, it nevertheless did itself proud for service groups on the limited and undisclosed invited list. Amongst the Americans there seemed to be a preponderance of West Point and Annapolis graduates. A standing invitation to Cunard Deck Officers was posted in our wardroom and I regarded my 'Supernumerary Deck Officer' classification on the articles as sufficient.

Delmonico's pre-eminence began in the 1870s during the heyday of such notorieties as Jim Fisk, Jay Gould, Andrew Carnegie, John D. Rockefeller, Commodore Vanderbilt and Pierpont Morgan. In his book *The Robber Barons* Matthew Josephson wrote:

> At Delmonico's, the Silver, Gold and Diamond dinners of the socially prominent succeeded each other unfailingly. At one, each lady present, opening her napkin, found a gold bracelet with the monogram of her host. At another cigarettes rolled in hundred dollar bills were handed around and consumed with an authentic thrill. One man gave a dinner to his dog and presented him with a diamond collar worth $15,000. At

a dinner costing $20,000, each guest discovered in one of his oysters a magnificent black pearl.

The Club was said to have been subsidised by groups of wealthy parents of the 'hostesses' who adorned the place. Located on the upper East side, it was surrounded by the apartments of New York's rich. Many hostesses were recent graduates of Ivy League colleges such as Smith, Radcliffe, Vassar and Wellesley, all strictly New England. The Club operated from 8 p.m. until midnight, with light refreshments including beer provided free of charge.

A noticeboard displayed invitations to private homes, both in the suburbs and in the country – it was simply a matter of arranging for a phone number to be called, of taking a train to a station, and there to be welcomed by your hosts. On account of the attractions of Manhattan, and the hospitality of the Seim family in Connecticut, I did not take advantage of these widely accepted invitations. However, I frequently visited the Club and formed a number of out-of-hours friendships.

During this period, Delmonico's most 'famous' resident was Peggy Hopkins Joyce. During the 1920s she was known as the 'Toast of the Town' and the 'Belle of New York' after becoming the leading showgirl in Earl Carrol's 'Vanities' and later Florenz Ziegfeld's 'Follies'. Manhattan playboys outbid each other for front row seats and she had become quite rich after several marriages. She was Damon Runyon's yardstick to measure the qualities of his Broadway dolls. Aussie Austin, then our junior first officer, tall, good looking, a splendid piano player and bachelor with a cultured accent, caught her eye in Delmonico's foyer one evening and never looked back. A few of us were occasionally fortunate enough to be asked to a party in her lavish penthouse. Although her beauty was beginning to fade, Aussie was kept busy as her escort when her 'English Captain' was in town. His wardroom stories of Manhattan celebrities were not to be missed. All this ended when Aussie married his attractive English wife, Jean, in March 1944.

Entertainment was available to non-commissioned ranks at other clubs. The British naval ratings and merchant seamen were poorly paid, but they were able to enjoy a similar type of hospitality at the Union Jack Club or Stage Door Canteen. Whereas the American servicemen attending clubs were usually in transit, the Cunarders kept returning time and again, and this enabled many officers and crew to make arrangements which gave them a break from shipboard life. The Anzac Club in New York catered for Australian and New Zealand Navy and Air Force personnel in transit to the U.K., and recreational facilities were provided for all ranks. U.S. troops serving in the Pacific were similarly entertained

When launched in 1913, the *Aquitania* was the world's largest and longest ship
and the Woolworth Building, in lower Manhattan, the world's tallest skyscraper.
Here an artist brings them together, showing the *Aquitania* gliding up the
Hudson towards Cunard's Pier 86.

when on leave in Brisbane, Sydney and Melbourne to the extent that
wartime disruption and limited facilities would permit.

Milne and I were fortunate in being accepted as honorary members of
the Harvard Club of New York City in West 44th Street. We had met by
chance in the St. Regis Hotel a Lieutenant Commander in the U.S. Navy,
Henry Reed. He invited us to lunch at his club where we were introduced
to a number of fellow members, and a week or so later we received invita-

The *Queen Elizabeth* is dwarfed by the skyscrapers of Manhattan as she lies docked at Cunard's Pier 90. 'All that life has to offer within the throw of a stone'. (Courtesy Andreas Feininger).

tions to take up honorary membership. The facilities included a swimming pool, squash courts, a gymnasium, bars, dining and reading rooms. The Club proved to be an invaluable retreat during the next two years. Life in New York, pausing only between 4 a.m. and 8 a.m., was hardly conducive to physical fitness, and consequently we made use of the pool and courts.

The contrast between the wartime U.S.A. and Britain was quite stark. Blackouts, food and clothing shortages with limited choices,

U.S. motor vehicle manufacturers converted many plants for the production of weapons. This typical advertisement was placed by Oldsmobile.

accommodation and transport difficulties, enemy bombing and subsequently rocket attacks on London, together with uniforms everywhere, all added up to a constant awareness of the war. In the United States, apart from occasional blackouts in the early months of 1942 when U-boats were enjoying their 'happy times' off the eastern seaboard, and also during air raid 'practice drills', lifestyles of the civilians were hardly affected. Thus although the horrible realities of war were not evident in such cities as New York, Washington or Boston, the Government and business did their best to focus public attention towards the conflict.

The press and radio stations gave full news coverage as far as censorship would permit, naturally with successes exaggerated and losses minimised. In the entertainment areas, newsreel featured war footage and Hollywood complied with plots featuring war heroes whilst the girlfriends and wives scorned the draft-dodgers back home. 'Don't Get Around Much Any More' remained on the top of the popular recording charts for many months. Advertisements for the purchase of War Bonds appeared with every turn of the head or the page, featuring 'Uncle Sam' in top hat with arm beckoning. The Government saw these investments as vital in soaking up huge amounts of surplus cash, generated by full employment, price control and overtime. The success of this campaign was evidenced by the absence of inflation and black markets.

The public was constantly reminded of the contribution made by women towards the war effort. Advertisements for recruits for the W.A.C.s, W.A.V.E.s and the Red Cross showed the girls hard at it, their faces aglow with pride and satisfaction. 'Rosie the Riveter' handled with ease heavy equipment, joining plates in shipping yards. Servicemen were invited to take part in comedy routines at the night spots and drew cheers when they announced their home state. Thus for us the luxury of being ashore in the U.S. was not altogether an escape from the thought that soon we would be back on the job.

Our return to New York on 9 June 1943 was the second of what would become a total of twenty-one visits, the remaining six westbound crossings being to either Halifax or to Boston. The heat and humidity of summer now blanketed the eastern seaboard, and when on the move outdoors, it became a matter of two shirts and two showers each day when possible, with our steward James being kept busy producing clean white uniforms. We were to remain in New York until 8 July, a period of just over four weeks. During the second week, the ship was vacated for three days for fumigation with cyanide gas, and all officers were accommodated at the Belmont Plaza Hotel on Lexington Avenue. Along with some others from the ship, I was invited to a cocktail party at Essex House, a forty-storey private hotel on Central Park South, an avenue known as millionaire's row with views across the Park. Later in the evening, we reciprocated by taking our hostesses – girls from Delmonico's who had used one of their parent's apartments for the party – to the nearby Persian Room of the Plaza Hotel for the supper show.

Ed Seim, the U.S. Gunnery Officer, introduced me to the Biltmore Hotel, an establishment then of quiet comfort and distinction adjoining Grand Central Station. The timber panelled men's bar attracted Ivy League commuters for those two or three whiskies after a hard day on Wall Street, before facing up to the train journey home to Westchester County. Here we ran into two deck officers from the *Queen Elizabeth*, which had docked that morning, and we relaxed to the sound of the palm court orchestra. Jay Gatsby could have walked in without a head being turned.

Next day the *Aquitania* sailed across the Hudson to the 1080-foot graving dock at Bayonne, New Jersey, where the ship was to be laid up for an estimated six days. It did not take long to discover what there was to know about dry docking and the news was all bad. For a start, a ban applied to the use of the plumbing system, and to perform one's ablutions it was necessary to patronise the dockside facilities. The ship's elevators were closed down, and although a walk from 'A' deck to 'F' deck, followed by a steep descent down a gangplank could be handled, the return journey several times a day was a bit thick. It was interesting to view the ship's rounded hull, the four huge propellers and rudder – but that fascination quickly wore off.

The difficulty in reaching Manhattan from this isolated area was another problem. Fortunately we learned from his tiger that the Cunard

Great care was exercised in allowing this 'Alien Seaman' ashore in the U.S.

car was calling for Captain Ford, and the Master agreed to give Milne and myself a ride. After two nights at the Belmont Plaza at our own expense, we trained with Ed Seim to spend a week with his parents at their home outside Bridgeport whose metropolitan area has been rated the wealthiest, not only in the State of Connecticut, but also in the whole of the U.S.

Ed Seim was an engineering graduate of the Massachusetts Institute of Technology, an excellent officer and a kind friend. I was to stay with the family many times and was always made to feel most welcome. Ed's father, Harry Seim, was the President of the Bryant Electric Company, a division of the Westinghouse Corporation. His plant was engaged in manufacturing components for the Navy and Air Force, and operated three shifts, seven days per week. He took us on an inspection tour of the plant and we were impressed by charts showing production figures, the few hours lost through accident and sickness, and the purchases of War Bonds. Industrial disputes were unknown.

The Brooklawn Country Club was a highlight of this and of subsequent visits. The manicured fairways were bordered by virgin New England woodland and the clubhouse provided additional sporting facilities and fine meals. Brooklawn hosted the 1987 U.S. Senior Open which was won by Gary Player from Doug Sanders. Apart from golfing, we motored around in the family Cadillac, with charming contemporaries of Ed's girlfriend squaring up the numbers. We made visits to Milford Haven on Long Island Sound where we swam and sailed. Little did I realise that forty years and two months later at Newport, just a few hours sailing away to the north east, Australian yachtsmen would wrest the America's Cup from the frantic grasp of the New York Yacht Club.

Returning to New York, we found the ship had been delayed in dry dock, and it was back to the Belmont Plaza. I had become friendly with a girl I shall here call Jenny who shared an apartment with two other girls on East 48th Street. She worked as a secretary in a Wall Street office and was on the roster at Delmonico's one or two nights a week. Jenny was frequently my companion when I visited the night-spots, and often we moved around as a group with one or both of the girls from the apartment and their respective boyfriends. The girls invited us on occasions to dinner parties, and my friendship with Jenny, combined with my membership of the Harvard Club, was to provide a welcome change from the surroundings of the ship.

One of the hectic evenings began with dinner at the Starlight Roof of the Waldorf Astoria, where Xavier Cugat was playing. At midnight we went to the Astor Roof where Harry James had the billing, and finally I was introduced to Jack Dempsey's Bar on Broadway. During this turn-around, I saw several Broadway plays, the show at Radio City Music Hall featuring, as always, the Rockettes, and I joined a conducted tour of the Rockefeller Centre which included the view from the summit of the 70 storey R.C.A. Building. On another visit to the Astor Roof, the Benny Goodman Quartet with Teddy Wilson, Lionel Hampton and Gene Krupa had replaced Harry James, and while we were having dinner, his group broadcast live for a half hour on the C.B.S. radio network.

On 6 July I made my first of many visits to Washington. The British Navy operated there under the name of the British Admiralty Delegation, and kept tabs on the movement of British ships and naval personnel in and out of the country. I caught the 8.30 a.m. streamliner out of Pennsylvania Station at 34th Street. This was a crack train called the Congressional Limited, and completed the journey in three hours and forty minutes with stops at Newark, Trenton, Philadelphia, Wilmington and Baltimore. The Navy met the expense of providing a chair in a first class car. On each side of a centre aisle, a single swivel arm chair spun in a complete circle, seemingly a considerable waste of space. Traditional Pullman porters unobtrusively were at hand to produce any requirements.

The enormous lengths of freight trains with hundreds of cars is a feature of the U.S. railroads which fascinates visitors. In wartime, the cars of the different railroad companies all became shuffled together, and it must have taken years to sort them out. In a single train, a panorama of romantic names flashed by the intrigued onlooker – Union Pacific ... Atchison, Topeka and Santa Fe ... Chicago, Burlington and Quincy ... Southern Pacific ... Denver and Rio Grande ...

The train ground to a halt and simmered down at Union Station a few minutes after midday. After surviving the initial blast of heat, I made my way to the British Admiralty Delegation offices where, after being asked a number of questions to ensure all was well aboard the *Aquitania*, we had a Gordons or two and then a nice lunch. I was scheduled to take the 5 p.m. train back to New York, but sufficient time remained for hurried visits to the buildings of Congress, the White House, Washington Monument and the Lincoln and Jefferson Memorials. This sampling was sufficient to whet my appetite for the visits which lay ahead.

I attended the sailing conference in New York the following day and we set out for the Clyde on 8 July. Sailors in port, particularly in wartime, tend to follow the tradition of concentrating on drinking, girls and spending their money in pursuit of that good time which in Manhattan, could hardly be described as elusive. You were expected to put yourself in a position of having no regrets for things left undone should something go wrong. Mae West said it best – 'Too much of a good thing can be wonderful.'

CHAPTER 9

The 'Race Against Time' Accelerates

The *Aquitania* made two round-trips to the Clyde from New York between 8 July and 23 August 1943, followed by a further five weeks in New York. The sailing conference on 7 July revealed that U-boat activity was increasing, although September came before the numbers of submarines approached the figures of the previous May. The US escort carriers, *Bogue, Core* and *Santee,* flying Wildcat and Avenger aircraft, had a number of successes against the 'Milch Cow' supply U-boats operating on the convoy routes to North Africa and in the Atlantic 'Gap'. Hitler demanded the production rate of U-boats to be increased from 20 to 40 a month, being determined to fight back after the heavy losses of the April and May period. This goal was never achieved but an average of about 30 was reached.

On the first trip, the passengers included 500 W.A.C.s (U.S. Women's Army Corps) whose presence guaranteed some mental diversion for the troops. The Atlantic was benign, but the long hours of daylight and in particular a number of cloudless moonlit nights made watchkeeping trying for the lookouts. The absence of surface escorts continued to puzzle troops and other passengers. Press photographs, newsreels and propaganda films, together with their understanding of the composition of all troop convoys, led them to expect that a rendezvous with escorts would lie just over the horizon. Doubts grew as the hours and then the days passed, but security would not allow a disclosure that these ships invariably proceeded independently. The presence of aircraft sweeping our track ahead for several hours on about three or four days of each crossing provided some reassurance that we had not been abandoned altogether by the shore authorities. On this particular crossing early morning air cover was provided for the last two days. Reference has been made earlier to a series of possible encounters with U-boat Captain Herbert Werner. Werner in *U-230* had sailed from Brest three days before our New York departure, headed for the Chesapeake Bay area. We had been routed well to the south of the most direct route and I estimate that on 12 July we would have passed not too far distant from Werner's track

Lieutenant Ewan
Scott-Mackenzie R.A.N.V.R. on
the bridge of HMS *Hurricane*.

in the Azores area. We arrived at the Clyde on 15 July with the usual escort of Spitfires as we sailed up the estuary. During the preceding two weeks seven U-boats were sunk in the Western Approaches, all by aircraft including two R.A.A.F. planes working in co-operation with the famed HMS *Starling*.

The day following our arrival I went on leave with a friend from Melbourne, Lieutenant Ewan Scott-Mackenzie. He had invited me to accompany him to visit his uncle, the Reverend Johnston Oliphant at the latter's manse in the estate of the Marquis of Linlithgow, located 20 miles west of Edinburgh in West Lothian. Scott Mackenzie was an executive officer in the destroyer HMS *Hurricane*, a convoy escort in the Atlantic. His father, a Surgeon Captain in the Royal Australian Navy, had taken part in the Battle of Jutland. The Marquis was appointed Viceroy of India from 1936 to 1943, and at the time of our visit had not yet returned to his domicile at Hopetoun House, a residence on a grand scale completed in 1680. The estate encompassed hundreds of acres, capturing magnificent views over the Firth of Forth and the Forth Bridge. We spent three days roaming the grounds which embraced a deer park, a polo ground and trout streams. The head gamekeeper sanctioned the shooting of rabbits for the table.

The *Aquitania* sailed for New York at 10 p.m. on 21 July 1943, the hour being in accordance with the practice of reaching the open Atlantic before daylight. Sailing times from New York varied little, the U-boat threat off the east coastline having declined since the tanker disasters of 1942. Our passenger list included 2000 German prisoners captured in North Africa, together with a naval draft despatched to commission new destroyers. These prisoners were isolated into manageable groups in the orlop decks, but were allowed on an open deck behind barbed wire to exercise and smoke for an hour or two each day. They were closely guarded by British soldiers with tommy guns very much at the ready – but the prisoners' demeanour did not suggest they were anxious to engage in an insurrection in order to steam back to Germany for another round of infantry warfare. Their manner, on the contrary, betrayed apprehension as their eyes swept the ocean searching for those U-boats they had been told infested the Atlantic. With few exceptions, they inhaled cigarettes continuously, suggesting they had not heard the habit was detrimental to their health! A number were allotted kitchen and cleaning duties. Many could speak some English and they were always aware of their destination.

This voyage led to a subsequent coincidence when in June 1973, my wife and I, touring by ourselves, spent an evening in the lounge bar on the upper floor of the Hotel Rossya, overlooking Red Square in Moscow. Eventually we became part of a convivial group of about ten – all Russians except for two eastern Europeans – and we busily engaged in buying each other drinks. These people were anxious to improve their English, and they made us feel quite welcome, both on this account, and also because I had several packs of Camels I had brought in from Singapore on an Aeroflot flight. There was a chap from Dresden in East Germany attending a convention, and I complimented him on his good English. He hesitated somewhat when asked where he had learned it, then replied he had been in the United States from 1943 to 1946. It transpired he had been captured in North Africa and had travelled to the U.S. in the *Aquitania* in July 1943.

On 24 July a 'Milch Cow', *U-459*, was sunk to the south of our position whilst on passage to Brest. Caught on the surface by a Leigh-Light Wellington, the U-boat crew fatally damaged the aircraft moments before its bombs were to be released. Before plunging into the sea, the bomber struck the U-boat, tearing away its guns and leaving on the deck two bombs set to explode at 30 feet. Slipping over the side, one bomb exploded beneath the stern, wrecking the rudder and causing a fire. Captain Mollendorf ordered 'abandon ship', set scuttling charges, and went down with his U-boat. A British warship saved 45 survivors, all from the U-boat except for the Wellington's rear gunner, Sergeant A. Turner.

Summer weather occasionally induced U-boats to rendezvous in the Atlantic beyond the range of Allied aircraft. (Courtesy German Federal Archives, Koblenz).

On the following day, 25 July, we received a signal of immediate priority which proved to be indecipherable. It was necessary to break radio silence for a corrected version, which ordered a change of route on account of four U-boats being in the area ahead. The following day we learned a fast unescorted merchant ship was torpedoed close to the route from which we had been diverted. A U.S. submarine was sighted crossing our tracks at dusk on 27 July. A warning had been broadcast, but taking no risks, the Captain gave it a wide berth. On 28 July we reached New York and unloaded the prisoners into lighters at the harbour entrance. They smiled for the first time.

We remained in port for seven days of which I spent three with Ed Seim at Bridgeport. Golf, swimming and country clubbing were the order of the day, with parties nightly at the homes of Ed and his friends. Back in Manhattan, we spent the remaining two days trying to cool off by visiting the beaches at Coney Island and Rockaway.

The ship sailed for the Clyde on 4 August, loaded down as usual with 8000 troops, including about 50 Australian airmen who had completed their training in Canada. At about 4 p.m. we passed the *Queen Elizabeth* on an opposite course, inward bound. On the second day out, at tea in the wardroom, one of the junior navigating officers mentioned that shortly we would be passing close to where the ghostly hulk of the 46,000-ton White Star liner *Titanic* lay below on the ocean bed. His grandfather had been a steward in the Cunarder, ss *Carpathia*, which on 14 April 1912 had heard the *Titanic*'s S.O.S., and was the first ship to reach the scene. Our navigator had heard the grandfather tell his stories dozens of times about the behaviour of the survivors during the two-day journey to New York. Recriminations and accusations were widespread amongst the 705 passengers and crew members saved out of the original total of 2218. Cunard and White Star had merged in 1934, and some of our officers had their own anecdotes which had been passed down. The water had been glass calm and the visibility clear when a lookout in the *Titanic*'s crows nest had sighted the iceberg at about 11.30 p.m. Shortly beforehand, a sudden drop in temperature had been noted on the bridge, but Captain Smith had pressed on at maximum speed. The order 'hard to port' was given too late to prevent 300 feet of the hull on the starboard side being opened to the sea. At 2.15 a.m., nearly three hours after the collision, the ship sank, drowning 1513 passengers and crew members. The original theory that a sharp edge of the iceberg had sliced the plates was disproved in 1986 by photos of separated plates where rivets had popped on impact. Only four of the 143 women travelling first class lost their lives, whereas 81 of the 179 women booked third class perished. All children except one in the first and second classes were saved, while 23 out of 76 in the third class were drowned. Cynics claimed that more than anything else to be learned from the catastrophe was the wisdom of travelling first class. The same lesson could well be applied to a troopship. Just make sure you become an officer before sailing. The pulling-away of only partly filled lifeboats added to the subsequent recriminations. The pay of crew members who survived – about two shillings per day – automatically stopped when the ship sank. For readers who enjoy gallows humour, there is the story of the parson rushing to the bridge of the *Titanic* and calling to the Captain: 'The passengers are panicking – what shall I tell them?' The Captain, mindful of the darkness, replied: 'Say we are within three miles of land.' The Chief Officer – standing nearby – frowned, and after the parson had raced away, asked the Captain why he had lied to the reverend gentleman. Replied the Captain: 'What I said is quite true – I just failed to mention the direction is straight down.'

The anecdotes in the wardroom gave us in the *Aquitania* something to think about. The *Titanic,* of similar size, construction and vintage, had sunk in a sea as calm as a mill pond with lifeboat accommodation for all passengers and crew. Everything was brand new, the crew, including the radio operators, well trained, and the liner remained afloat for almost three hours before sinking. The first rescue ship, the *Carpathia*, arrived at 4 a.m., four and a half hours after the collision, yet in spite of all these rather favourable circumstances, slightly less than one third of the total of passengers and crew was saved. The discovery of the wreck further prolonged public fascination with this tragedy. Then came the film!

Back in the *Aquitania* – on 9 August at about 11 p.m. the radar picked up a contact about 4 miles dead ahead. We turned away hard to port, and the radar showed the contact moving with us. Continuing to turn we changed course to west-north-westerly. The contact followed, but we shook it off after about 30 minutes and resumed our original course.

On 5 August 1943, the day after we had sailed from New York, Winston Churchill had set out from Gourock for Halifax in the *Queen Mary*, escorted by a number of cruisers. The Prime Minister was accompanied by all his chiefs of staff and a large entourage, to attend the first Quebec conference with President Roosevelt. When Churchill wished to send a signal, one of the escorting cruisers, for security reasons, would divert 50 miles or so from the route to transmit, and then rejoin the convoy. Churchill changed plans and returned to Britain after the conference in one of the cruisers of the squadron after the *Queen Mary* had been immobilised in Halifax for 28 days. In spite of secrecy precautions, almost every Haligonian was reported to have turned out to welcome and later to bid farewell to the Prime Minister at the dock. Three U-boats were sunk during our crossing, two by aircraft from USS *Card*.

The *Aquitania* remained in the Clyde from 11 August to 16 August, and during this period I spent two nights at the Caledonian Hotel at Dunoon, a resort which overlooks the anchorage from the north-west side of the estuary. Bicycles were available for hire and I rode several miles down the coast, making the most of the last of the summer weather. On the return crossing, we carried 1500 Royal Air Force trainees destined for Canada and arrived at New York on 23 August. The scheduled stay of five weeks was to enable all the outstanding work to be completed, and for the ship to be prepared for continuous service through to the following April.

Milne and I had ourselves well organised when the ship was in port. Lieutenant Commander Hobday took over the discipline and supervision of the signalmen and coders, leaving us free to come and go as we wished. Surprisingly, I did not find the matter of money any great problem. The rates of pay for Australian officers were about midway between the British and U.S. scales, and being domestically unburdened, I escaped pay deductions for dependants. As the result of some administrative error – or so Cunard later claimed – Milne and I were not being called upon to pay for our messing. Seagoing was a way of life to save money, and my only expenses afloat were for the rationed liquor, cigarettes, chocolate and tipping. Officers were allocated a weekly ration of a bottle of whisky or gin, plus a case of U.S. beer. Whisky cost $1.20 or six shillings, and gin 80 cents or four shillings per bottle. I cannot recall the price of the beer, but it was virtually a give-away, which we Australians, used to a stronger brew, claimed it ought to have been. U.S. cigarettes cost 5 cents per pack, the same as chocolate bars. Merchant Navy officers and crewmen received a 'War Risk Allowance', rising to the equivalent of 80 dollars per month – a necessary addition to their meagre rates of pay. In the 1930s a Cunard First Officer received about 5 dollars per day – when ashore and between ships, this was reduced to about 50 cents.

Apart from the occasional trip to London or Edinburgh, there was little on which to spend money in Britain. Thus I would return to New York with the jingle of money in my pocket, financially equipped to follow my inclinations within reason. Price control, officer club facilities, the waiving of cover charges at night-clubs and reduced prices for theatre tickets, were all contributors to an agreeable lifestyle. As things turned out, I spent most of my time ashore with Americans, but had little difficulty in keeping pace with their spending habits. Max Frost, an Australian Purser with Cunard, and myself were invited to use the golfing and other facilities of the Rockland Country Club in New Jersey – about an hour's drive from Manhattan, and I became a regular visitor. Many Australians are horse racing followers, and I occasionally attended a meeting at Belmont Park. Located on Long Island, about 20 miles from Manhattan, it is regarded as the premier racing complex in the U.S.A.

The National Tennis Championships were contested during the first week in September, and I watched play on the last two days at Forest Hills on Long Island. The performers included Jack Kramer, Frank Parker and Pancho Segura. One of the younger hostesses I had met at Delmonico's Club, Sarah, persuaded me to take a busman's holiday, and we travelled by riverboat up the Hudson to Poughkeepsie where she had just completed her final year at Vassar, a leader amongst New England's ladies' colleges. On the way we had passed Sing Sing Prison and the West Point Army Academy.

The *Queen Elizabeth* docked on 10 September and her Assistant U.S. C.O. Troops Major Frank Rollins, who was serving in the *Aquitania* when I first joined her in Sydney, threw a party for his friends from both ships at his parents' home at Van Cortland Park. Also invited were a number of members of his fraternity at Princeton where he had been studying at the outbreak of war. Over a hundred guests assembled and I expect his neighbours wondered where he had collected this hotch-potch of Yorkshire, Lancashire, Scottish, Cockney, Irish, Welsh, West Country and Australian accents. On Thursday evening, 30 September, 8000 troops including about 200 Australian airmen and 300 W.A.C.s embarked, and we sailed at 10 a.m. next morning. The refitting programme had now been completed and seven long, cold months of continuous Atlantic crossings lay ahead.

During the period covered by this chapter, from 7 July to 30 September 1943, thirty-two U-boats were sunk, twenty-six by British and U.S. aircraft and six by British ships. Carrier aircraft claimed six. An estimated 500,000 tons of Allied shipping was lost in the North Atlantic. At this point of the war the three Cunarders would have carried close to 300,000 troops to Scotland, having made some twenty-five eastbound crossings. The contribution of the *Aquitania* at that stage was smaller on account of a late start.

CHAPTER 10

New German Naval Technologies Bring Allied Response

At the sailing conference on 30 September 1943, the submarine plots showed that the number of U-boats operating in the Atlantic had continued to increase after the summer recall. The long hours of daylight had ended, and the accumulated production of submarines during the previous three months had been moved out into the Atlantic from the Baltic shipyards. Crew members who had survived the spring onslaughts had been recuperating in Norway and at the French Atlantic ports, and now were resuming their inevitably brief careers. Sailors in the newly commissioned submarines were usually aged less than 21 years, with the commander being under 30.

U-boats were now supplied with a new type of 'smart' acoustic torpedo which the Germans called the 'Wren' (named 'Gnat' by the Allies). The conventional torpedo was steam driven, leaving a 'track' or 'wake', and had alternative settings giving it a capacity to travel 15,000 yards at 28 knots, 10,000 yards at 34 knots or 6000 yards at 46 knots. These torpedoes were kept on course by gyroscopes, and so could be set to travel in a straight line, while others 'searched' in a pre-set pattern. Torpedoes could also be set to explode at the end of a run should they miss or stop short of the target.

The 'Gnat' was propelled by electric batteries which brought the advantage of eliminating the self-revealing wake when it performed its special function of homing in on the tone produced by a ship's propellers. Two sound receivers were inserted into the 'Gnat's' head which registered the propeller noises. The torpedo's rudder would automatically change position to direct the missile towards the side where the noise was the louder, thus chasing the stern in an eel-like fashion. A disadvantage was its limited range and reduced speed. Some months later the Allies partly countered the 'Gnat' with the introduction of the 'Foxer', an expendable device trailed by an escort and which emitted a noise designed to be more attractive to the torpedo than the vessel's propeller tone. It was not practicable for a liner to employ this protection.

Very long range Liberators of R.A.F. No. 120 Squadron based at Aldergrove, Northern Ireland. The importance of their role cannot be overestimated. (Courtesy Imperial War Museum, London)

Experience taught that some degree of immunity from the 'Gnat' developed when the speed of the escort vessel was below 8 knots or in excess of 24 knots. This knowledge was only of limited help to the escorts of a convoy whose speed was usually within the danger limits. However, if a U-boat had been detected by ASDIC, the attacking vessel could stalk it at a speed below 8 knots with some expectation that a 'Gnat' would not be attracted by its propellers.

We also learned at this sailing conference that in late August and early September, twenty-four U-boats equipped with receivers capable of detecting Allied 10 centimetre radar transmissions, and supplied with the new acoustic torpedoes, had established interception lines across the routes of convoys ONS 18 and ON 202 which had sailed from Liverpool and the Clyde. By 19 September, these convoys had closed within 90 miles of each other in the vicinity of 650 miles west-north-west of Ireland. U-boat sightings made by Liberator aircraft from Iceland, together with the interception of radio transmissions by the surface escorts, indicated that at least fifteen U-boats had been homed in around the convoy. At dawn on 20 September, the frigate HMS *Lagan*, when investigating a reported sighting, was struck in the stern by a 'Gnat', the

The Focke Wulf Condor could range well out into the Atlantic from both France and Norway. (Courtesy Air Force Museum, Wright Patterson Base, Ohio)

explosion killing twenty-nine members of her crew. The crippled ship was taken in tow and eventually reached Britain. The same day, two freighters were torpedoed and sunk, and their crews were scooped out of the water by the rescue ship *Rathlin*.

Admiralty now decided that the two convoys should be merged, and their combined escorts totalling seventeen vessels were placed under Commander M. J. Evans in HMS *Keppel*. By nightfall, all sixty-six merchantmen were in station. The time had come for the U-boats to begin their onslaught, but furious activity on the part of the escorts prevented them from closing on the columns of ships. However, the Canadian destroyer *St. Croix* and the corvette HMS *Polyanthus* were sunk by acoustic torpedoes with heavy losses of life. Next day *Keppel* rammed and sank *U-229*, and was able to continue her role despite a damaged bow.

Liberators from Newfoundland and Swordfish aircraft from the escorting merchant aircraft carrier *McAlpine* were now covering the convoy, but the U-boats hung on determinedly. On 23 September, in fog and cloud, U-boats and escorts exchanged torpedoes and depth charges whilst aircraft flew overhead – the airmen desperately hoping the visibility would clear. Shortly before midnight and during a break in the weather, HMS *Itchen* sighted a fully surfaced U-boat. The frigate set out

133

in hot pursuit, blazing away with her 4in guns while keeping the submarine fixed in her searchlight. The escort vessel looked set for a kill but the acoustic torpedo fired by the U-boat homed in on its target. The explosion broke the frigate into two parts, both of which quickly went down. Earlier this ship had rescued from the water the survivors of both the *St. Croix* and *Polyanthus*, and only three crew members from all three ships were finally rescued. During the next four hours, three merchant ships were torpedoed and sunk, and next morning the loss of another ship occurred. Against these casualties, three U-boats were destroyed and several others were believed to be damaged. By this time the convoy had come within range of continuous daylight air cover from Newfoundland, and the U-boats dropped back to reform their interception lines. Continuously over four days, this heavily escorted convoy had been attacked and harassed by fifteen U-boats, and in the process had travelled nearly 1000 miles.

Aquitania left New York on 1 October and on our third day out, at about 11 a.m., a Liberator patrolling at about three miles on the port bow signalled it had sighted a U-boat. The ship turned hard away to starboard whilst the aircraft flew out about three more miles on the port beam, and depth charges could be seen exploding in the distance. By this time, the plane could not afford to expend more fuel and returned to base. Another Liberator arrived about an hour later, but the fate of the U-boat remained unknown.

The route had been scheduled as far south as practicable on account of the submarine activity to the north. The daily U-boat report showed a rectangle of ten U-boats we could not avoid, but on the afternoon of 4 October we were diverted further to the south, delaying our entry into that area. Three Liberators in turn had covered us that day. The same evening, our radar was out of action for three hours. On 5 October we passed the liner *Orion* travelling unescorted on an opposite course. Two Grumman Wildcats from a U.S. carrier flew over in the afternoon and flashed a good luck message. These aircraft were almost certainly from the escort carrier USS *Card*, whose aircraft on the previous day had sunk *U-422* and *U-460* at 43-18N 28-58W and 43-13N 28-58W, probably within 200 miles of our position. It is of interest to note that the aircraft sweeping the tracks of the independently-routed liners were always land based and were never provided from escort or support groups which frequently included other U.S. carriers such as *Bogue*, *Core*, *Santee*, *Block Island* and *Wake Island*. Only small bombing types with a limited range could be flown off these ships and were probably regarded as unsuitable for the protection of these troopships. For our part, we would have welcomed even a Grumman Wildcat.

German JU 88 fighter bomber. Although of limited range, it claimed many successes against Allied shipping in the Western Approaches area and along the Gibraltar convoy routes. (Courtesy Air Force Museum, Wright Patterson Base, Ohio)

At 1 a.m. on 6 October we received an 'Immediate' diversion and at 10 a.m. an 'Emergency' diversion, the latter being transmitted four times in succession from Whitehall Radio. Our Petty Officer Telegraphist had heard nearby U-boat transmissions about twenty minutes beforehand. Captain Ford ordered the troops to boat stations, and the men remained mustered for about three hours. No explanation was given over the loud-speakers, although earlier the troops would have heard the gunners' alarms sounding action stations. The Admiralty report that afternoon positioned a U-boat where we had passed at 10 a.m. and revealed that we would have moved directly into a group of three U-boats about midday had it not been for the diversion. The plot indicated that during the night ahead, the ship would be passing through a block of about six submarines.

At 10.30 the next morning, I was writing a letter when the gunners' alarms sounded, followed by the order over the loudspeakers – 'all troops off the boat deck'. I shot up to the bridge and saw an aircraft which had been identified as a Focke Wulf Condor, approaching from astern in the classic fashion at an altitude of about 300 feet. Every gun on the ship blazed away, even the 6in guns aft. When about 1500 feet astern, the pilot turned away to port – the ship in the meantime having gone hard to star-board. There was no indication that the Focke Wulf had been hit, nothing having been seen to be shot away. The aircraft, followed by a hail of fire, flew off out of range, and then shadowed like a shark beyond a reef for about a half hour, during which time its radio transmissions could be heard. Presumably the fuel situation then compelled it to return to its base in Normandy, as it must have been operating at the limit of its range. We immediately broke radio silence to report the incident, and within a half-hour the ship was directed to change course to the north-west. The troops were ordered to remain below on the grounds that attack from the air was more probable than a U-boat encounter. They were issued with K-rations ostensibly to sustain themselves should they end up in lifeboats or rafts, or more likely, in the water. At approximately 2.30 p.m. we ran into a fog which restricted visibility to about a half mile. It remained until nightfall, and although maximum-strength U-boat transmissions were heard late in the afternoon, nothing was seen. Air cover from Plymouth arrived at first light the next morning and the gunners remained closed up at action stations all day.

On 8 and 9 October, further to the north, an inward bound convoy was assailed by an estimated fifteen U-boats. The enemy succeeded in sinking only one merchant ship, but also sank the Polish destroyer *Orkan*, a blow to the limited naval contribution of that ally. Allied aircraft sank three U-boats. No further incidents occurred and *Aquitania* arrived at Gourock at 4 a.m. on Saturday 9 October.

At the sailing conference on 12 October before our next departure from the Clyde, Captain Ford expressed his concern that the ship had not been provided with air cover on 5, 6 or 7 October, a period when the ship had been in particular danger. The Greenock Commander stated that the allocation of the V.L.R. Liberators to Coastal Command was insufficient to supply the air cover obviously needed, but pointed out that many hours of flying would have been involved just to reach these areas, leaving little time for patrolling. He claimed that several shore based aircraft would be required to supply full daylight coverage. Captain Ford did not seem particularly impressed. He said he had heard on the BBC news on 8 October that 1000 bombers had been over Frankfurt the previous night, and suggested that an allocation of say two to protect the *Aquitania*, leaving 998 for Frankfurt, would have made more sense. The Commander regretted that the distributions between Bomber Command and Coastal Command were matters for the Allied High Command.

While he was at it, Captain Ford stated a special case for the *Aquitania* by comparing her vulnerability with that of the two *Queens* which he had commanded. Admitting that at times the *Queens* carried nearly twice the number of troops as the *Aquitania*, the slower speed of the latter, about 22 knots as against about 30 knots, provided an added coefficient of danger which was probably of a geometrical rather than an arithmetical differential. These were hardly his exact words which of course I cannot recall, but this was the gist of his argument. He also pointed out that the

The final moments of a U-boat after being depth charged to the surface. Its conning tower was then raked and wrecked by gunfire. (Courtesy U.S. Navy).

length of the *Aquitania,* of just over 900 feet, made her a target for a torpedo only slightly less difficult to hit than the *Queens* with a length of about 1020 feet. Captain Ford seemed to have been implying that the *Queens* received preference in the provision of air cover which might have been expected in view of the ages and values of the ships involved, apart from the troop numbers.

Looking at German records relating to losses of U-boats in the North Atlantic, it would be unfair to claim that the Air Forces were inactive during this crossing. On 4 October four U-boats sunk; 5 October one; 8 October three sunk. All were destroyed by Allied aircraft, six being shore-based and two flown off the U.S. escort carrier *Card.* The failure of the Germans to press home the air attack on 7 October emphasised that their air force placed importance on a spotting and shadowing role as well as an attacking role in the Atlantic. Most attacks were within 300-400 miles of Ireland, and although the Luftwaffe was in a position to release bombs on shipping up to 800 miles out into the Western Approaches, they did not always do so. In order to achieve the maximum range and to allow for shadowing, only a limited number of bombs was carried, and the aircraft were not generally equipped to carry torpedoes. The Luftwaffe

This Allied air base in Iceland provided vital cover for convoys taking the northerly Atlantic route. (Courtesy U.S. Navy National Archives).

usually flew in the Atlantic the two-engined Dornier Do217, the Junkers Ju88, the Heinkel He111 and the long range four-engined Focke Wulf Fw200 Condor. After 1940 the latter aircraft were based in Norway, Belgium and France.

Some evidence of the further reluctance of the Luftwaffe to press home attacks on well-armed shipping was provided by the experiences of Captain Walker's Second Escort Group. On several occasions his sloops drove off Ju88's with anti-aircraft fire – the aircraft turning away before reaching a position to drop their bombs. On the other hand, a large troopship would have been a glittering prize, and a German pilot worth his stuff should have taken the chance. Nevertheless, the Condors sank many freighters, particularly those sailing unescorted.

The Germans developed an air-to-surface missile glider bomb known as the Hs293 – British sailors called them 'Chase me Charlies'. The gliders were about 11 feet in length and weighed approximately 1700lbs, being propelled by hydrogen peroxide. A bombardier directed the missile by remote radio control after it had been launched at a speed of about 250 miles per hour. Many merchant ships were sunk by this weapon, but its greatest prize was the Italian battleship *Roma* after it had surrendered to the Allies earlier in 1943. Our first warning of the 'Charlies' came at the previous sailing conference in New York in September 1943. We were instructed to improvise, as a make-shift countermeasure to the glider bomb, an electric razor of the type which operated on the same frequency – with the object of jamming the targeting. Accordingly, a razor was kept in the chartroom, to be turned on

Avenger aircraft from USS *Core* achieved many successes against U-boats. (Courtesy U.S. Navy National Archives)

pending identification of an approaching aircraft. Normally the use of these razors was banned on account of the possibility that a U-boat might home-in on its frequency.

The glider bomb was the ideal weapon to launch an attack on a troop-ship, and apart from the razor trick, the only defence was to try to shoot the missile down. A bizarre episode was reported from the Bay of Biscay when after a razor had been switched on, the 'Chase me Charlie' turned about and set out after the releasing aircraft. Allied bombers were directed to attack the plants which manufactured glider bombs and this tactic limited their production.

On 12 October we sailed from the Clyde for our first visit to Halifax, carrying approximately 5000 civilians and service personnel. Our third possible encounter with Herbert Werner occurred during this crossing. In his book *Iron Coffins*, Werner describes having sailed from Brest in *U-230* on 4 October supplied with acoustic and looping type torpedoes. The deck was fitted with eight guns and a new antenna which could receive radio signals at a depth of 30 metres. On 12 October, *U-230* reached its designated position at 58N 28W and on 16 October torpedoed four merchant ships, and in the process was attacked by four destroyers and a Liberator. The *Aquitania* had passed through this general area on 15 October. Remaining in this position, Werner awaited a convoy, or anything else which happened to pass. On 26 October, he stated he fired five torpedoes into another convoy, striking two merchant ships. The same day the *Aquitania* would have sailed through that section of the Atlantic on her return from Halifax, making the then total of possible encounters with Werner four. Werner claims that six U-boats were operating in this interception area, and that his vessel was the only survivor. During this month approximately 140,000 tons of shipping was lost, mostly in the North Atlantic.

A number of U-boats were active off Nova Scotia, and continuous air protection was provided during the last two days, although air cover had not been available on three of the first four days. Yet sixty B-17s had been shot down over Germany in one particular daylight attack on Schweinfurt. During this crossing six U-boats were sunk, and an additional four during our return to Scotland. Aircraft bagged six, and the corvettes the remainder, including two by HMS *Vidette*.

Landfall at Halifax was made at dusk on 18 October but immigration delayed our going ashore until the following morning. The city is built on a peninsula measuring about four miles by two miles, inhabited by a population of about 75,000. The deep harbour provides sanctuary for the largest vessels and the ship was able to tie up alongside the dock. The most memorable event to occur in Halifax happened in 1917 during the First World War, when the French cargo ship, *Mont Blanc*, collided with a Norwegian ship, *Imo*, during passage through the 'narrows'. The French vessel was laden down with T.N.T., acid and petrol, and this exotic combination produced an explosion which almost wrecked the town, killing about 2000 people and injuring a similar number. The anchor shaft, weighing 1000lbs, was hurled 2 miles and houses 60 miles away were shaken.

The visit of the *Aquitania* was tranquil by comparison. The two first class hotels – the Nova Scotia and the Lord Nelson – served excellent meals, but not only was it impossible to buy a drink before or after dinner, the meal itself was an exercise in temperance. Nova Scotia fell under the influence of settlers from Scotland and puritan New England, and their descendants still seemed to have the upper hand. However, there were billiard tables at an 'Anzac Club', squash courts, and two or three movie theatres. After embarking U.S. and Canadian troops, we sailed for Scotland on 23 October. Air cover remained until dusk but Liberator protection scheduled for the following day was cancelled due to poor visibility. The same evening a radar contact at about 8000 yards, combined with the movements of the contact following our sudden change of course, indicated the presence of a submarine on the surface ahead. The afternoon U-boat report had shown that the ship would be passing through a rectangle of six predators. Air cover was not again provided until 28 October, when a Catalina patrolled for five hours.

In *Hitler's U-Boat War*, Clay Blair revealed the following:

U-129 commanded by Richard von Harpe aged twenty-six sailed on October 12 1943 to patrol the United States East Coast from Cape Hatteras to Florida. En route on October 26 Von Harpe came upon the huge and fast ocean liner *Aquitania* but was unable to get off a shot.

My diary entries show that the *Aquitania* had sailed from the Clyde for New York on 23 October. This would be consistent with our route having converged with Von Harpe's on passage from a north German port or Bergen fourteen days after he had sailed for U.S. waters south of Cape Hatteras. The diary for the actual sighting date of 26 October reads 'now entered tough area – next 48 hours most dangerous'. This comment would have been based on the p.m. Admiralty U-boat report. A 1963 US Navy publication based on German records reveals that *U-129* was scuttled at the French port of Lorient on or about 20 August 1944 when still under the command of Von Harpe. Presumably the boat had been damaged in action and had not been repaired in time to escape before the arrival in Lorient of General Patton's Third Army from Normandy seven weeks after the invasion.

The ship arrived at the Clyde on 29 October. The weather was cold, and during the turn around I remained in the Gourock-Greenock area, filling in time playing some golf, and putting to good use the wait for the lighter at the Bay Hotel. The local W.R.N.S. officers organised a dance at Greenock and a number of us from the ship stayed overnight at the hotel.

We sailed from the Clyde just before midnight on 4 November, my tenth crossing. An estimated thirty U-boats were at sea but foul weather throughout the crossing prevented the arrival of any air cover. A number of signals advised the expected time of arrival and the type of plane, but the flights were cancelled due to storms and poor visibility. On the day after we sailed, action stations were sounded when an aircraft was briefly spotted through a break in the clouds – probably belonging to the U.S. Ferry Command. Our high-frequency direction finder detected strong U-boat transmissions on our port bow on 7 November, and we turned hard away. Heavy seas were running and our radar failed to make contact suggesting a U-boat was partly submerged. Within a half hour an emergency diversion signal was received indicating that two or more shore monitoring stations had obtained cross bearings on a reporting enemy.

Another diversion signal on 9 November again lengthened our route. This coincided with a gale which had already compelled the Captain to reduce speed and to abandon zigzagging. In addition to all this a further signal in the late afternoon proved to be in a code we did not hold. No option remained other than to break W/T silence. The reply revealed that our call sign had been used in error and that the signal was not intended for us. During that night we were advised we would be covered by a U.S. Army Air Force Catalina in the morning, but it failed to appear, without any signalled explanation. This crossing had highlighted the limitations imposed by the North Atlantic weather on air protection. Nevertheless, another ten months were yet to pass before any surface escort would be provided, and then intermittently for a few hundred miles out into the Western Approaches.

The tidings of winter were evident when we arrived at New York on 12 November after an absence of nearly six weeks. The leaves had fallen, the crowds were well wrapped up, and Christmas decorations had made an appearance on Fifth Avenue. Jenny, who studied the entertainment columns of the *New Yorker*, was ready with the latest information as to who was performing at which hotel or night club. I went golfing at the Rockland Country Club, and as a further concession to physical fitness, played squash and swam at the Harvard Club. Sarah had taken employment in a small, rather sophisticated book shop in 52nd Street, west of Fifth Avenue, and she loaned me copies of best sellers. In contrast with Jenny she did not drink, and steered me to theatres and inexpensive restaurants as distinct from nightclubs.

On 17 November the ship sailed for the Clyde, the passengers including about 800 U.S. army nurses and 2000 black soldiers. The temperature was below freezing point as we steamed down the Hudson – the coldest I had ever experienced. The following day an R.C.A.F. Catalina swept ahead from dawn to early afternoon. A diversion re-routed us far to the north. The afternoon U-boat report revealed that a ship had been torpedoed close to where we had passed the previous afternoon. A Liberator from Iceland had covered us from midday to dusk on 21 November. Overnight a gale estimated at force 9 combined with a following sea produced rolls estimated in excess of 20 degrees and forced the abandonment of zigzagging – not a matter of great moment since an attack in this weather would be unlikely. On the 5th day a convoy to the south was assailed by six Ju88s with glider bombs, the type of air attack we were particularly anxious to avoid. During this crossing four U-boats were sunk, namely *U-211*, *U-536*, *U-538* and *U-648*, all about 1000 miles west of Ireland. Arriving at Gourock on 24 November, the surrounding hills were covered with snow. The following day I met Scott-Mackenzie in Glasgow, and we again travelled to Linlithgow to stay with his uncle. I had bought supplies of tea, sugar and coffee in New York – an inexpensive but very welcome addition to the rationed supplies at the manse. Mackenzie had been transferred from HMS *Hurricane* and was about to take up an appointment in HMS *Bicester* in the Mediterranean. The Marquis of Linlithgow was now in residence at Hopetoun House after his return from India as Viceroy. The hospitality of the Reverend Oliphant was quite unstinting.

The *Aquitania* sailed for New York on 29 November with a draft of British merchant seamen to crew Liberty ships which Henry J. Kaiser was launching at the extraordinary rate of up to three per day. At the sailing conference, the R.N. Commander disclosed that an inward bound convoy was coming under attack in the Western Approaches, and this proved to be Convoy SL 140 which had been shadowed by ten U-boats. Walker's Second Escort Group was summoned to assist the Fourth Escort Group and the attack was beaten off.

A gale blew up the morning following our departure when we were about 50 miles north of Ireland, and slowed us down to about eight knots. At about 9.30 a.m., a signalman on the wing of the bridge sighted a floating mine at a distance of about a quarter of a mile and almost dead ahead. The order hard to port with full speed on the starboard propellers was given, and the bow came around in time to miss the mine by an uncomfortable 50 yards. About a minute later another mine was sighted within the same distance on the port beam and some questions were asked later as to why this had not been spotted earlier. The Captain refused to allow the gunners to fire at the mines out of concern that our hull might be damaged by the explosions. Had the ship been making her usual 21 knots, we may well have struck the first mine before the alteration to course had taken effect.

Early in the war, the Germans had laid extensive minefields at the entrances to British ports, especially off the east coast where at one stage the Port of London was almost closed. The magnetic mine, laid by aircraft, was detonated by the magnetic effect of a ship passing above it. These mines were countered by ships being 'degaussed', a procedure whereby cables were wrapped around its hull and subjected to an electric current. The Cunarders were thus equipped but the 'horned monsters' sighted on this occasion must have broken away from distant moorings and would explode on contact. On 6 August 1942, the *Queen Mary* narrowly escaped disaster when about 200 miles north-west of Ireland. The vibration of her propellers set off an acoustic mine, sending up a tremendous explosion about 400 yards astern. This created a geyser of water which reached a height of about 300 feet.

We had been routed far to the north and close to Iceland – darkness was setting in at about 4 p.m. and lasting until about 10 a.m. On the second night out from the Clyde, a clear light appeared on the port bow, and the absence of any registration on the radar screen was disquieting.

Presumably an improperly blacked-out ship or a neutral vessel was responsible and our radar may have been subject to a temporary aberration which occurred occasionally with the early model sets.

On 2 December, shortly before dawn, the ship received an emergency signal ordering an alteration of course, and at the same time advising that bearings on a U-boat transmission indicated our position had been reported. At the time, we were passing through a rectangular block of ten U-boats. The same afternoon, a gale of about force 10 blew up, and at reduced speed we overtook stragglers from a scattered ONS convoy. A merchantman requested us by lamp to call up the Commodore on our radio telephone, explaining its own equipment had failed, but our Captain quite properly refused.

My diary reminded me of the fact that on the evening of 4 December I had invited three young Irish priests, on passage to Quebec Province to take up parish appointments, to join me for a drink in my cabin. I had come across them in the afternoon on the boat deck, huddled together against the biting wind, and as usual for passengers, sweeping the horizons with their eyes. After they had relaxed with a couple of whiskies, they asked about my religion, and were surprised the invitation had come not only from a non-Catholic, but also from something of a sceptic. They wanted to know how I came to terms with the job without faith, and seemed to regret this brief meeting would give no opportunity for them to do something for me.

The towers of Manhattan rose into view about midday on 6 December. Washington Radio botched the forward transmission of our expected time of arrival signal, and New York had not alerted tugs. The ship was unable to dock until 5 p.m. and after a period at anchor, we moved slowly up the river. The 'brownout' over Manhattan had now been lifted, and as we passed Battery Point, I clambered up the seventy or so steps of the ladder inside the foremast to the crowsnest. The view was quite spectacular on this cold, clear evening, as lights were being switched on all over the city. From that time onwards, I had an even greater respect for these particular lookouts who were required to sit out an Atlantic gale experiencing 20 degree or more rolls.

During the period covered by this chapter, 30 September to 6 December 1943, thirty-eight U-boats were sunk in the North Atlantic. Escort vessels claimed fourteen, land-based aircraft seventeen, and carrier aircraft seven, including four by USS *Card*. Thirty of these U-boats were sunk whilst the *Aquitania* was at sea during her six crossings. The percentage of sinkings by ships, as against aircraft, increased towards the end of the period on account of the onset of winter with reduced visibility, and longer hours of darkness. Overall U-boat losses were of course in excess of the above figures, taking into account other combat areas such as the South Atlantic and the Indian Ocean. Total Atlantic shipping losses in 1943 reached an estimated 2,200,000 tons, an average of 183,000 tons per month.

Whilst the concentration of this chapter has been on the movements of the *Aquitania*, the experiences of the *Queen Mary* and *Queen Elizabeth*, and indeed of the other half-dozen or so smaller but fast, independently-routed troop transports, would have been similar. Their crossings were completed without any surface escort and presumably they received the same limited amount of air cover depending on availability, distances, weather and the perceived enemy threat. As in the case of the *Aquitania*, there were no reports of 'observed U-boat encounters', the outcome of which would have been highly predictable. U-boat transmissions at irregular times combined with position fixing by cross bearings established that these ships were sighted at times by the enemy, whereas sightings from a ship of the infinitely smaller enemy object were rare. Radar, particularly at night, was a critical protective factor.

Until September 1944, when destroyer escort was provided at times for several hundred miles in and out of Britain, the only visible outside protection evident to troops and passengers were aircraft intermittently patrolling ahead. The ship's officers were aware of the efforts of the Allied navies in destroying U-boats attacking convoys and in organised hunting, but generally the only naval vessels seen by the troops were within harbours. The role played by the Allied air forces in protecting these otherwise unescorted liners is briefly outlined here.

The first Consolidated Liberators arrived in Britain in September 1941 and, equipped with Anti-Surface Vessel Radar, patrolled between Iceland and Britain. These aircraft could effectively protect shipping up to 700 miles from base, after allowing a worthwhile period for patrolling. They carried twenty-five depth charges filled with the new Torpex explosive. However, these aircraft numbers were reduced by planes being taken over by Ferry Command for the carriage of V.I.P. personnel across the Atlantic. Early in 1943, the Mark III long range Liberator was patrolling over the Atlantic. Extra fuel tanks had been fitted into some depth charge bays, increasing the range and extending flight duration to about 17 hours. Recommended attacking tactics included taking advantage of the sun and cloud, avoiding approaching from a low height until within 6000 yards of the U-boat, and preferring to attack from dead ahead or astern. Additional precautions included evasive turns and switchback height changes if the boat was surfaced and was fighting back.

The introduction of the Leigh Light and 10 centimetre radar, which unlike early A.S.V. radar, could not be detected by the U-boat's

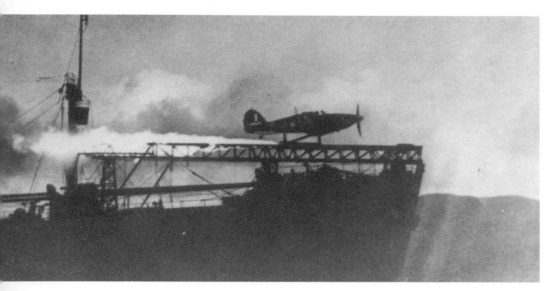

A Hurricane fighter being catapulted from an American ship to intercept an enemy aircraft shadowing the convoy. (Courtesy Imperial War Museum, London).

'Southern Cross' aerial, further strengthened the attacking capacity of Coastal Command and other Allied aircraft. By 1943, aircraft used against U-boats from the Allies' Atlantic bases included Liberators, Catalinas, Wellingtons, Sunderlands, B-17s (Flying Fortresses), Halifaxs and Whitleys. The Liberators had the greatest capacity to remain with these ships the longest, and eventually they became our protection almost exclusively. The crewmembers of the Mark III Liberator numbered on an average nine – the captain, co-pilot, flight engineer, three radio/radar officers, one radio/radar mechanic, and two navigators/bomb aimers. In order to gain the maximum range, this aircraft, fully loaded with fuel and bombs, which gave an overall weight of about 8 tons, adopted an air speed averaging 135 knots, based on 'maximum aerodynamic efficiency'. The height of the patrolling aircraft varied from about 5000 feet down to about 2000 feet, depending on the weather and to some extent on the captain's tactical preference. The greater height provided an extended radar and visual coverage, but involved a time delay in descending to an attacking position. When hunting the enemy at night as distinct from daylight escorting, and using the Leigh Light in conjunction with radar, these aircraft flew between 500 and 1000 feet.

During the course of protecting the unescorted liners, the aircraft reached out up to some 30 miles ahead depending on the speed of the ship. The distance from the ship was greatly reduced as the beam position was approached, the range of the torpedo being the determining factor. The ship's zigzag pattern was ignored, the patrolling being based on the mean track provided before take-off.

The aircraft's radar played the major role in the detection of a surfaced U-boat, particularly in poor visibility. The liner would alter course sharply, responding to a warning, while the aircraft attempted to reach the U-boat before it dived. Frequently we did not see our protector again and were left only to speculate as to the outcome. Any feelings amongst crew members that they might have been deprived of an opportunity to witness a killing were hardly widespread, particularly for those who had been torpedoed earlier in the war. Radar enabled aircraft to locate the liners without difficulty at the beginning of a patrol, with the large Cunarders appearing on the screen at up to 70 miles.

In 1941 a joint R.N.-R.A.F. committee had ordered four merchant ships to be equipped with catapults and Hurricane fighters as C.A.M. (Catapult Armed Merchant) ships, to sail with convoys and to protect them against bomber attacks. As mentioned elsewhere, it has continued to remain a mystery why one of the surplus Hurricanes was not fitted to the foredecks of these unescorted troopships where space was ample. A Focke Wulf Condor or a U-boat surfacing ahead could have been a fair target for one of these fighters. Such an exercise was a grim prospect for the pilot who was likely to be beyond the range of a land base and with the best prospect of ditching in the water or parachuting to the surface with the knowledge that the ship would not stop. However, there was no shortage of brave volunteers in the Allied air forces.

Coastal Command took part in the daily scrambled phone conference with Admiralty, the Western Approaches Command and Bletchley Park, when the current U-boat disposition was estimated and intelligently guessed. The patrolling program for the following 24 hours from Britain, Northern Ireland, Iceland and Canada was largely determined as a consequence. The independently-routed ships were advised, usually three or four hours in advance, when to expect air cover. One reason was a precaution against the ship attempting to shoot the aircraft down should recognition confusion occur. Cancellations were also advised. Only on rare occasions would a relieving aircraft take over from the first in the 'gap' area, where many hours of flying to reach it were required. Usually the aircraft arrived close to first light, with fuel limitations forcing it to detach about midday. Allowing for the days without any air cover, it may be a fair guess to say we received this protection for about 25 per cent of daylight hours. The scheduling of these flights reflects the tendency for the enemy to patrol actively on the surface in the mornings, to lay submerged listening to hydrophones during the afternoons, and to replenish air and to recharge batteries again when prowling on the surface at night.

One aspect is certain – the sight of a patrolling aircraft had a notice-able relaxing effect on the troops, and also on the cipher officer for that matter. Thus the Allied air forces were seen as the Great Protectors of the Cunarders and their kindred, and their efforts undoubtedly saved the lives of innumerable men in the Atlantic.

CHAPTER 11

The Winter of '43-'44 – The Stormiest in Memory

This stopover in New York lasted six days. Jenny and I with others had dinner at the Lincoln Hotel where Count Basie and his orchestra were playing. The first night ashore always called for a big splash and later we caught the midnight show at El Morocco. Next day the ship was again scheduled for fumigation and Cunard, being unable to book sufficient accommodation at the Belmont Plaza Hotel, suggested Milne and I use the British Navy's resources to ease the problem. We moved into the Barbizon Plaza, a good hotel close to Central Park, and remained there for three days. I saw two plays with Sarah and on the Saturday her parents took us motoring to Oyster Bay and Westhampton on Long Island. I had called at the Anzac Club, my mailing address in New York, and found a Christmas cake from home had arrived. It had survived the tropics and there was nothing to suggest its interior had been probed by the F.B.I.

We sailed on Sunday 12 December. With the temperature down to 10 degrees F., ice had formed around the ship, but the current ran freely in mid-stream. On 18 December, the ship ran into a severe storm and some damage occurred when a quartering sea caused tables and chairs to capsize. We reached Gourock on 19 December, and I remained on board for most of the three days rather than brave the rain and snow. Fifteen airgraphs awaited me – the first mail for two months. Captain Ford returned after a trip off and Maurice Hobday, the British gunnery officer, went on leave. We cipher officers were well overdue for a spell based on the system operating for all others aboard, but it continued to remain our policy to ignore the subject on account of the risk of being replaced permanently. Although unknown to us at the time, it will be seen later that Admiralty may well have had no record of us.

I was good and ready when we sailed a few minutes before midnight on 22 December – Scotland can be 'strictly for the birds' in mid-winter. Christmas Day found us slightly north of the 60th Parallel, close to Iceland, and this was to be my first white Christmas, with the decks

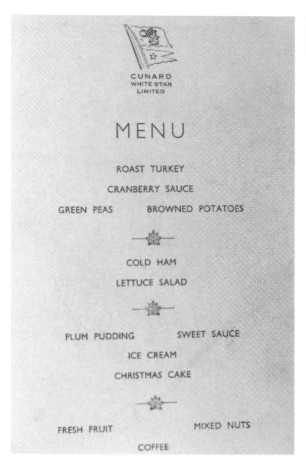

CUNARD
WHITE STAR
LIMITED

MENU

ROAST TURKEY

CRANBERRY SAUCE

GREEN PEAS   BROWNED POTATOES

COLD HAM

LETTUCE SALAD

PLUM PUDDING   SWEET SAUCE

ICE CREAM

CHRISTMAS CAKE

FRESH FRUIT   MIXED NUTS

COFFEE

The troops' Christmas Dinner menu was the same for all ranks.

covered in snow during the five hours of daylight. Cunard took all the steps to observe the ceremonial rituals, hanging appropriate decorations in the lounges and dining rooms, and serving lashings of traditional fare. I understand the Divine service was conducted by the staff captain – the rule of the master not leaving the immediate vicinity of the bridge area in wartime being always observed. Although a questionable morale booster, at church services they always sang: 'Oh hear us when we cry to thee, for those in peril on the sea'. However, I believe they were spared 'Nearer my God to thee', claimed to have been sung as the *Titanic* went down.

King George sent a Christmas message addressed,

To all the seamen of the Merchant Navy and Fishing Fleets, and especially to those who must spend Christmas Day away from Home.

The message consisted of three paragraphs of unstinting praise for the efforts of these men. In the evening, Milne and I invited the two elderly elevator operators, Don and Starling, to our cabin for a Christmas drink after they came off duty. They had served with the company for about 45 years and told us this was the first drink they had ever had in a stateroom – which I suppose was not surprising. The Australians had undermined the caste system. Starling was always addressed by his surname – as was considered becoming for his status – but somehow Don was always called by his Christian name. Nobody knew why. Elevators were for the use of ship's officers only – not for those in transit.

Approximately six hours earlier during mid-afternoon, the 26,000-ton German battlecruiser *Scharnhorst* sailed from her base in a Norwegian fjord, like ourselves close to the 60th Parallel, to intercept convoy JW 55B, bound for Russia, and which was escorted by three British cruisers, with destroyers and corvettes. Our radio operators had noted a considerable increase in the volume of traffic being broadcast by Whitehall W/T in London, and this continued for the next 36 hours. The initial indicator groups revealed the messages were in 'Flag' cipher, that of the highest secrecy and held only by flagships and a limited number of shore author-ities. The low volume of traffic gave the enemy little opportunity of breaking these codes which were not on issue to us. We remained igno-rant of the action until the news was released by the B.B.C. two days later.

The *Scharnhorst* located the convoy in the twilight about 9.30 a.m. on Boxing Day, but was driven off by the cruisers, which, in company with destroyers, set out in pursuit. Ships of the Home Fleet commanded by Admiral Sir Bruce Fraser, flying his flag in the battleship *Duke of York*, had been steaming a parallel course 200 miles to the south of the convoy, and the *Scharnhorst* sailed into the trap. A running fight followed, since described as the 'Last Battle of the Dinosaurs'. After being struck by an estimated thirteen 14in shells, twelve 8in shells and eleven torpedoes, the German slowly laid over and slid beneath the surface. British ships then moved in and scooped up 36 survivors out of a crew of nearly 2000 from the freezing water on this dark arctic night. Death came quickly at the 60th Parallel, a fact which did not escape us.

Hitler's U-Boat War reveals another sighting of the *Aquitania* at this time:

Detached from 'Coronel' [name of U-boat group] on December 16 1943, *U-543* proceeded towards Newfoundland with orders to hunt ships and also to broadcast weather reports twice daily. On December 27 Kapitanleutant Hellriegel reported he had chased the big, fast ocean liner *Aquitania* in vain. Alerted to the presence of this boat by Enigma decrypts and Huff Duff, the Canadian authorities mounted a massive hunt for three hundred miles east of the coast of Newfoundland.

Presumably Ultra had gathered sufficient material that day to enable a rapid decrypt of the U-boat sighting signal by radio to Germany and had relayed the information to Canada. The 'Huff Duff' refers to a High Frequency Direction Finding fix by Allied listening stations on the U-boat's position. My diary entries show that the *Aquitania* was westbound about two and a half days out of New York when this sighting occurred. The entry for that day was innocuous: 'Beautiful morning sun shining. Passed large convoy on starboard side in afternoon. Catalina escort for short time'. *U-543* escaped on that occasion, then managed a better-than-average survival period of another six months. On 2 July 1944 when SE of the Azores at 25-54N, 21-36W, and whilst still under the command of Hellriegel, she was sunk with no survivors by an aircraft from the escort carrier USS *Wake Island*.

Chunks of ice from upstate New York were floating down the Hudson and the air had a knife-edge when the *Aquitania* returned to New York on 30 December. The *Queen Elizabeth* had arrived a few hours earlier and I boarded her for dinner with Ed Seim before he moved his gear back to our ship. He had temporarily relieved a gunnery officer there. With the other U.S. gunnery officer from the *Queen Elizabeth*, John Kissel, we had the usual first night ashore, taking the three girls from the apartment to the midnight show at the Rainbow Room. The views over Manhattan from the sixty-fifth floor of the R.C.A. building with the huge Christmas tree in Rockefeller Plaza below, all added to the occasion.

Having spent Christmas at sea, the celebration of the New Year in New York came as some compensation. Jenny had made a booking for dinner at the Cafe Loyale on Fifth Avenue, and shortly before midnight we moved on to Times Square to witness the action. The traffic in Broadway, Seventh Avenue, and in the nearby cross streets had come to a halt, and convivial pandemonium prevailed as strangers joined hands to dance in circles, whilst others snaked around in conga lines. About one man out of two seemed to be in uniform, as were a percentage of the women. Crowds of soldiers and girls swarmed in and out of 'Roseland' – the most popular dance hall in New York.

The question of 'security' in New York was something of a problem, and this was brought to mind when Sarah asked why I had been in town for two days before contacting her. It eventuated she had heard the name of my ship mentioned at Delmonico's months earlier, and had now arranged for a friend working on an upper floor of the Chrysler building to phone her whenever the four funnels were seen steaming up the river or docked at Pier 86. The sudden influx of officers wearing Cunard uniforms into Delmonico's was a sure sign that one of the 'monsters' had arrived, and by the same token, the uniform's abrupt disappearance indicated a Cunarder had sailed or was about to sail. A crew member being driven back to the ship by friends had to consider whether he should be dropped off a few blocks from the pier, rather than be delivered to the gates. Asking a taxi driver to take you to Pier 86 could bring the comment: 'It looks like the *Aquitania* will be sailing in a few hours – when passing a short time ago I noticed she was raising steam'. Docking within a few minutes walk of the heart of Manhattan was fine in peacetime, but it rendered the slogans 'The enemy is always listening and watching' and 'Loose lips sink ships' something of a mockery. The Silent Service could cope with the listening problem, but the watching was beyond control. Shipboard contractors with deadlines became aware of sailing dates, and New York's skyscrapers were potential watchtowers for spies or alleged neutrals. Nevertheless, docking in midtown Manhattan had a wide range of compensating advantages, and our crew had no complaints whatsoever.

An interesting comment on troopship security was made by a leading participant in the 'Watergate Saga', Gordon Liddy. Interviewed on a U.S. network T.V. programme, re-telecast in Australia on 30 March 1995, Liddy was asked could he kill a person if he believed U.S. security was at risk. He gave just one example. If he knew a person was about to disclose a sailing time and date of a troopship out of New York, he 'would have no problem in shooting that person'. Well said, Gordon!

The ship was iced in when we sailed on 2 January, and the sound of cracking accompanied the initial movement as she responded to the straining lines from the tug boats. The *Queen Elizabeth* followed our wake in line astern, and she remained there until nightfall at about 4.30 p.m. A U.S. Navy Ventura had been sweeping the seas ahead for both vessels, and on the aircraft's departure, the *Queen Elizabeth* quickly surged away.

The Admiralty had routed us far to the north, slightly above the 60th Parallel and the closest we were ever to approach towards Cape Farewell on Greenland, the southern entrance to the Denmark Strait, or Iceland. The weather was foul and galleries of ice hung from the ship's railings. It was intriguing to watch waves break over the bow and literally freeze to a halt. With the scuppers frozen over, the build-up of deck ice must have weighed many tons. Ice also clung to the rigging and the deckhouse, with the falling of rain, sleet and snow serving to aggravate the position. Ice also formed around the gun mountings and it was necessary to operate their mechanism regularly to prevent freezing up, and also to keep the barrels free from clogging. Smaller ships on Russian convoys encountering this weather for weeks at a time could become in danger of capsizing due to an excessive topweight of ice, and the crews had to set to with axes and hammers to break it away. Warning of this danger was provided by a

Frozen spray covers the decks and rigging of the German liner *Europa* during a peacetime winter crossing. (Courtesy New York Times)

ship hanging over for an excessive period – 'they rolled, lay on the roll, and then rolled a little more'.

The gun crews stationed on the *Aquitania*'s foredeck were at times taken off watch when the plunging bow began to throw back the waves, all water, and not just spray. On four occasions, signals were received advising that air cover, due to arrive at first light, was cancelled on account of poor visibility. On 10 January the coast of Northern Ireland was sighted and the ship anchored in the Clyde late that afternoon after the Spitfires had put on their welcoming display for the troops. I spent two days at the hotel at Dunoon, but the weather prevented any worthwhile outdoor activity. The *Aquitania*'s programme was well established, but this did not prevent rumours being circulated by the crew from time to time regarding faraway destinations. Anywhere but the cold North Atlantic would do. Our stewards occasionally engaged in discreet fishing expeditions which were met with a smile and a shrug.

I had been invited by one of the junior deck officers to accompany him home on his three days of leave. He lived in the Lake District of Westmoreland, south of Windermere, and I had previously met his sister in Gourock. I received similar invitations from other merchant officers from time to time, but made a practice of declining. A visitor placed a strain on the family food supply, and his presence interfered with those brief opportunities for families to get together. The position differed in New York where the turn-arounds were of longer duration.

During periods of subdued activity in an area believed to be free of U-boats, I would often chat with one of the deck officers on duty on the bridge. It became clear that many had mixed feelings about their career prospects when the war ended. Cunard had lost passenger liners and cargo ships and out of the crew members fortunate enough to be saved, some had joined other shipping lines, but would probably wish to return to Cunard. Further losses were likely to be experienced and our crew members had some anxiety regarding the number of appointments likely to be on offer. These conversations brought forward accounts of the conditions which prevailed in the majority of merchant ships prior to this war and led to my understanding as to why I was so often asked about life in Australia, a taste of which many of these men had experienced when trooping Australians to the Middle East. A look at some of these pre-war conditions could give some insight into the minds of those officers in whose hands the lives of so many troops were placed.

Sailing with Cunard was something apart from the wartime experience of the average merchant sailor, but some of our officers had made it the hard way. Leaving school at an early age, they regularly sailed off to some remote outpost of the British Empire. However, a number of shipping companies would indenture youths directly out of school as midshipmen, and train them from the beginning to become officers. After an initial period of some weeks ashore, the following years at sea would be interspersed with attendances at shore establishments such as the technical college at Liverpool, where courses included navigation, seamanship and ship construction. After four years the midshipman could sit for his Second Mate's certificate, and that of First Mate after another four years. Two years later, with further seagoing experience and additional courses, the examination for certificate of Master could be taken. The British Blue Funnel Line put their midshipmen through the Outward Bound Sea School at Aberdovey in Wales, and the one month's course included mountaineering, rowing, and generally a spartan life.

The Cunard Company had a policy of encouraging its officers and certain crew members to join the Royal Naval Reserve. In the event of war, Cunard ships were likely to be taken over by the Government, and membership of the R.N.R. could assist captains and officers to retain their appointments. In peacetime, a liner captained by an R.N.R. officer, and at the same time carrying at least seven officers and ratings who were members of the R.N.R., was entitled to fly the Blue Ensign alongside the House Flag.

Officers and crewmen seeking R.N.R. status were required to undergo initial training courses in the Navy in some areas of learning not normally encountered in their training such as proficiencies, disciplines and techniques of war including gunnery, tactics and communications. Attendance at refresher courses was necessary about every two years. The officers of the Royal Navy were generally recruited from a different segment of society, but it could be expected that these courses would help break down what outsiders regard as a British preoccupation with 'class'. As a member of the Volunteer Reserve, the old joke was repeated to me time and again.

> The officers of the Royal Navy are gentlemen but not seamen, the officers of the Merchant Navy are seamen but not gentlemen, while the officers of the Reserve are neither.

The conditions under which crews of merchant ships sailed before the Second World War were rather dreadful, although considerably better in passenger liners. After the First World War, the British parliament passed regulations relating to health, accommodation, food and safety. But these were only 'recommendations', and were unenforceable in law. Many seamen claimed that owners operated a blackballing system, exchanging lists of malcontents who were unable to understand always being turned away. Bedding and clothing were continuously wet in some loose-plated hulks, with food often of the poorest quality. Their own could not always be trusted – a few unscrupulous captains served their own interests by purchasing inferior stores in foreign ports. Statistics kept by the London School of Hygiene and Tropical Medicine found the death rate of seamen below 55 years was double the national average, with tuberculosis being the major killer. After the Second World War, powerful unions redressed the balance, frequently to the great inconvenience of passengers as both Cunard, and particularly the French Line, can attest.

On a few occasions strains surfaced between the services, and one particular incident remains in my memory. Entering the wardroom for tea one afternoon in late 1944, I found a guest, a British merchant service officer on passage, sounding off about the Royal Navy. He claimed to have been a survivor from a Russia-bound convoy in July 1942 which was ordered to scatter, and which had its naval escort withdrawn when under attack from the Luftwaffe and U-boats. He claimed only ten of forty merchant ships reached port and he virtually accused the Navy of cowardice. The matter was revived the following March when one of the deck officers returned from leave with a copy of the London Sunday Express dated 25 February 1945. A front page article headed 'Convoy Charges Untrue' stated that the Admiralty,

> described as entirely without foundation reports in the American press concerning the conduct of British naval vessels escorting a convoy to Russia 2½ years ago.

It went on to refer to allegations by a repatriated Baltimore seaman that thirty-four ships had been sunk.

The story of Convoy PQ17 is well-known, even to the extent of the making of a T.V. play based on the collective guilt felt by a group of Royal Navy officers in one of the escorts. PQ17 consisting of thirty-four ships, had assembled at Iceland and sailed for Archangel on 27 June 1942, escorted by twenty-two R.N. vessels. A force of two battleships and seven cruisers with destroyer screens were in the area bottling up the *Tirpitz*. After four days' sailing the Luftwaffe sighted and began to attack the convoy. Admiralty Intelligence reports indicated the *Tirpitz* was raising steam, and from his Admiralty bunker, Admiral Sir Dudley Pound signalled the Escort Commander, Captain John Broome: 'Immediate – owing to threat of surface ships the convoy is to disperse and proceed to Russian ports'. The outcome of the total withdrawal of the protection was the sinking of twenty-three out of the thirty-four freighters together with huge quantities of vital weapons and supplies. And the *Tirpitz* did not in fact sail. Such matters are not easily explained to merchant seamen, and it was not surprising that these men at times displayed a watchfulness and caution in dealing with the Navy. Being an Australian, I believe I was seen as being outside the system, and was able to retain friendships which continued after the war.

On 14 January 1944 we sailed for New York. The U-boat situation was typical for this time of the year, with gales preventing the enemy employing wolf pack tactics. For this reason, Admiral Doenitz had again moved his main patrol lines further east to within about 300 miles of the west coast of Ireland, taking advantage of the flying restrictions on Coastal Command operations brought about by the seasonal conditions. An estimated thirty U-boats were forming interception lines in this area, but the tonnage of merchant ships sunk declined to 43,000 during the month. On 12 January 1944, Admiralty announced the loss of the destroyer *Hurricane*, struck by an acoustic torpedo in the North Atlantic. This had been the ship in which Ewan Scott-Mackenzie was serving when I had initially stayed with him at Linlithgow. He had been transferred to the Mediterranean three months before the sinking.

This enormous mass of water, photographed from the bridge of Germany's 50,000-ton *Bremen*, must have caused a massive list to port. (Courtesy New York Times).

The westbound crossing was memorable on account of the 'Great Gale'. Looking back on the storms I had experienced both before and after this particular crossing, it exceeded by far any other in its intensity. On the second day out, Sunday 16 January, at about 2 a.m., I felt the ship beginning to plunge and by daylight at 9.30 a.m., Captain Ford had reduced speed from our normal 21 knots to 5 knots. Shutters enclosing lower promenade decks were being torn away and standee bunks were ripped from their fixtures. Our course at that point was approximately due west, but it having become essential to head more directly into the huge waves, we had altered to west-north-west. Zigzagging was out of the question and by the morning of the 17th, we were 24 hours behind schedule and about 100 miles to the north of our route. The barometer descended close to 28 inches, but by late morning the seas had dropped slightly as the weather began to lift, and speed was increased to about 10 knots.

During the night the gale again intensified, and by daylight of the 18th it had reached its height. Winds approaching 100 m.p.h. slammed towering, sky-climbing combers down on the foredeck. The iron railing surrounding the bow was torn off, lifeboats and rafts were carried away, fixed steel ladders disappeared and the hospital was flooded. The ship was carrying only about 2000 passengers which was just as well, as many standee bunks on B deck had become tangled masses of iron and canvas.

The glass sank below 28 inches and speed was reduced to about three knots – dead slow with nothing more than steerage way. A 'North Atlantic Snorter' if ever there was one.

The watch officers agreed that this was a full gale – all of force 12. The vessel would suddenly yaw up to 10 degrees followed by the quarter-master hastening to correct the course. A repeat performance in the opposite direction was just as likely to occur. The foredeck buried itself into each passing wave, and then angrily threw aside tons of water as the bow rose. It was easy to understand how smaller ships, less stoutly con-structed, could break their backs as they balanced on a crest before pounding down into the next trough. Liberty ships met their fate in this manner on a number of occasions, although steering aslant could reduce the danger. The visibility changed from minute to minute as thick dark clouds, driven by the tempest, scudded by. The lookouts continued on the alert in their search for U-boats through the whirring clearview screens, but it must have been difficult to avoid a preoccupation and a fascination with the storm itself. Fortunately, the cold was not excessive and icing did not become a problem.

An intriguing aspect of the gale was the fact that the entire ship, 902 feet in length, fitted completely into the trough between two waves with some distance to spare. You could stand on the bridge 60 feet above the water, and only the next oncoming wave would be visible ahead, extend-ing downwards almost 100 feet from crest to trough. At the same time, the crest of the previous wave could be seen, already clear of the stern. It followed there would have been at least 1200 feet between crests which must have taken days of hurricane force winds to build up, the same dis-tance as a testing par 4 golf hole! When the *Queen Mary* was being designed, the team initially assumed that the distance between crests did not span more than 600 feet, with 800 feet being an absolute maximum. However, additional information subsequently submitted indicated that gaps of over 1000 feet had been reported, and this was quite consistent with our observations.

After the ship rode slowly up a crest and had begun the downslide, the four screws would break the surface, evidenced by the vibrations from the accelerating shafts. All decks were declared out of bounds to passen-gers, and it was impossible for the crew to attend to damage on the foredeck. A glowing and flickering around the masthead and other pro-jections developed, and this was explained by old hands as being the ghostly electrical phenomenon known as 'St. Elmo's Fire' – to be seen only in extreme weather conditions.

During the afternoon of 18 January, a message from Admiralty required us to report our position, course and speed. This was unusual

A huge wave, viewed from *Aquitania*'s Promenade Deck, slopes perhaps 100 feet from crest to trough. (Courtesy New York Times)

yet hardly unexpected in the circumstances, and we signalled a position 50 hours behind schedule and nearly 200 miles to the north of our specified route. The calculation was by dead reckoning and later proved to be fairly accurate. Our navigator had found it impossible to obtain a fix during the previous 48 hours, the sun, stars and the horizon all having been entirely shrouded. His problem was further compounded by the uncertainty as to the drift, and the difficulty in steering the attempted course. The instant electronic satellite fix was then only science fiction stuff.

Barely 100 miles had been covered in the previous 24 hours. The gale continued during the 19th although the Captain had been able to increase speed to 6-8 knots. Concern mounted about supplies of fuel and water, but by late afternoon on the 20th, the gale had almost blown itself out and we were able to work up to normal speed. Fortunately no convoys were in transit in this sector of the Atlantic, and we had the brunt of the storm largely to ourselves. Running out of fuel can have disastrous consequences. In 1873 the White Star liner *Atlantis*, short of coal, changed destination from New York to Halifax. Within sight of the harbour but out of fuel, she sank with the loss of 546 lives.

It was of interest to hear the bridge officers discuss the gale at tea that afternoon. Over 100 years of combined seagoing experience would have been present, but not one recalled having seen waves of these dimensions previously. Some claimed to have encountered stronger winds and others steeper seas, but it was the overall height of the waves and distances between crests which were so memorable. Never was there any suggestion – either during or after the storm – that the ship had been in danger, a confidence hardly shared by many passengers. The damage was basically superficial, and in spite of her many protests in the form of creaking, groaning, vibrating and thumping, the Old Lady, proclaimed to be unrivalled as a seaboat, showed she was more than a match for anything the Atlantic could contrive to test her. On the eighth day, speed was reduced on account of a growing fuel shortage, the one thing every wartime strategy aimed to avoid.

Ed Seim, the U.S. gunnery captain, wrote in his log:

> The worst weather in the history of the detachment was encountered. For 12 hours, no one was allowed on the top deck side because of a hurricane. No one was allowed on the foredeck for a week. The foreward guns were in bad shape from the weather.

Milne and I had dinner with Captain Ford the evening before we arrived in New York. He was full of praise for the ship and his quartermasters, and relieved that the damage had not been more extensive. The vessel was again becoming weather-scarred and rust-stained, but it would be many weeks before the grey paint again could be spread. We arrived in New York on 25 January, four days behind schedule, which might have been a record of sorts for a ship of this size. It is significant that *U-972* was the only U-boat listed as lost by the German High Command during this crossing, and it was described as 'missing'.

The following day Mr. and Mrs. Seim entertained Ed, Alec and myself at Le Café Chambord on Third Avenue. This restaurant was then regarded as the finest place to eat in all Manhattan. Writing in 1953, novelist Evelyn Waugh, also a noted gourmet and traveller, described it as 'the best restaurant in the world'.

Another evening we made one of our occasional visits to an Irish bar, also on Third Avenue. The place projected a genuine Irish atmosphere – not created for tourists, but flowing from its own patrons who all seemed to be locals and not very well off at that. A character from Limerick sawed away at the fiddle for drinks and as the night advanced, he would stop and curse every time trains on the elevated railway outside thundered by, causing the suspended lights to swing in the haze of smoke, spiked with the smell of alcohol and food. His speciality was 'If You're

Irish Come Into the Parlour'. To capture the atmosphere we would drink Jameson's, and towards the end of the night joined in the singing of 'East Side, West Side, all around the Town'. We had some great times, always out of uniform. It was typical James Joyce atmosphere – only Molly Bloom was missing.

The *Aquitania* sailed on 29 January 1944, again taking the cold uncomfortable northern route near Iceland. On the third day we were overtaken by a north-westerly gale coming in on the port quarter. Under these circumstances, the predominant movement became that of rolling, as distinct from pitching, which happens when heading into the wind. The *Aquitania* was not equipped with modern stabilisers, and the rolls of up to 25 degrees were much more disconcerting than any pitching movement. A following sea is disturbing for the inexperienced traveller in that the ship will tend to remain laid over on what seems an alarming angle for many seconds, producing the fear that it may never regain its trim. It is a motion inducing seasickness more than the pitching movement and some troops would struggle up on decks in the hope the cold fresh air might do something for them. A young man from mid-America, never having seen the sea, conscripted into the army to fight a war he may not know much about, horribly seasick, imagining the ship to be followed by submarines, was an unhappy sight. All would be different a few days later, when the ship was sailing smoothly up the Clyde with the sun shining, the cattle grazing on the gentle hills. Now a smile lit his face as he contemplated the pleasures of London lying in wait.

On the second last day about midday, three aircraft identified by the bridge as Dorniers commenced to make lazy circles outside the range of the guns. One began a low run from astern but pulled out when we threw everything at it. We immediately reported to Admiralty and were advised that fighters were being despatched. The aircraft departed heading towards the Luftwaffe base at Stavanger in Norway, but about an hour later another began to shadow and could be heard transmitting, presumably attempting to 'home-in' U-boats. The ship then ran into fog which remained until nightfall. We received a signal advising that the fighters had been cancelled on account of the weather.

On the final day we steamed on a wide circle down the west coast of Scotland through the Minches and Outer Hebrides, giving the area north of Ireland as wide a berth as possible on account of U-boat activity there. The weather was clear and sunny, we had a Sunderland patrolling ahead and were within sight of the coasts of the Western Isles for most of the daylight period. I had never seen troops so happy at sea, and little scope remained for the additional relief, usually evident when at Gourock, the boom defence net closed behind us on 5 February.

Firing of depth charges. (Courtesy Imperial War Museum, London).

The enemy never made any known attempt to penetrate the defences of the Clyde by using midget submarines with the object of placing limpet mines on the hulls of warships or transports. The Italians used limpet mines to severely damage the British battleships *Valiant* and *Queen Elizabeth* at Alexandria in December 1941, and they also sank ships with these mines at Gibraltar on a number of occasions. The British were successful with this type of attack on the *Tirpitz* in a Norwegian fjord, on Italian cruisers at Palermo, and on a floating dock at Bergen. The trip back to New York after a three-day turnaround was uneventful, although on the second day out, a convoy to the south was attacked. The enemy lost seven U-boats during this crossing, all north of the 49th Parallel. The locations had ranged up to the 60th Parallel and between the longitudes of 12 to 18 degrees west.

During February 1944, Captain F. J. Walker, the Commander of the Second Escort Group based in Liverpool, added to his renowned exploits. Walker sailed from Liverpool on 29 January 1944, the same day the *Aquitania* had sailed from New York for the Clyde. His Group now consisted of HMS *Starling, Wild Goose, Woodpecker, Magpie* and *Wren*, and during the next twenty days they hunted to destruction six U-boats, and captured the entire crew of *U-264*. Walker had developed an extraordinary talent for anticipating the movements of a submarine. Following a sighting of a U-boat by an aircraft, or a report of a torpedo attack, Walker in *Starling* could sail for several hours to the general area, and then gain an ASDIC contact against all expected odds. The *Wild Goose* was the specialist in the actual detection, and on this particular voyage extending over 7000 miles, she made the initial contact with four of the six U-boats sunk. The first success occurred on 1 February with the destruction of *U-502*, and the second took place six days later when the Group was escorting the inward bound convoy SL147, consisting of eighty-one ships. Eighteen escorts, including two merchant aircraft carriers, protected the convoy. It was estimated that by 9 February – the day the *Aquitania* set out for New York – the number of U-boats shadowing had built up to twenty-seven. In the evening, *Wild Goose* made a contact and then directed *Woodpecker* which sank *U-762* with twenty-six depth charges. The following morning three 'Gnats' exploded at the end of their runs close to *Kite*, *Wild Goose* and *Starling* without causing damage.

The most spectacular incident of Walker's voyage occurred on 10 February when at about 9 a.m., lookouts on *Starling* saw several hundred yards away the streaking track of a conventional torpedo with a partly surfaced U-boat in the background. Walker immediately gave the order to turn hard away and at the same time fire depth charges at the minimum depth setting. Two explosions occurred almost simultaneously close to *Starling*'s quarterdeck as the depth charges set off the torpedo. By some miracle, the ship was not damaged, and it was only quick thinking by the Captain and the disciplined response of his crew which saved the vessel. After four more successes against U-boats, the group finally set sail for Liverpool. Just before midnight on 20 February, when the ships were steaming line abreast, without any warning the stern was blown off *Woodpecker* by a 'Gnat'. When she finally sank after seven days in tow, all the ship's company was saved. The destruction of these U-boats was the result of a systematic procedure which gave the enemy little chance of escape once located. Statistics showed that an average of four hours elapsed before destruction occurred after the firing of 106 depth charges. Walker and his crew received a heroes' welcome including an official signal: 'Johnnie Walker still goes strong'. In fact Walker was suffering considerably from the stresses of war, and he died on 9 July as the result of a cerebral thrombosis. Vessels under his command were credited with having sunk twenty U-boats.

At the funeral service for Captain F. J. Walker C.B., D.S.O.*** R.N. in the Liverpool Cathedral, the Commander in Chief, Western Approaches, Admiral Sir Max Horton concluded his address:

> Not dust, nor the light weight of a stone, but all the sea of the Western Approaches shall be his tomb.

HMS *Starling* returns to a triumphal reception at Liverpool in February 1944 after the Second Escort Group led by Captain Johnny Walker had bagged six U-boats.

Walker's biographer, Terence Robertson, wrote:

> In the late afternoon, the destroyer reached the edge of the great, rolling ocean and here under a darkening sky with the wind strong enough to fleck the grey-green waves with white, the weighted coffin was tilted over the side into the waiting sea.

I had neglected to contact Sarah on the previous turnaround, and realising her spy in the Chrysler building would have told her the ship had called, I anticipated trouble when we reached New York on 16 February. I visited the Commodore to see what could be had in the way of theatre tickets, and there I hit gold. A few months earlier, 'Oklahoma!' had opened at the St. James theatre to rave notices, being hailed as at least equal to the previous all time great musical – 'Show Boat', originally staged in 1927.

After the show, we crossed town to the Stork Club for supper. The Stork shared with El Morocco a reputation for attracting the leading celebrities of café society. Apart from film stars, notables whose presence was now and then reported included the Windsors, Madame Chiang Kai-shek, Jack Dempsey, Babe Ruth, Jack Kramer, Ernest Hemingway, Tennessee Williams, Mayor Fiorello La Guardia and Frank Sinatra – the last strictly without bodyguards. Elliot Roosevelt and Humphrey Bogart were reported to be banned – perhaps the management had heard that a club becomes distinguished, not by whom it lets in, but rather by whom it keeps out. If any celebrities were there that night, we did not notice them.

The two extended turnarounds of the previous summer had become distant memories and my pay-book was becoming inflated. On the next day, our last, we saw a matinee, 'Arsenic and Old Lace', followed by dinner at Le Pavillon, a Fifth Avenue restaurant rated next to Le Chambord for excellence. That helped to cut back my balance. Gentlemanly requirements naturally barred contributions by the lady. The books provided by Sarah for the next voyage were John Steinbeck's *The Grapes of Wrath* (1940 Pulitzer Prize winner) and Maynard Keynes' *The General Theory of Employment Interest and Money*. The latter, a gift, was intended as and proved to be a preparation for my final year of economics which lay ahead. What a combination of books – the first described the sickness, the second, for many, the cure. We sailed on 21 February 1944.

CHAPTER 12

The Hectic Months Preceding D-Day

The most carefully guarded secret of the war was probably the ability of each side frequently to decrypt the other's ciphered signals with varying delays. At times, the Allies were decoding German messages to and from U-boats within 24 hours of transmission. The operation was known as 'Ultra', the name being based on the most restricted signal classification, 'Ultra Top Secret'. Although known to few for many years, it has become apparent that a major protection for independently routed troop transports was the selection of the route, and of its subsequent adjustments, during passage. These decisions were made by Admiralty, which leaned heavily on the information provided by Ultra.

The daily A.I.G. 331 U-boat situation report, referred to in Chapter 7, was couched in general terms. It was sent to all Allied warships and troop transports in the Atlantic in the second top grade cipher, and any decrypting by the enemy was unlikely to betray the Ultra operation, since direction-finding bearings alone could explain the knowledge. The evidence points to the Germans having remained largely unaware of the success of Ultra throughout the war.

British intelligence had been working on the breaking of German codes well before the war. Subsequent successes arose from gaining possession in Warsaw in 1939 of the German cipher machine known as 'Enigma', and the receipt during the same year of the scheduled forward settings of the machine's three drums for a number of months. The capture of the enemy weather ship *Munchen* in the Atlantic in May 1941, with its Enigma machine and future drum settings, was followed by another similar success during the same month. Allied ships had depth-charged *U-318* to the surface. It was boarded before sinking and an Enigma machine of higher classification with drum settings was removed. These events enabled immediate decrypting before the next drum setting programme had been distributed and brought into operation.

At the outbreak of war, the British had established the Ultra operation at Bletchley Park, a Victorian mansion in Buckinghamshire. The participants were mostly civilians, as distinct from service personnel, and these

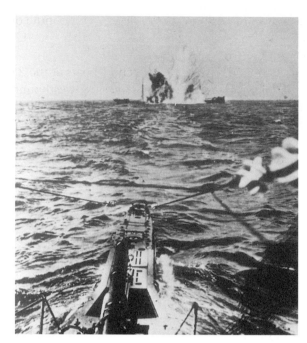

Torpedoing of an unescorted merchantman, photographed from the U-boat conning tower. (Courtesy Imperial War Museum, London)

teams of cryptologists were drawn from mathematicians, statisticians and scientists. The secrecy provisions of their employment extended indefinitely into the future, and it was not until almost three decades after the war had passed before books on the subject began to appear. Apart from the interception of signals to and from U-boats, additional information used by Ultra included direction finding bearings, sightings by Allied aircraft and shipping, details of ASDIC contacts, and even the recognition of individual keyboard styles of U-boat radio operators.

On 8 March 1943, the Germans introduced an improved Enigma machine, with the number of drums increased to four. This change had the effect of initially preventing, or considerably delaying, Allied decrypting, but with increasing skills, data banks and enemy traffic combined with brilliant guesswork, Ultra was again operating with its former success by the end of 1943.

An illustration of the above is given by an examination of four randomly-selected Admiralty papers relating to signals based on Ultra information during December 1943. They bore the classification 'Most Secret Message' – 'To be kept under lock and key – Never to be removed from the office'. Ultra-based signals were subjected to an extended moratorium, but have become available for inspection at the British Public Records Office in Kew, Middlesex. They give an indication of the then brief decrypting delays.

1 December. Exact details given of positions to the degree and minute of an area being patrolled by twelve U-boats and advised another four U-boats would join on 6 December (in 5 days time).

3 December. Details of a patrol line formed by sixteen U-boats at the 25 degrees west meridian for 'night operations against a slow westbound convoy'. This was convoy ON 214.

17 December. This signal provided a specific example of almost instant decrypting. It stated that at 1937 hours the previous day nine U-boats were adjusting their speeds to arrive at a particular area (exact position given) at a.m. 20 December (three days ahead).

20 December. This signal corrected the above figure to twelve U-boats and advised the enemy was expecting a convoy which would be subject to German air reconnaissance.

These successes could be attributed in part to the long hours of darkness when U-boats were usually surfaced, thus providing transmitting opportunities for lengthy and frequently unnecessary messages. These signals gave both Ultra and direction-finding stations additional material, which, however, diminished as days lengthened and as schnorkel-equipped boats needed to spend less time on the surface.

The Americans co-operated closely with Bletchley Park after entering the European war. They were already conducting a similar operation in Rockefeller Centre, New York, with a team of cryptologists led by Colonel William Donovan. Up to that point, the Americans were reading many of the Japanese coded signals.

The Germans had monitored British naval traffic between the wars, and in 1936 succeeded in breaking their codes, which were based on books, with periodic changes in the reciphering tables. During the early years of the fighting, this decrypting continued with varying delays, and at times enabling wolf packs to intercept convoys. In April 1943 the British introduced new ciphers combined with the more frequent replacement of reciphering tables. A delayed decrypting still took place but the information was generally too stale to be effective.

The Battle of the Atlantic entered another phase early in 1944. The successes of the long-range Liberator aircraft against the German submarines, together with the theoretical closing of the 'Black Hole' or 'Gap', continued to make running battles between submarines and convoy escorts an unprofitable exercise for the Germans. In practice, the 'Gap' remained for the liners in that an aircraft could not stay with the ship for sufficient length of time to justify a sortie into the mid-Atlantic. The 'wolf pack' tactics had been wound down slowly as U-boats were progressively fitted with a new device of Dutch origin known as the 'Schnorkel'.

U-boats under construction in Krupp's yards at Kiel. The rate was progressively increased until 1944 and then maintained. (Courtesy German National Archives, Koblenz)

The mounting U-boat losses were partly the result of attacks when surfaced at night, while recharging their batteries and replenishing the air supply. As early as 1942, a number of British Wellington bombers had been fitted with 'Leigh Lights', named after their inventor, Squadron Leader Humphrey de Verde Leigh R.A.F. The beam would floodlight a surfaced submarine at the final moment as the aircraft zoomed in on a radar contact. These lights were subsequently fitted to other Coastal Command aircraft, including Liberators, enabling them to sink U-boats in transit through the Bay of Biscay between the French ports and the Atlantic Gap. In 1944 the use of parachute flares producing two million candlepower was introduced, the technique being to release one or more above a U-boat on the first attack.

At this stage of the war, all U-boats had been fitted with the radar countermeasure Metox, which provided a directional warning by detecting radar transmissions from an approaching aircraft. It had been designed in Paris by the French for Germany. Metox was subsequently rendered ineffective by the Allied development of centimetric radar, which Metox could not detect. There was, however, a limit to the number of times a U-boat could keep on surfacing and submerging in rapid succession before exhausting its batteries and air supply. The Schnorkel became a partial solution to this problem. Constructed of twin tubes

Kapitanleutnant Peter Cremer commanded U-boats from December 1941 until June 1944. His photograph of this Atlantic gale highlights the discomforts experienced by crews when their U-boat was surfaced. Peter Cremer was one of a small group of 'Great Survivors' for a period of this length.

contained within a single outer casing, it was hinged to the deck just forward of the bridge. The U-boat was able to proceed at about 4 knots at periscope depth using her diesel engines, and at the same time could recharge her batteries and replenish the air supply. The intake tube was constructed to periscope height whilst the outlet tube, at a lower level, discharged the burnt gases clear of the intake. Both surface craft and aircraft experienced difficulty detecting a periscope or Schnorkel by radar unless the sea were particularly calm. When proceeding in daylight, trimmed down to Schnorkel depth, a U-boat trailed a foaming wake and exhaust fumes which, in reasonably calm weather, could be spotted by a lookout with a keen eye.

These Schnorkel boats patrolled British coastal waters and the inner Western Approaches rather than in Mid-Atlantic. Crews found living conditions unpleasant, frequently experiencing a sudden reduction in air pressure when waves rose over the air intake causing a temporary closure of the valve. When operating near the coast, the crews languished in their bunks by day to conserve air until the nightly prowling for targets began. The human endurance factor had the effect of limiting the period of the patrols, although less travel time was involved in reaching the areas of operation. Transmitting by radio was restricted on account of these

The strength of a North Atlantic gale demonstrated by this extraordinary photograph of the *Queen Mary* in mid-ocean. The bow has plunged deeply beneath the green water which may well have reached the height of the bridge. (Courtesy F/Lt Joseph Collins, radar officer with 59 Squadron R.A.F. September 1943 to June 1946)

prolonged submerged activities, and many days could pass without a U-boat reporting to base. The detection of U-boats thus became less frequent, and further complications for the Allies arose from the difficulty in distinguishing between a wreck and a U-boat when an ASDIC contact was obtained in shallow coastal waters. The loss ratio of submarines was accordingly reduced by the installation of Schnorkel.

Additional advantages accrued to the enemy by operating U-boats close to British harbours. The shipping lanes converged as major ports such as the Clyde, Liverpool, Bristol, Plymouth and London were approached, and the chances of a U-boat sighting a target increased proportionately. In spite of the benefits of these coastal and Western Approaches operations, Doenitz also maintained submarine patrols in both the Gap and in the Halifax areas. One purpose was to draw off Allied aircraft and escort ships from the expected invasion areas, and the U-boat persisted as a threat across the width of the Atlantic throughout the remainder of the war. In March 1944, a submarine withstood a hunt for a record period when the First Escort Group kept a U-boat below the surface for two days and one night – over 38 hours. The morale of the U-boat commander had not been impaired as he demonstrated on surfacing, by torpedoing and sinking the frigate HMS *Gould*. The U-boat was in turn sunk by HMS *Affleck*, which then set about rescuing the surviving crewmembers of *Gould*.

Allied anti-submarine aircraft now employed a device known as a sonar buoy. After sighting a U-boat, an aircraft would drop a buoy above where the enemy had dived. The buoy would then transmit information relating to the depth and direction of the enemy. Two or more buoys could provide a better fix on the U-boat's position, course and speed.

In February 1944 the unescorted troop shuttle service schedules were unbalanced when the *Queen Elizabeth* had to spend six weeks in the Bayonne dry dock to rectify damage when struck by a freak wave when westbound for New York. Proceeding with little more than steerage way in mountainous seas, the bow buried itself into an enormous mass of water. The foredeck was crushed down several inches, opening up large cracks, decks below buckled, and glass in the wheelhouse shattered, cutting communications wiring. All the damage was the result of one particular wave, but the gale itself apparently did not equal the proportions of the prolonged storm experienced by the *Aquitania* the previous month.

Between 21 February and 25 April 1944, the *Aquitania* made three round-trips to the Clyde, with the final leg ending at Boston. These six crossings followed the previous patterns with the usual diversions and the frequent provision of air cover outside the Gap. On 5 March, the fourth day of a return journey to New York, we ran into a heavy storm. A signal was intercepted from a Liberty ship about 50 miles away, reporting it had broken in two. Another vessel was standing by and presumably the endangered crew was rescued. The temperature climbed to 60 degrees as we sailed across the Gulf Stream, but snow was falling on the decks the next day as we approached New York. By this time we had completed ten round trips or twenty crossings, and had been on the move constantly since the beginning of the previous October. At this stage, the *Aquitania* would have carried about 80,000 troops to the U.K., whilst the combined contribution of the *Queens* would have reached approximately 400,000.

Alex Milne had been unwell for several weeks and the ship's surgeon, 'Doc' Rust, had urged him to apply for a trip off. He suffered from attacks of dermatitis and a U.S. medical officer ashore now insisted he be admitted to a naval hospital on Long Island. After discussing the position with Captain Ford and with Maurice Hobday, I told the shore authorities that I was confident I could carry on alone for at least the next voyage, after which it was expected Milne would return. The volume of work was no great problem, and Maurice Hobday, with the assistance of the Chief Petty Officer Telegraphist Robertson, could have coped with non-emergency ciphering in the event of my own incapacity.

We arrived back at the Clyde on 21 March and I was more than ready to give London another whirl, spending four days away from the ship. I put up at the King George and Queen Elizabeth Dominion Officers' Club at 46 Grosvenor Street, between Grosvenor Square and New Bond Street. The building was a Georgian home of large proportions with priceless fittings including a divided grand staircase. 'Bed, breakfast and bath, seven shillings and six pence ($1.50), lunch two shillings, tea one shilling and dinner three shillings and six pence'. A bath meant there was one up the corridor. The clubs for 'non-commissioned officers and men' usually charged two shillings and six pence for bed and breakfast. Notices pinned to a board invited those with the time and inclination to visit country manors, where I was told by other Australians the hospitality was excellent.

London had changed since my visit the previous May. The atmosphere was now electric, fired with the anticipation of the invasion of Europe, and with the chance of victory within the year. Streets teemed with servicemen, and if some were apprehensive about the impending invasion, their girlfriends did their best to direct their minds elsewhere. Theatres and restaurants were packed, particularly with G.I.s who had no wish to be launched into eternity with their pockets stuffed full of pound notes.

I tracked down a steak at Simpson's, and on another occasion had dinner at the Carlton Grill. Whilst touring the 'City' to visit the heavily blitzed Guildhall, the Royal Exchange and St. Paul's Cathedral, I dropped in at the Old Bailey and watched a fellow being tried for forging food ration tickets. He did not seem to be going too well when I left.

On arriving back at the ship, I found Captain Ford had been replaced by Captain Cyril Illingworth, whose previous appointment had been Captain of the *Queen Mary*, and who had been in command when she collided with HMS *Curaçoa* in 1942. The new Captain began his seafaring career under sail running between Liverpool and Rangoon. He joined Cunard in 1910, and in the First World War served in the battleship HMS *Valiant* at the Battle of Jutland. He became a Captain in the Royal Navy Reserve and was another of Cunard's fine officers. Captain Illingworth was featured on the cover of *TIME* magazine on 11 August 1947, when he was again Captain of Cunard's flagship.

The return trip to New York followed the northern route. U-boats in the Gap were able to take advantage of the longer hours of daylight, but the patrol lines began to thin on account of a proportion of the submarines returning to base, being retained to participate in repelling the impending Allied invasion. We arrived in New York on the evening of 3 April, and the following day I visited Alex Milne in hospital where he was up and about, but insufficiently recovered to return to the ship. That night Jenny and I had dinner at the Starlight Roof at the Waldorf Astoria, and later we moved on for a splendid night of jazz at Cafe Society

Uptown where Teddy Wilson and Hazel Scott were packing them in. A colleague from Navy Office Melbourne, Lieutenant Charles Plummer, had been ciphering his way between Liverpool and New York in the unescorted Dutch troop transport *Nieuw Amsterdam*. Attempts to meet at Delmonico's continued to be thwarted by our differing schedules and I learned on my return to Boston on 6 June that he had been transferred to another ship in the Pacific. This proved to be our fastest turnaround to date, our departure on 6 April taking place within two and a half days. The ship had docked at Pier 90 on account of some problems at Pier 86, and the *Queen Mary* was due to disembark passengers at Pier 90 within hours of our hurried departure. We passed her on an opposite course shortly after leaving harbour.

On 12 April at about 9 a.m., I decoded an emergency signal ordering us to change course immediately, and to proceed at maximum possible speed for three hours on account of U-boats having been fixed directly on our track. The same signal advised that two Liberators were being sent from Iceland. Captain Illingworth was shaving and he shot up to the bridge, his face covered with soap. After sounding action stations for the gun crews, he ordered all troops to boat stations where they were required to remain for the next three hours wearing life jackets. Shortly after 11 a.m. the Liberators found us and they remained to 3 p.m. – the limit of their fuel endurance.

Lieutenant Charles Plummer of the *Nieuw Amsterdam.*

During the afternoon of 13 April, we passed two heavily-escorted outward bound convoys north of Ireland and by lamp exchanged pleasantries with the commodores. Fewer ships now lay at anchor in the Clyde on account of an exodus to the invasion ports on the south coast. *Hitler's U-boat War* records the following fantasy (at least as far as the two hits were concerned) of a U-boat commander:

> The new *U-385* commanded by Hans-Guido Valentiner, age twenty-three, sailed from Norway on April 5 1944, fitted with Fliege search radar. Southbound near Iceland on April 13, Valentiner attacked a destroyer of a small convoy with a t-5; it missed. Two days later he fired a three torpedo salvo at what he described as an 'Empress' class ocean liner but it was in fact the monster liner *Queen Mary*. He claimed 'two hits' and 'two boiler explosions', but *Queen Mary* was not in fact hit. On that day and in that place she reported a heavy 'underwater explosion', perhaps a premature or some other torpedo malfunction.

Captain Bisset in his book *Commodore* reported that the *Queen Mary* had sailed from New York on 10 April taking a particularly long route near Iceland (actually 4069 miles) and this would be consistent with the above convergence. *U-385* was later sunk by an aircraft of 461 Squadron R.A.F. operating in conjunction with HMS *Starling*, on 11 August 1944 just off Lorient. This was just nine days before the port fell to the Americans and presumably Valentiner had set out to escape to Norway through the Western Approaches.

On 16 April, the *Queen Mary* arrived carrying over 13,000 troops – a peak number for that season of the year and an indication of the congestion caused by the storm damage to the *Queen Elizabeth*. We sailed for Boston the following evening.

We were routed well to the south for a change, and this offered hopes of warmer weather. On the second day out the ship passed uncomfortably close to a floating mine which presumably had broken free from some distant mooring. At dusk on 20 April, when for the first time the ship was actually within sight of and abeam with the Azores Islands, Lieutenant Commander Hobday, leaning against the taffrail, sighted a periscope and wake about 800 yards dead astern. It had not been reported earlier by other lookout stations, nor had the radar picked up any contact. Hobday concluded that the U-boat had lain submerged during the day, and was in the act of surfacing for its nocturnal patrolling, or had heard our engines on its hydrophones, when the sighting was made. Within a few seconds the periscope disappeared into the twilight.

The same evening at the contract bridge card game, an elderly radio officer, something of an amateur maritime historian, mentioned that earlier in the day we would have passed close to where possibly the greatest unsolved mystery in seagoing history was discovered. He was referring to the *Mary Celeste* incident when the 280-ton U.S. half-brig, bound from New York to Genoa with a cargo of 1700 barrels of commercial alcohol, was discovered at 3 p.m. on 5 December 1872 drifting, undamaged, and without a soul aboard. The master, his wife and baby daughter and the crew had vanished without trace, and speculation as to what occurred continues to the present day. I decided not to embarrass this elderly friend by asking how did it come about that he had been aware of the ship's position close to 38N 27W. In reality, there was very little that crew members did not discover about sailing dates, destinations and very roughly the route being taken.

On 25 April 1944, we tied up at Commonwealth Pier in Boston following two beautiful days of clear weather. Confirmation was then received that the ship would be refitting for about eight weeks. The *Aquitania* had made eighteen crossings during the previous twenty-nine weeks covering about 65,000 miles. By this time a considerable amount of maintenance work had accumulated due to storms and continuous travel since the previous fall. Hunks of several layers of grey paint were breaking away in places, revealing Cunard house colours. It was time for a pause.

The period covered by the two previous chapters from 7 December 1943 to 25 April 1944 included probably the worst stretch of stormy winter weather throughout the war. The long hours of darkness, together with cloud and fog, greatly limited the periods when air cover could be provided for convoys or for these liners. On the other hand the discomfort experienced by the crews of a surfaced U-boat during these storms restricted enemy activity. U-boat losses in the North American – U.K. shipping lanes totalled fifty-two, with ships accounting for thirty, whilst aircraft destroyed fifteen, a discrepancy compared with earlier figures being due to the weather. The remaining seven submarines were lost due to collisions, sinking mines and unexplained disappearances, probably storm damage. U-boat production would have exceeded losses by about thirty. Thirty of these U-boats were sunk whilst the *Aquitania* was at sea during the twelve crossings she made in this December-April period.

CHAPTER 13

A Boston Refit Allows Travel Opportunities

I had read a couple of books on Boston from the ship's library, and I must say it was with enthusiasm that I stepped ashore. Historically, it is perhaps the most interesting city in the country, being the centre of a culture which produced Hawthorne, Emerson, Thoreau and Longfellow. A number of seats of learning such as Harvard, Massachusetts Institute of Technology, Tufts, Wellesley and Radcliffe colleges were established around this area of New England.

Things got away to an indifferent start. Hobday, always prepared to supervise the gunners and communications ratings when the ship was in port, was laid low and admitted to hospital. About six weeks earlier I had developed a persistent cough and my uniforms began to hang rather loosely. Dr Rust packed me off to the same hospital for a chest X-ray, Milne still remained in hospital on Long Island, and all told it was beginning to look as if the Royal Naval representation in the *Aquitania* was in bad shape.

Every morning it became my lot to think up duties for the sixty ratings, but fortunately our two permanent service Chief Petty Officers were well versed in this sort of exercise. In peacetime, that was what the Navy was partly about. The hands were set to painting the gun positions, and when they had finished, why, they set to and painted them again. In the mornings I inspected quarters, went through the work scheduled and occasionally, not always without twinges of conscience, dealt out some mild discipline for offences against Naval regulations, such as when a U.S. shore patrol would deliver a rating in a condition less than sober.

An officer's club – similar to Delmonico's in New York – operated at the Statler Hotel where theatre tickets and holidays with private families were on offer. Young ladies of solid upbringing, some from the better Beacon Hills Brahmin families, welcomed servicemen to the club. The Copley Plaza Hotel featured a carnival-style diversion called 'The Merry-Go-Round Bar', where you could sit at a table circling slowly around the bar core and sum up the other patrons at the stationary outer tables. In the adjacent 'Oval Room', Pola Negri, from the days of silent films, had the star billing.

A message arrived from the British Admiralty Delegation in Washington, stating that I was required to attend a five-day refresher course. Working hours were short and I was able to visit in a leisurely fashion the memorials, monuments, museums and libraries which I had skimmed over or missed altogether on previous occasions. Other diversions included dinner with an R.N. Captain and his W.R.N.S. wife at their home in Chevy Chase, Maryland, and an evening with the Australian Naval Attaché.

In preference to returning to New York or Boston on the Friday, I decided to spend the weekend at Harper's Ferry in West Virginia where the Civil War is regarded by some historians as having begun. Located about 60 miles west of Washington, the resort is where the Potomac and Shenandoah Rivers meet. The New York Times had described it as 'One of the U.S.A.'s five great small towns'. The Hilltop Hotel was poised on a high bluff at the point of confluence of these rivers and I had a room with a splendid view.

A member of the staff of the Chilean Embassy in Washington and his wife were staying at the hotel, and they kindly invited me to join them motoring down the Skyline Drive into the Blue Ridge Mountains of Virginia. The road follows a ridge at about 3500 feet and passes through the Shenandoah National Park, providing frequent views of that river which is as beautiful as its name and the song. A profusion of apple blossom bathed the hills of what has been termed Virginia's hunt country.

The Chilean couple drove me back to the Capital on that Monday morning, and in the afternoon I travelled by train to New York where I remained for two days. The time had now come to put in an appearance back at the ship, and on returning to Boston I found all to be well, and that Maurice Hobday would be released from hospital the following week. The gun crew and communications ratings appeared to have suffered no harm from the absence of their officers.

The Seim family again invited me down, and Ed and I visited Bridgeport on the Friday for an extended weekend. The weather was not yet sufficiently warm for swimming in Long Island Sound, but we played some golf and on the Sunday drove across into the Catskill Mountains. Ed Seim had just been notified of a permanent transfer to the *Nieuw Amsterdam* but I was to meet him again several times at Gourock, in New York, and also at his home. This Holland-America Line vessel was manned by a Dutch crew with the exception of the gunnery and communications personnel.

Two Jewels from the C.P.R. Crown – The ill-fated *Empress of Britain* passes beneath the Chateau Frontenac.

The refitting of our ship would not be completed for a further four weeks, and I made arrangements to spend ten days in New Hampshire, to be followed by a visit to Canada. The village of North Conway had been recommended and I booked into a small private hotel. Essentially a ski resort about 150 miles north of Boston, North Conway is close to the Maine border. I played golf each morning, and in the afternoons there were always invitations to go driving with other house guests. These excursions centred on the White Mountains, an area abounding with lakes and peaks and views of exceptional beauty. We also visited Bretton Woods where the historical International Monetary Conference was to begin six weeks later.

I left North Conway on 2 June for Montreal. My fellow train travellers were devouring newspapers with headlines forecasting the invasion of Europe to be imminent. At Montreal, I managed a room at the Ritz Carlton and later that night, I ended up with a group at the night club called El Morocco, which failed to display the zebra striped decor of its splendiferous Manhattan namesake. The orchestra played 'The Last Time I Saw Paris', preceded by an introductory reference to the impending invasion, and the vocalist generated some applause amongst the largely French-speaking patrons. One sensed that in Quebec Province, enthusiasm for the war effort hardly equalled that in their neighbours. Posters and placards were scarce and opposition to conscription was strong in sections of this French-orientated community. This had not been the case in Halifax, Nova Scotia, where the British heritage was more dominant.

The next day I travelled by train to Quebec and stayed overnight at the Chateau Frontenac, the principal centre together with the Citadel, for the two Quebec conferences involving Churchill and Roosevelt. In those days it was one of the world's 'Great Hotels', with its unique architecture, its French cuisine in the Jacques Cartier dining room, and its commanding position over the River St. Lawrence. I expect it still retains its ranking.

I was awakened about 5 a.m. on Monday morning by the pealing of church bells, and penetrating the hotel from all directions, the noise continued until breakfast. Surely 'Operation Overlord' was en train with La Belle France being in the process of Liberation. Mais non, it was explained that the church bells were rung in that fashion daily, and that the locals had stoically acquired the knack of not hearing the bedlam. I had left my razor at the hotel in Montreal and underwent for the first time the unnerving experience at the Chateau barbershop of being shaved by a Frenchman with an appearance of singular ferocity, brandishing a cut throat razor. I suspected his sympathies lay with Vichy but I slipped away unharmed – at least physically. Escaping to Montreal the same afternoon, I left for Boston the following morning.

Hastening along the railroad platform, I picked up a copy of the *Montreal Gazette*, and on unfolding it in the train was confronted with the banner headline – 'INVASION LAUNCHED – CANADIANS, BRITISH AND AMERICANS LAND IN FRANCE – MONTGOMERY LEADING'. The paper also announced three recent sinkings of U-boats by the Canadian Navy in the North Atlantic, the destroyer *St. Laurent* having achieved the latest successes.

During my absence, Alex Milne had returned to the ship, but within a few days the skin rash again erupted, and he was admitted to a naval hospital in Boston. I visited him the following morning and was sorry to learn he was going to be repatriated to Australia. I initially informed the Captain and Maurice Hobday that Milne, who had been absent since March, would not be returning, and I was instructed to pass this information on to the shore authorities with an expectation that a replacement would be provided. Nothing then happened but we assumed another cipher officer would be awaiting our arrival at Gourock on 29 June. The naval authorities at Greenock knew nothing about the situation, although they had been informed the previous March that Milne was temporarily in hospital. No indication was given that they intended to do anything about it.

Neither the new skipper, Captain Illingworth, nor Hobday was fussed about the position, nor was I for that matter. Presumably I had done the job alone satisfactorily since March. A replacement had not turned up by the time we sailed and from then until war's end nothing changed. Nevertheless, on reflection, I should have taken whatever steps would have been necessary to bring about Milne's replacement.

From the end of 1943 until the beginning of the invasion, the transportation of troops across the Atlantic reached its climax. In addition to the Cunarders, including the *Mauretania*, the other independently routed ships, namely the *Empress of Scotland*, *Île de France*, *Nieuw Amsterdam*, *Pasteur* and *Andes*, were all making their contribution. These ships sailed from Halifax, Boston, New York, Hampton Roads and Charleston, to Liverpool and occasionally to the Clyde, with the ports in southern England such as Bristol, Plymouth and Southampton remaining too vulnerable to air attack.

The numbers of United States liners were also increased with temporary transfers from the Pacific Theatre. The majority of tonnages ranged from 25,000 for the *West Point,* down to about 18,000 for the *Mariposa,* with speeds varying from 17 knots for the *Argentina* and *Brazil* to the *West Point's* 24 knots. Other U.S. transports included *Mt. Vernon, Wakefield, Monticello, Hermitage* and *Uruguay.* The *Wakefield* had burned at sea off Halifax in 1942 but was later salvaged and recommissioned. A number of these U.S. sailings entered the Mediterranean, reinforcing troops fighting in Italy. The slower ships, and those bound for Italy, usually proceeded in convoy.

CHAPTER 14

The Invasion – U-boats Flee the French Atlantic Ports

Hitler had instructed Doenitz to assemble as many U-boats as feasible to assist in repelling the invasion, and when the landings occurred in Normandy on 6 June 1944, approximately fifty submarines sailed from their bases in the Biscay ports and another twenty set out from Norway. During the first four days, thirty-six sightings of U-boats were reported, six being sunk and another six damaged. The skies over the invasion areas swarmed with patrolling Allied aircraft, and only a few Schnorkel-fitted submarines penetrated the invading fleets. Allied losses from submarines were only three ships, and the U-boats played little part other than diverting some Allied aircraft from France. U-boats unequipped with Schnorkels found the task of reaching the invasion area almost impossible, the waters being illuminated at night by aircraft equipped with Leigh Lights. However, Admiral Doenitz, in his memoirs, claimed thirty U-boats fitted with Schnorkels took part, of which twenty were destroyed, while 762 crewmen were lost. He also claimed twenty-one Allied vessels were sunk and seven damaged. I expect the truth lay somewhere in between. On 24 August Doenitz recalled all submarines from the invasion area, and ordered the majority to return to the Atlantic.

Coastal Command had continuously swept the seas north of Scotland and west of Ireland, interrupting the passage of the U-boats sailing from their Norwegian base at Bergen to the invasion area at Normandy. Between D-Day and the end of June, a Canadian squadron sank five U-boats north of Scotland. The Allies estimated that twenty-one submarines were lost by the enemy during June and that in the first six months of the year, a total of 122 U-boats was sunk, off-setting the commissioning of 115 new vessels.

By early August the U.S. forces of General George S. Patton's Third Army were streaming south from the Normandy coast towards the Biscay ports of Lorient, Brest and St. Nazaire, and after the breakthrough at Avranches on 4 August, a hasty evacuation of submarines loaded with men and equipment began. The long journey of escape to Norway via the west of Ireland then north of Scotland, continuously harassed by aircraft, must have been an ordeal under jam-packed conditions, but the majority reached their destinations.

The *Aquitania* sailed from Boston on 22 June. At the sailing conference the map showed the U-boat patrol lines were below previous strength in the 'Gap' area, but Captain Illingworth was warned that the western and central sections were by no means clear of the enemy. We were particularly cautioned of dangers in the coastal areas of Britain from patrolling Schnorkel-equipped craft, and from other U-boats in transit between the French ports and Norway. The ship was assigned a fairly direct route close to the great circle, but during passage we had the surprising number of seven diversions, which confirmed all the warnings. On the fourth day, at the northern extremity of our route, the sun dipped only briefly below the horizon. Air cover was provided for the last two days of the crossing. As we sailed up the Clyde, the summer sun added colour and beauty to the scenery. German records subsequently revealed that during this seven-day crossing, six U-boats were sunk in the Atlantic shipping lanes, the majority close to west coast ports of the U.K.

On 24 June, two days after the *Aquitania* had sailed from Boston, the 365-foot Japanese submarine *I 52*, whilst on the surface in rendezvous with a U-boat, was sunk by an acoustic-guided torpedo dropped by an Avenger aircraft from the carrier USS *Bogue*. This huge submarine had sailed from Japan for occupied France the previous March carrying two tonnes of gold bars (now valued at U.S.$25 million) together with scarce materials and drugs. She carried a crew of 94 and 14 scientists, and the intention was to exchange the cargo for radar technology to combat radar equipped U.S. aircraft in the Pacific. The purpose of the rendezvous, which took place in the mid-Atlantic 1200 miles west of the Cape Verde Islands, was to collect fresh supplies and to be fitted with a radar detector to warn of the presence of Allied planes as the French coast was approached. On coming under attack, both submarines dived, but the Japanese craft, after being fully submerged, was struck by the torpedo, the fact being recorded on a tape in the Avenger's cockpit. Whilst the U-boat escaped, the Japanese boat sank at a depth of 600 fathoms. Ironically, the French Atlantic ports were overrun six weeks later, thus sparing the Japanese Captain considerable problems. A long article in *The Times* of London dated 19 July 1995 set out in detail the success of a Mr Paul Tidwell, a Vietnam veteran, in locating and photographing the wreck on 2 May 1995, after years of research and the use of techniques which located the *Titanic* and *Bismarck*. Mr Tidwell 'believes the Japanese Government will not lay claim to the gold'.

Captain Fall directing the Quartermaster aboard the *Queen Elizabeth.* (Courtesy Imperial War Museum, London)

We arrived at Gourock on 29 June and sailed for New York on 3 July. Large amounts of mail had accumulated, the first to be delivered in over two months. I took the opportunity to visit Ed Seim in the *Nieuw Amsterdam* which had arrived from New York. Captain Illingworth was due for leave, and he was replaced by Captain Fall, also a Royal Naval Reserve Captain who had already commanded both the *Queen Mary* and *Queen Elizabeth.* We had expected to return to New York almost empty but shortly before sailing, about 2000 German prisoners of war from Normandy arrived – part of the 500,000-strong Seventh Army. Many exhibited symptoms of shock, and our guards had little to worry about. The westbound voyage was trouble-free, but it was not much of a tonic for the prisoners who looked the unhappiest collection ever assembled. However, the view of the Manhattan skyline certainly worked wonders for the demeanour of those whose turn it was to be exercising in the deck compound when we arrived on 10 July. The enemy lost four more U-boats during this crossing, one success being gained by a Sunderland of 10 Squadron R.A.A.F.

The next round trip took us away from New York from 15 July to 2 August, and during the turnaround in Scotland, three U.S. staff members and myself hired bicycles and pedalled down the south-east bank of the Firth of Clyde to the resort of Largs. During this eighteen-day mid-summer period only three U-boats were sunk in the Atlantic, reflecting the

"DAMN IT ALL THEY'LL EXPECT US TO WORK EVERYDAY NEXT"

CODING OFFICE

HARTLEY.

Freedom in port and at sea from scheduled watch keeping duties occasionally drew good-natured comments from our Cunard colleagues. Radar Officer John Hartley chose this method. (Courtesy John Hartley)

withdrawal for the invasion. However, R.A.F. and U.S. aircraft destroyed nine in the Baltic area, including four in port at Kiel and Bremen.

Alex Milne visited us shortly after the ship arrived back in New York on 2 August. He was living in style in the Barbazon Plaza Hotel waiting to hear something about his passage back to Australia – his skin trouble having cleared up again. The Navy was meeting his hotel bills and providing a special shore allowance for New York – he concluded the Admiralty was still working on the mystery of these two Australians. Sarah and I saw two Broadway shows, 'Mexican Hayride' at the Winter Garden, the Mecca of comedians, and 'Catherine Was Great' starring – you guessed it from the name – Mae West. Broadway was having its greatest boom, with money available to provide costuming and sets rarely before seen.

The ship sailed from New York on 6 August 1944, with our passenger list including about 500 Army nurses whose boat station was the promenade deck outside my cabin. A number of the comments overheard as the girls found themselves looking through the windows at my luxury accommodation were amusing, and occasionally of the type only nurses could get away with back in those days. During this round trip extending over seventeen days, in contrast to the previous experience, twelve U-boats were sunk in the North Atlantic with *Bogue, Vidette,* and *Starling* all having successes.

B.B.C. Radio broadcasts and ship's newspapers (2 cents) kept troops posted with the latest on all fronts.

The departure of Alex Milne involved no change in the cipher department work schedule. I would be awakened usually between 2 a.m. and 4 a.m. on three or four nights each crossing to decipher a signal relating to the times of arrival and departure of air cover. I would visit the cipher office before and after breakfast, and spend perhaps an hour making amendments to various naval publications, adjustments which had been supplied at the previous sailing conference. A visit to the bridge then followed when I would discuss briefly with the senior watch officer the U-boat report of the previous afternoon, and the dispositions which I had plotted on the chart. Next were a few words with the naval signalman on duty followed by a visit to the radio shack to discuss any problems with our Chief Petty Officer Robertson and the Chief Radio Officer, George Parsons. The coder on duty was well aware of this routine and I could be immediately contacted at the beginning of the transmission of any signal addressed to the ship.

Lunch with the British gunnery officer Hobday and his two U.S. counterparts was a relaxed affair, with the dining room uncrowded. Eastbound, the travelling officers had to make do with a sandwich as did their men, whilst westbound passengers were served three meals a day. Between 2 p.m. and 4 p.m. nothing was expected of watchkeepers not on duty. They climbed into their beds or bunks, not to be disturbed until shortly before 4 p.m. By this time they were about to report on duty, or were sufficiently refreshed for night rosters. Tea was served in the wardroom at 4 p.m. with a gathering of deck officers not on duty. Passengers of 'distinction' including civilian V.I.P.s or senior service officers were occasionally invited. Towards the end of a crossing when we were more likely to be in the mood, the trooping officer would 'procure', as someone incorrectly put it, a few girls from travelling W.A.C.s, W.A.V.E.s, W.R.E.N.s or nurses.

I found the daily work programme could be handled by one cipher officer assisted by the three watchkeeping coders and Petty Officer Telegraphist Robertson in the background. Whilst ciphers, as distinct from codes, were to be handled only by officers, that aspect would be cast aside in an emergency.

The communication arrangements in the *Queen Mary* and *Queen Elizabeth* were somewhat different as far as I could tell. The staffs included W.R.E.N. officers and coders who were exchanged after two round trips. These rapid replacements drew an official protest from Captain Fall when he was master of the *Queen Elizabeth*, who complained the cipher office had become something of a training ground. Neither Captain Fall nor Captain Ford, who were in positions to compare the differences in the arrangements between the *Aquitania* and the *Queens*, ever suggested that our staff should be increased. I like to think that our slimmed down operation worked equally as well. On this subject, I was told unofficially at Greenock that the *Aquitania* would have to find a few extra knots before any girls came our way.

Apart from the aspect of duties, which were congenial enough, life aboard was comfortable and conducive to pursuing other interests. The day began with good old James, the Cunard steward of about 40 years service, bringing the tray of tea. I never used the jug of hot water or the sugar but he insisted upon providing them – it just would not have been right otherwise. I tactfully brought up the subject of the thin slices of buttered bread. He insisted this was a Cunard custom which extended back well beyond his experience, that practically all the passengers, well, the British ones anyway, appreciated this delicacy of palate, and he felt confident that, given the chance, it would become for me a habit I would never abandon. Eventually I found one or two small slices not altogether displeasing.

James looked after the laundry, purchased my requirements at the canteen, and delivered the whisky and beer in accordance with the ration.

U-boat sinking by the stern following depth charge attack by Sunderland aircraft in the Western Approaches. (Courtesy Imperial War Museum, London).

Whenever required, he was Johnny-on-the-spot. I tipped him in keeping with the wartime practice which for travelling officers was one dollar each for cabin and dining room stewards for the crossing. Shortly before the war ended he was found dead from natural causes in his cabin, and, along with others he had served so well, I wrote to his family.

The British Commander of Troops, Colonel Heppenstall, was a keen chess player, a proficiency at which was encouraged by the army as a sure-fire aid to winning battles. We had a loose arrangement to play between 11.30 a.m. and 12.30 p.m. subject to the exigencies of our respective services – as he would have put it. I played deck tennis after tea when the weather was favourable, otherwise it was a matter of walking on deck, reading, writing letters or bringing the diary up to date. Recorded music was played over the ship's speakers for an hour between 4 p.m. and 5 p.m. and the B.B.C. news was also broadcast, although at times the quality of the reception was poor.

Dinner at 7 p.m. was the usual practice although the table was available also for the 8 p.m. sitting. The liquor ration would stretch to two or three drinks per day, and now and then I invited a passenger or two to join me before dinner, a gesture appreciated in an otherwise dry ship. In the evening, the ship's staff arranged a movie or a concert in the lounge, but these were crowded, and I preferred to play bridge. The movies, both British and Hollywood, proved the adage that truth is the first casualty of war and humour the second. My cabin, now with Milne leaving and having ample room for the tables and chairs, was the venue for cards and the players were usually drawn from the U.S. gunnery officers, U.S. trooping staff or the Cunard radio operators. 'Doc' Rust sometimes had a rather high stake poker game going in his cabin with U.S. officers, and I occasionally filled in, particularly when in the Clyde in winter.

I occasionally talked with travelling servicemen through the range of ranks, from professional men to those who had never nailed down a job, and I rarely came across any who had met an Australian before. I followed politics and found these discussions of interest leading up to the 1944 election when Thomas Dewey, Governor of New York, won the Republican nomination by 1056 to 1 (General MacArthur). The majority of our U.S. staff with whom I mixed came from upper income families, and strongly objected to Roosevelt's social and economic policies. I won quite a number of useful bets when Dewey scored less than 100 electoral college votes. I can attest that betting on politicians sure beats horses. In 1958 I drove up the Hudson from New York to Hyde Park, and visited Roosevelt's former home, now a museum, and his grave.

When the ship turned around in the Clyde between 13 and 16 August 1944, the capture of Paris was imminent. The U-boat ports of Brest, Lorient and St. Nazaire had fallen, and in Italy, Florence and Pisa had been re-taken with their treasures intact. V-1 flying bombs were buzzing in on London, and Hitler was threatening to launch his V-2 rockets on that city. The British press could always be relied upon to bolster our successes. On 9 August, London's *Daily Mail* excelled itself. Under the heading 'ALLIES TRAP FLEET OF U-BOATS – ATLANTIC BATTLE NEARLY OVER', the paper reported;

> German U-boat warfare in the Atlantic has been cut more than 75% by the break-through into Brittany, and the Battle of the Atlantic is virtually finished.

It went on to say over 100 U-boats would be lost or left stranded in the Atlantic without a base. In fact the British 'Official History' estimated the total U-boat fleet at 437 during April-June 1944 and 396 during July-

September 1944. These figures hardly amounted to a 75 per cent reduction.

We arrived off Halifax on 22 August, carrying 500 women and children, but fog prevented our entry into the harbour, and we weaved around in circles throughout the night. The ship remained here for six days, and I took the opportunity to spend three days at Kentville, a resort close to the Bay of Fundy, about fifty miles west of Halifax. Private hospitality was available through service clubs, but I have something of a kink about retaining control over my own activities. Canadian Pacific operated a splendid hotel at Kentville, complete with an excellent golf course, and well up to the standards they maintain at the Chateau Frontenac at Quebec, Chateau Lake Louise, and at Banff Springs. At dinner on my last night, the management produced champagne to toast De Gaulle's triumphal march into Paris that day.

Canada played a leading role in the defeat of Hitler. She had declared war on Germany on 10 September 1939, only seven days after Britain and Australia, and her first contingent of troops arrived in the U.K. in December of that year. Their strength had reached five divisions by D-Day, and the Canadian First Army under Montgomery's command was in the forefront of the landings in Normandy. Vast quantities of food and munitions were shipped across the Atlantic, and the construction of ships and participation in the Empire Air Training Scheme were all major contributions. Many Australian airmen who crossed the Atlantic in the Cunarders had completed their training in Canada. The scheme put through a total of 137,000 Empire flyers. As was the case with the Australians in the European Theatre, every Canadian who served was a volunteer.

At the outbreak of war, the Canadian Navy consisted of six destroyers and five minesweepers. The force expanded over the following years to reach about 400 warships, mostly corvettes, manned by some 90,000 seamen. Whereas Australian sailors serving in the Atlantic were dispersed widely amongst British ships and with limited recognition, the Canadian vessels were manned exclusively by their own national crews, which generated an independence not always relished by the Royal Navy. Canada became responsible for the campaign against the U-boats in the western segment of the Atlantic, and her navy and air force operating out of St. John's in Newfoundland, and also Halifax, had outstanding successes. The presence of an R.C.A.F. Liberator, sweeping the horizon ahead of the *Aquitania*, was on those occasions a welcome reminder of the Canadian effort. Unlike members of the Australian Navy in the war at sea, some Royal Australian Air Force personnel were able to retain a distinct identity by serving in three R.A.A.F. squadrons in Coastal

This spectacular photograph was taken from the second of two R.A.F. Mosquitos, swooping in to attack and sink a U-boat in the Western Approaches. (Courtesy Imperial War Museum, London)

Command, namely R.A.A.F. 10, 461 and 455. Six hundred R.A.A.F. members served with the R.A.F. Coastal Command Liberator squadrons as individuals, and several thousand in the overall Command.

We sailed from Halifax on 26 August and the contingent included Canadian troops to maintain the replacement of casualties in Europe. During the following ten days, Canadian warships had notable successes against the U-boats with HMCS *St. John*, *Swansea*, *Dunver* and *Hespeler* all despatching victims to the seabed. At this stage Schnorkel equipped U-boats were active to the north, west and south of Ireland, and we had Liberator escorts during most of daylight for the final two days. On the last night, the Captain ordered all personnel to sleep in their clothing, following the receipt of a signal emphasising the danger.

An indication of the enemy activity during this period was given in a letter written to his family by U-boat commander, Graf Matuschka, who was making his first foray in *U-482*, a Schnorkel-equipped boat.

> After our first patrol we have returned in good shape to the north. Our task led us west of England, and has given us quite unusual success. On August 30th 1944, the boat sank the American turbine tanker *Jacksonville*, on September 1st the corvette *Hurst Castle*, and on September 8th the motor ship *Pinto*, and the British Steamer *Empire Heritage*.

U-482 was only one of several Schnorkel boats having a high old time in the North Channel and inner Western Approaches. However Matuschka and his crew did not last long. On his next patrol, he torpedoed the Norwegian tanker *Spinanger* and almost gained position for a shot at the aircraft carrier HMS *Thane*. Shortly after the Second Escort Group put an end to another German submariner's brief career.

Whilst the *Aquitania* was being refitted in Boston between 26 April and 22 June, twelve U-boats were sunk in the Atlantic. Following our departure from Boston and until 4 September, we completed seven crossings, and twenty-three of the U-boat sinkings which took place during that period occurred whilst we were at sea, out of a total of thirty. The proportion of successes by ships, namely twenty-two, had increased significantly, reflecting the release of warships from the invasion area combined with additional requirements of aircraft by Bomber Command. The Schnorkel greatly lessened the ability of aircraft to detect U-boats at sea, though the boats were still suppressed by the presence of aircraft. The fact remains that U-boats of the time were very slow when submerged. During July an R.C.A.F. airman, Flying Officer J.A. Cruickshank, flying a Catalina within the Arctic Circle, had his aircraft shot down whilst in the process of sinking a U-boat. After a series of heroic efforts to save his aircraft and crew, Cruickshank died. He was posthumously awarded the Victoria Cross.

Captain Sir James Bisset, the master of the *Queen Mary*, had been busy during the five months from February to July. He made twelve crossings and reported carrying 74,504 troops eastbound to Britain, with each voyage averaging six days. Shortly after sailing from New York on 1 July, he received a personal message from Queen Mary to commemorate the tenth anniversary of her launching of this vessel which bore her name, and which had spent almost half her life in wartime service. The *Queen Elizabeth* had re-entered the shuttle service in March following extensive damage repairs and was keeping pace with her sister Cunarders.

CHAPTER 15

Surface Escorts in UK Waters

The *Aquitania* passed through the boom at Gourock shortly after dark on 4 September 1944, and as the anchor chain rattled down, the vast shape of the *Queen Mary* was visible, outlined against the hills of Dunoon. The following morning when I made arrangements to travel to London for six days, I became aware of an unusual amount of activity afoot at both Gourock and Greenock. Two large lighters were tied up at the Gourock pier, spruced up officials were bustling around, and a number of V.I.P. limousines queued up at the Greenock Station. I learnt on my return from London that the *Queen Mary* had sailed that above-mentioned evening for Halifax, carrying Winston Churchill, Mrs. Churchill, the First Sea Lord Admiral Cunningham, and Chiefs of Staff, Brooke, Portal, Ismay and Metcalf together with an entourage of 195 officials. Cunard Commodore James Bisset, the Captain of the *Mary*, described the ship as being 'escorted by cruisers and destroyers in relays' which was hardly surprising in view of the U-boat activity. The Prime Minister was on his way to attend the second Quebec conference, and the British party subsequently returned in the *Queen Mary* from New York 'under a U.S. naval escort which was relieved in mid ocean by British cruisers'. The quotations are from Commodore Bisset's book.

On arrival in London I again stayed at the Dominion Officers' Club in Grosvenor Street. The action in the West End was now more subdued, the streets being less crowded with servicemen than previously on account of the invasion. The V-1 flying bombs had been landing on London regularly during the preceding days and weeks, and my visit coincided with the launching of Hitler's latest advanced weapon.

On 8 September I had tippled away the evening at the Codgers' Club, a pub off the Strand near Australia House, frequented by Australian Navy types. Later, when travelling by taxi back to Grosvenor Street, the driver asked whether we had heard loud explosions earlier in the evening. We replied in the negative, suggesting V-1s were responsible, but the driver claimed the noise was of an entirely different character. In fact this happened to be the night of the first German V-2 rocket attacks on

London. One landed in Chiswick and the other in Epping, at opposite ends of the City. These mysterious explosions – resembling thunderclaps – could be heard all over London, and I incorrectly assumed the several I later heard were V-1s.

An official shroud of silence was imposed, and two months elapsed before Churchill revealed the explanation. These rockets with a 1-ton warhead travelled at a speed of 3500 m.p.h. giving no advance warning, and there was no prospect of shooting them down in flight as could be done with the V-1. Over 2000 V-2 rockets fell on greater London and more than 5000 residents were killed. The Allied armies eventually over-ran the launching sites of both types of weapons.

I spent most days exploring London. The number of historical places seemed limitless, and having learnt to find my way around, I was able to accomplish a great deal. I travelled down to Brighton in Sussex – a sea-side resort populated by retirees who were continuously disturbed by wave after wave of bombers heading for the French coast. Another day I spent at the horse races at Windsor where England's leading jockey Richards – later Sir Gordon – unfortunately failed to ride a winner.

The British children were the greatest beneficiaries of the 'invasion'. The G.I. could buy chocolate, ice cream, cakes, donuts, oranges, bananas, fancy biscuits and canned juices at his canteen – luxuries gen-erally unavailable to British families. For the girls there was perfume, scented soaps, and of course nylon stockings which, I was told, were occasionally handed over, one now and the other later. A triumph for a family was the daughter's acquisition of a G.I. as a regular boyfriend, thus gaining for her family indirect access to a U.S. canteen. On the other hand, the establishment of a U.S. camp in a district was forecast to be a prelude to a liquor and taxi drought.

The British introduced 'Welcome Clubs' where hostesses were avail-able for what the club name suggested. They were similar in intent to Delmonico's in New York, and many regarded them as especially neces-sary in London where ladies of negotiable virtue successfully continued in business. The largest club was the Rainbow in the Piccadilly Circus area. The wartime mixing of the populations could be looked upon as a great success, evidenced by nearly 100,000 British brides migrating to the U.S. after the war. In Australia about 15,000 girls married U.S. ser-vicemen – about a similar proportion of the population. It would be true to say that the travelling troops whose best hopes were a good time in England were not let down by the British.

We sailed at 4 p.m. on 13 September for New York, and for the next 24 hours were escorted by the destroyers HMS *Nubian* and *Serapis*. This was the first occasion we had had surface escort either in or out of

Servicemen's clubs in London helped distract thoughts from what lay ahead across the Channel.

Britain, and it highlighted the continuing ability of Schnorkel-equipped U-boats to operate in coastal waters, and also the first apparent avail-ability of, or willingness to provide, destroyers for our protection and rescue purposes. The initial course led us south through the Irish Sea, and darkness had set in before we altered to the south-west to pass through the narrow St. George Channel between Wales and Ireland.

U-boat Kapitanleutnant Herbert Werner headed *Aquitania*'s way for the fifth time. Since our joint presences in the same area on 26 October 1943, Werner had made a foray into the Mediterranean, and several into the Bay of Biscay where his vessel was damaged. Whilst the crew await-ed repairs, he describes his officers and men being well looked after by the local French girls whose contribution to the 'Resistance Movement' seemed to be directed more towards movement than resistance. On 7 September 1944, Werner sailed from Bergen in command of Schnorkel-equipped *U-973* under orders to rendezvous with three other submarines west of Ireland for a four week period. On 13 September, the

Aquitania emerged from the Irish Sea into the Atlantic at about the same day as Werner would have arrived. 'Near encounter' number six would have occurred on the last day of our return journey on 4 October, when Werner set out to return to Bergen.

During the following months we were frequently escorted by destroyers through coastal waters and the inner Western Approaches. These warships took up their stations about three miles ahead, one on the port bow and the other in the equivalent starboard position. All three ships maintained the same zigzag pattern, but now and then a destroyer darted off to investigate an ASDIC contact. We would turn hard away, and the dropping of depth charges frequently followed. No chances were taken, and I expect a number of wrecks were disturbed. Depending on the distance, these explosions could send severe shudders through the *Aquitania*, which had not been designed to withstand the concussion. Destroyers did not have the range to accompany us far out into the Atlantic when beating at over 20 knots. When engaged in normal convoy duties, these ships were usually able to refuel from a merchant tanker.

The discomforts suffered by the crews of these smaller ships were all too obvious. As often as not, a heavy sea would be encountered west of Ireland, and the destroyers faced the task of attempting to keep ahead of the liner. A troopship maintained speed on the basis that destroyer protection did not compensate for the added danger involved in slowing down. The tenacity with which these escorts attempted to keep their stations in heavy seas drew our admiration. They were notoriously 'wet' in that they leaked when the bending of their hulls opened the riveted plates. In very rough weather a destroyer might be compelled to turn about, the limiting factor being the risk of damage. If this point were reached, with exchanges of regret, thanks, and good luck all round, the destroyers would peel away, heading at reduced speed back towards the Clyde, Londonderry, Liverpool or Milford Haven, rolling perhaps 30 degrees in a quartering sea. A cruiser, with its greater range and capacity to cope with heavy weather, was the ideal escort for a troopship, but one never came the *Aquitania*'s way. The Navy seemed to prefer to operate in pairs, groups, or not at all, and two spare cruisers might have been hard to come by. After all, I suppose containment of the *Tirpitz* had to dwarf all other considerations, or so it seemed.

The daily U-boat reports showed a notable increase in the numbers of submarines patrolling the North American – U.K. shipping lanes with the majority in the eastern waters. German losses were being limited by the protection offered by the Schnorkel and the commanders avoiding the strongly-defended convoys. The faster, independently routed ships could afford the time taken to avoid the more direct lanes sailed by the slow convoys either by steaming north close to Iceland, or taking the southern route nearer to the Azores. Accordingly, the U-boats gained some prizes in these fringe areas at a reduced risk to their own safety.

The long, hot summer had passed and the leaves were turning when the *Aquitania* arrived in New York on 21 September. A delay of several hours occurred before docking, both on account of fog, and the unloading of 3000 prisoners into tenders in the Lower Bay. The transports were now bringing home on leave members of the U.S. Army Air Corps who had completed a specified number of sorties over Europe – usually thirty. These airmen wore leather jackets with bombs painted on the back to signify the actual number of missions flown. The majority had taken part in daylight raids, often involving up to 1000 bombers deep into Germany, harassed both ways by fighters and ack-ack fire. It was no farewell to arms for all – like other Allied pilots, some were called upon to exceed the thirty missions.

The painted jackets were a reminder of the wartime custom in the U.S. of families having members serving overseas being issued with emblems to fasten to their front doors, or to hang in lighted windows. A blue star was attached for each family member abroad. U.S. Army Captain, Buster West, the liaison officer for troops messing, had one of these emblems stuck to the door outside his cabin, displaying a sense of humour not always appreciated by other Americans who have always been less relaxed about their patriotism than the British or Australians. A prankster superimposed a gold star over the blue star to signify the serviceman was dead, but Buster confirmed his sense of fun by leaving it undisturbed. And this was well before M*A*S*H.

During this visit Sarah and I saw Elizabeth Bergner in the play, 'The Two Mrs. Carrols' and we made a day trip to Atlantic City on the New Jersey coast. An extravagance was dinner at the Colony restaurant. The pace in Manhattan had begun to slacken with the numbers of servicemen thinning and the published casualty lists growing. The queues behind the silk ropes at the night-clubs had shortened.

We sailed on 27 September and the second day out brought something of a disturbance when two cases of spinal meningitis were diagnosed amongst the troops. Each person on board was required to swallow four sulphur tablets, with the doctors somehow managing to come up with the 36,000 pills. Only one further case was reported.

On the fifth day we received a signal advising the ship would overtake within visual range during the afternoon an inward bound convoy, the senior escort being HMS *Highlander*. This destroyer had distinguished herself earlier in the war by depth charging and sinking *U-32*, four days after the U-boat had torpedoed and sunk the liner *Empress of Britain*

A rescue ship equipped to haul survivors aboard and to treat injuries and burns.
(Courtesy U.S. National Archives, Washington)

north-west of Ireland. An executive officer in *Highlander* was a friend from Melbourne, Lieutenant Arthur Webb.

About 3 p.m. a forest of masts rose above the horizon and as we closed on this large convoy, and after receiving Captain Fall's permission, I told our signalman to call up *Highlander* by lamp to advise Webb that a Lieutenant Satchell wished to communicate with him. With the assistance of our respective signalmen, we had exchanges by lamp for about five minutes and arranged to meet the following Friday. Webb was heading for Liverpool, and we agreed on Edinburgh as being the most suitable place for a rendezvous.

The convoy, plodding along at 10 knots, extended over about fifteen square miles. We exchanged greetings with the Commodore's ship sailing at the head of the centre column, the position normally taken by that vessel. A convoy commodore was usually a retired senior naval officer or a merchant mariner who had commanded a large passenger liner. He bore the responsibility for the conduct of the masters of the individual ships, supervised station keeping, and ensured zigzag patterns were observed. The policing of blackouts, of the emission of excessive smoke, and of the daylight dumping of rubbish were also part of his duties. In heavy weather stragglers became his concern, and in the event of a U-boat attack, the operations of the rescue ships, which were fitted with equipment to scoop men out of the water, came within his jurisdiction. However, over-all control of the convoy remained the responsibility of the naval officer commanding the senior escort. In the event of an attack, he gave direc-tions such as alterations to course or to scatter, and his vessel always handled ship-shore communications.

In 1943 when I first crossed the Atlantic, convoys were classified as 'fast' or 'slow'. A fast eastbound convoy from the U.S.A. or Canada to the U.K. was designated HX, and depending on the weather and other vari-able factors, could average about 11-12 knots. These sailings averaged about once weekly. On the return journey in ballast, an ON designation was given to the fast convoys.

About every eight or nine days a slow convoy identified as SC sailed from the U.S.A. or Canada with an average speed down to 8-9 knots, whilst on the return journey the designation was ONS. The fast convoys consisted of about sixty ships with the numbers increasing towards the end of the war, whilst the slow convoys were made up of about forty ves-sels. Both convoys sailed in a broad formation with a sixty-ship convoy being about six miles in width and two miles deep. However, rough weather could considerably distort these formations. The independently routed troop ships were designated as AT 'convoys' when eastbound and as TA 'convoys' returning to North America. All convoys were given a number to follow the lettered designation.

Late in the afternoon of 3 October, we effected a rendezvous with the destroyers HMS *Impulsive* and PS (Polish Ship) *Piorun*, and under air cover they escorted us through the Schnorkel area to Tulsa Rock. We reached the Clyde on 5 October, and I met with Arthur Webb at the North British Hotel in Edinburgh three days later. On returning to the ship, I was pleasantly surprised to find that Captain Battle, who had been in command when I had originally joined the ship in Sydney, and who had helped Milne and myself retain our appointments, had returned to the *Aquitania*.

The *Aquitania* had now completed thirty-three Atlantic crossings since May 1943, of which seventeen were eastbound, carrying some 8000 troops, making a total of about 135,000. The *Queen Elizabeth* and the *Queen Mary*, having begun their shuttles in the latter months of 1942, had carried about 650,000, making a total of approximately 785,000 troops for Britain's 'Three Proudest Liners' by October 1944. The *Queen Elizabeth* had achieved the largest total on account of the *Queen Mary* being recalled to the Middle East in the early months of 1943. The speed advantage of the *Queens* over the *Aquitania* was offset by longer

During the final months of the war, the *Queens* carried a limited number of wounded Americans on the Westbound crossings as shown here in the *Queen Elizabeth*. (Courtesy Imperial War Museum, London)

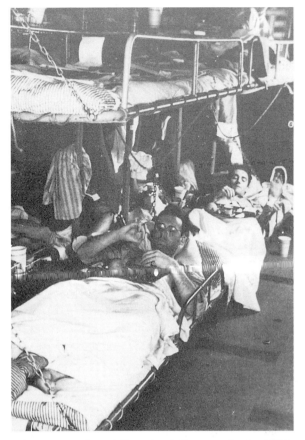

turnarounds, but the abandonment of avoiding the full moon in the U.K. waters for the *Queens* accelerated their troop delivery.

The brief periods in port provided little relief from stress for the merchant seamen and the permanent military staffs. In New York, the crews were engaged in the loading of stores, and maintenance work which could not be carried out at sea. They were required to assist contractors in specialised repairs, and in the case of the *Queens*, for example, in the conversion of a number of standee bunk areas to cot accommodation for the wounded on westbound crossings. Regular troops enjoyed this comfort travelling east. The permanent staffs were occupied with arrangements for the next troop intake involving vast amounts of paperwork.

The mounting casualty lists in Europe, with the consequent need for reinforcements, all added to the sense of urgency. It must be admitted that the communications staffs and gunnery crews largely escaped these pressures in port and, in my own case, apart from the excursion to Washington, I was free to spend my time ashore until the sailing conference. On the other side at Gourock, the atmosphere was more relaxed with fewer passengers and stores to be loaded. The threat of air attack maintained pressure for an early departure, apart from our tight schedule, and the necessity to use tenders was a deterrent for those of us with ideas of going ashore frequently. Thus leave after six months, or about every seven round-trips, was nothing more than the crew members needed and deserved.

We sailed for New York on 9 October. On the fourth day out the radar broke down in the early evening, and was not restored by radar operator John Hartley until about 10 p.m. A surface contact off the starboard bow at about three miles was made on the initial sweep. The night was heavily overcast and the visibility poor. We turned hard to port and the radar indicated that the contact changed course to follow, but we gradually pulled away.

An event, amusing in hindsight, occurred. A ship, vividly painted in Orange, Green and White of neutral Eire, appeared over the horizon on the port bow, and our British gunnery officer Maurice Hobday decided to give his men down aft an exercise in gun laying. When the Irishman of some 6000 tons came within range, distances and bearings were progressively relayed from the bridge to aft control. Suddenly the ship, and in particular Hobday, were shaken by the simultaneous firing of both 6in guns. This was followed by an agonising wait of the several seconds it took the projectiles to carry to the target area. Two splashes, uncomfortably close to the cargo ship, indicated the aim was good but not quite true. The neutral vessel turned hard away and our signalman, operating his lamp, offered apologies in exchange for abuse. As it turned out, a wiring defect in the communication system had prevented the after gunners receiving the initial instruction that they were to engage in aiming only. We heard nothing further, and I expect any formal protest by the Irish would have ended in an Admiralty waste paper basket. Had Winston Churchill heard of the incident, he may well have recommended decorations.

During this voyage I was accosted on deck by a chap in civilian clothes with a West Country accent who said he was a merchant navy engineer on his way to join a ship at Hampton Roads. In those days one would occasionally come across characters who claimed they had fought with the International Brigade against Franco in the 1936-39 Spanish Civil War, and some were phoneys who sought the kudos and the free drinks which went with the recital of heroic deeds. This chap gave me that pitch, claiming to have jumped ship in Bilbao in August 1936, made his way to Madrid and joined the Brigade. He had horror stories of the two-year siege and of his escape to Barcelona in late 1938. I remained somewhat sceptical, but by this time he was in my cabin and alone on his second whisky. Then to my surprise he produced a dog-eared photograph of a group including himself in army uniform in what he claimed was the Plaza del Ray in Barcelona. I concluded he had been there and at any rate, his stories were worth a couple of whiskies. One first hand description of fighting in the Spanish Civil War was given by a correspondent for the Manchester *Guardian*. This woman reporter mingled with front-line Republican troops, and at the end joined refugees from Barcelona. The lady was none other than Nancy Cunard, great-granddaughter of Sir Samuel himself, and daughter of Mayfair society hostess Lady Emerald Cunard. Her participation was heroic stuff.

The evening before we arrived in New York, Captain Battle invited me to join him at dinner. Earlier in the voyage he had expressed his regret at the departure of Milne, but also his satisfaction that his representations on our behalf to remain in this ship had succeeded. He had been surprised that I was the only cipher officer aboard but seemed content with the position. The Captain reminisced about the whale of a time he and Captain Bisset had when in Sydney together between 27 February and 22 March 1943 as masters of the *Queen Mary* and *Aquitania*. Invitations galore from city, golf and racing clubs had poured in, together with theatre and sporting event tickets. Residents of harbourside mansions and grazing properties sought them as houseguests – it must have been a triumph for a Sydney socialite to produce one if not both to mingle with her guests and to point to their ships through her windows. Little wonder that Commodore Sir James Bisset settled in Sydney on his retirement in 1948, living with a view across the harbour through the heads. Captain Battle praised the performance of the destroyer escorts during the first day of our voyage, particularly their compliance with the zigzag pattern and their success in maintaining their position ahead in spite of the seas having risen close to the acceptable limit. He forecast that cruisers would be escorting these liners all the way across before the end of the year. The master was hardly in a position to compete as a host with Cunard's famed gourmet, Sir James Charles, but his tiger had the facilities in his pantry to add skilled touches to the fare served in the dining room. In addition, he produced one small bottle of fine wine.

CHAPTER 16

U-boats Change Tactics – The Shuttle Presses On

The *Aquitania* arrived in New York on 16 October 1944. The duration of each Atlantic crossing was now on average slightly shorter on account of the U-boat concentration having shifted partly away from the 'Gap' into the Western Approaches and British coastal waters. The ship was thus able to travel closer to the most direct, i.e. the great circle, route, and the number of diversions per crossing were now down to about two or three. During the October-December period of 1944, U-boat sinkings totalled twenty-seven against the commissioning of sixty-seven new submarines.

The Germans hoped to reverse the trend of the Atlantic war by the introduction of their new Type XXI and Type XXIII U-boats. Features included an ability to remain at sea for longer periods, and a capacity to dive below 800 feet, out of the probable range of depth charges. Another feature was a torpedo firing system which enabled the missile, released at a depth of 150 feet, to home-in on the enemy. Above all, the maximum underwater speed was increased to about 18 knots allowing the U-boat to escape the many hunters, and also to intercept, while submerged, all but the fastest ships.

The Allies were well aware of this German building programme and they launched air attacks on the Baltic shipping yards and the networks of canals along which pre-fabricated sections were moved. The German army desperately attempted to defend the yards against the advancing Russians, and the U-boats were progressively sailed to Norwegian ports where unfinished work was completed and crew training continued. It was not until February 1945 that the first Type XXIII was commissioned, and April 1945 before the Type XXI became operational.

The increased distances from their Norwegian bases such as Bergen, Trondheim and Hortin in Oslo Fjord as against the lost Atlantic ports, combined with the additional stresses placed on the crews of those operating under Schnorkelling conditions, reduced the period U-boats spent in the actual combat areas by over a week. U-boat commanders were now being instructed to employ surprise tactics such as firing the torpedoes from inshore when attacking in coastal waters rather than from seaward, and to escape towards the coast rather than out to sea.

The Allies began to lay deep minefields in the British coastal areas in the latter months of 1944 to combat the Schnorkel-equipped U-boats, and the mines were set to be detonated only by vessels proceeding at a depth of more than 100 feet. A number of German submarines were lost or damaged by this tactic, which had the effect of restricting the movement of the enemy, and lowering the morale of the crews. The captains were now instructed to observe more strict radio silence, and for weeks at a time the German command could remain unaware of the location, fate or successes of a U-boat. At the same time, this radio embargo prevented the Allies determining the disposition of enemy submarines by obtaining direction-finding bearings. The Germans had again changed their codes, and the cryptologists' contribution to the Admiralty reports was further reduced.

Coastal Command reported on the Schnorkel,

> It has become clear that while we had succeeded in keeping the enemy under and had thus greatly limited the power of his attack, he, by his skill with the Schnorkel and with the aid of radar warning devices, had succeeded in eluding us. The situation is indicated by the reduction which is seen in the totals of sightings and attacks during the autumn months (1944) when between 50 and 70 are known to be at sea.

The German 56,000-ton battleship *Tirpitz*, sister to the *Bismarck*, had been disabled in late 1943 in Norway's far north Alten Fjord by Royal Navy volunteers in midget submarines and by Fleet Air Arm aircraft. With the enemy's only other surface menace of note, the 11in gun pocket-battleship *Admiral Scheer* and the heavy cruiser *Admiral Hipper*, she remained the only possible threat to the Royal Navy. This menace was not being taken lightly in view of the strength of the forces which had to be mustered from both the Home and Mediterranean Fleets to sink the *Bismarck* in May 1941. On 12 November 1944 R.A.F. Bomber Command launched an attack by R.A.F. Lancasters which pounded to destruction the most dreaded man-of-war ever to put to sea. The *Tirpitz* had immobilised heavy units of the Home Fleet at Scapa Flow and at Rosyth throughout the war, but her career had in fact been one of little combat. She never accomplished anything much in action. Perhaps the forecast of Captain Battle that cruiser escorts for the Cunarders would soon become available, would now turn out to be correct. We would have to wait and see.

Nazi Battleship *Tirpitz* being attacked by Albacore aircraft from Royal Navy fleet carrier *Victorious* off Norway. The tracks of three torpedos are visible in the upper section of the photo – all missed. (Courtesy Imperial War Museum)

During the four months between 16 October 1944 and 15 February 1945, the *Aquitania* completed eight crossings. The winter at sea proved to be less tempestuous than that of the previous year, although we averaged about one moderate gale per crossing. During our visits to New York spanning these winter months, Sarah endeavoured to extend my cultural horizons, and we saw a number of operas at the Metropolitan including 'Carmen' and 'Il Trovatore'. The New York Philharmonic Orchestra played regularly at Carnegie Hall under Arthur Rodzinzki, supported by an up-and-coming Leonard Bernstein.

I had discovered there was more to New York than nightclubs, theatres, restaurants, and bars. Lower Manhattan had many attractions, all the more accessible if you avoided appearing as a tourist. My small wardrobe of civilian clothes enabled me to mingle with the

Artist's impression of the torpedoing of the *Lusitania*. Note the large hole beneath the bridge reflecting the view that the ship was struck by two torpedoes. (U.S. Library of Congress)

Manhattanites without receiving the attention usually drawn by a foreign uniform. The mixture of races in the Lower Manhattan area offered a miniature world tour within a few square miles embracing the foods, smells, languages, clothing, variations of skin colourings and facial features of many countries. Members of all races gathered at such places as Paddy's Market, Little Italy, Greenwich Village, Battery Park, and the Union, Madison and Washington Squares, the last named being a magnet for children and chess players. The Bowery had its deadbeats and a visit to Chinatown on the Lower East Side was an inexpensive way to savour the Orient. This area, bordering the East River, also sheltered a Jewish ghetto whose population disappeared into the garment district of Seventh Avenue by day.

Alex Milne caught a ship back to Australia from San Francisco after a prolonged stay in New York, having failed to persuade the doctors to allow him to return to the *Aquitania*. He had done his best and his bed in Cabin A10 still awaited him. I spent several more days with Ed Seim and his family at Bridgeport when one of our turnarounds coincided with the *Nieuw Amsterdam* being in port. Whilst briefly in dry dock in December, new propellers were fitted to the *Aquitania*, designed to increase her speed by about 1 knot.

An Atlantic incident of interest occurred on 17 December 1944. King George VI had appointed his brother, the Duke of Gloucester, to the post of the Governor-General of Australia. Their Royal Highnesses, the Duke and Duchess, together with an entourage and other assorted passengers, sailed from Liverpool on 16 December in SS *Rimutaka*, shielded by an escort of enviable strength for a small liner, and consisting of the cruiser HMS *Euryalus*, two destroyers and five frigates of the Eighteenth Escort Group. At about 11.15 p.m. on the evening following the departure, and when proceeding on a south-westerly course south of Ireland, one of the frigates, HMS *Nyasaland*, registered an ASDIC contact indicating a U-boat ahead on the *Rimutaka*'s port bow – a fine developing situation for a shot, and one which an unescorted trooper might not have survived. The alarm was raised, and all other vessels hauled around to the north while *Nyasaland* pressed forward to the attack. On the second firing of depth charges an underwater explosion erupted, and a large patch of diesel oil indicated the fate of the U-boat. The Duke proceeded in safety to Australia.

On the seabed close to where the *Rimutaka* had passed, and on the route taken by the *Aquitania* when proceeding south of Ireland, lay the shell of Cunard's *Lusitania*, the victim of one of the most controversial sinkings in the history of naval warfare. The disaster which occurred on 7 May 1915 had become part of Cunard crew folklore – steeped in bitter memory. It is of interest in this context to note the difficulty of saving lives even under the most favourable conditions. The sea was calm, the sun shone, and the water was not unduly cold. Although the final resting place was within fifteen miles of the Irish coast, only 764 passengers and crew out of a total of 1962, or 39 per cent, were saved. *U-21* had struck home with a single torpedo, but the position was aggravated by a second explosion, now believed to have been caused by coal dust in an empty coal hold. The danger had been increased on account of the maximum speed of the ship being cut back to 18 knots by the shutting down of one of the boilers to save fuel before the departure from New York for Liverpool. Captain William Turner had been advised that a U-boat was in the area and had swung out lifeboats beforehand. However, only six of the 48 boats were found to be afloat, the steep list to starboard being the inevitable cause. Admiralty had dispatched the cruiser *Juno* from nearby Queenstown to speed to the rescue, but when within view of the lifeboats and swimmers, she was ordered to return to port, Admiral Fisher fearing the cruiser may also become a victim of the U-boat. Eventually fishing vessels and other

Above left: Captain Turner, master of the *Aquitania* on her maiden voyage, proudly wears the full dress uniform of a naval reserve officer. Above right: A change for the worse a year later. The captain walks the streets of Queenstown, the day after the *Lusitania* sank, wearing a shrunken uniform and borrowed cap.

small craft arrived. It is not surprising that merchant seamen have long memories.

Meanwhile, to return to the Second World War, I spent New Year's Eve 1944 at St. Enoch's Hotel in Glasgow, on my way to St. Andrews. Hogmanay is an occasion of considerable moment in Scotland, and I found myself, and the bottle of scarce whisky I had brought along, well involved. Even the required consumption of haggis was unable to spoil a memorable night. The next morning, somewhat the worse for wear, I continued on to the east coast resort and university town of St. Andrews, also the seat of the world's most famous golf club, the Royal and Ancient. The 'Old Course', the most renowned of the four layouts, would be the first choice of golfers worldwide to have had the experience of playing. When golfing journalists and top players combine to rank the world's leading half-dozen courses, it is always included along with, I might add, Australia's Royal Melbourne. It was my good fortune to have a letter of introduction to the secretary, and he allowed me to make use of the clubhouse.

The *Aquitania* remained for ten days in New York in mid-January 1945, and I spent a week at a skiing resort in the Poconos Mountains of Pennsylvania, about 120 miles west of Manhattan. The Split Rock Lodge on Lake Harmony provided top class accommodation and I found the skiing excellent for the learner, with optional slopes of moderate gradients. The lodge was packed with holiday-makers, mostly girls on account of the war, and the snow was abundant with temperatures down to zero. On departure, I queried my account – it being only about half what I had expected. The manager insisted it was correct, but I suspect this was another example of wartime hospitality.

On returning to the ship I received a nasty jolt. A message from the purser invited me to stop over in his cabin for a drink before dinner. He poured me a stiff one, ushered me to a comfortable chair, then gently broke the news. According to his audit staff, I owed Cunard a substantial sum representing nearly two years of 'messing', a liability which I strongly contested, explaining that in any event, I could not readily lay my hands on the amount involved. I was due to visit Washington the next day where, I was told, a letter would be sent to Melbourne, that the matter was not of sufficient importance to justify a signal, and that indications were the war would be over before any reply was received. The purser said this step should satisfy the auditors and that is how the matter still rests.

A contributor to the *Strand Magazine* once wrote,

> The chief purser of a ship as big and as important as the *Aquitania* has to have the acumen of a Chancellor of the Exchequer, the resources of a Maître de Hotel, and the bland persuasive guile, the swift response to atmosphere of a master diplomat.

That was Purser Hurley all right. I subsequently came across another job description. Douglas Reeman in his book *Rendezvous South Atlantic* described a senior decoding officer as having 'an untouchable and unreachable position – it suited him very well indeed'. Well, it was not quite that good!

On the morning after our return to the Clyde, I was having morning tea in the wardroom when one of the third officers suggested I accompany him sightseeing to Durham and York. Rain was threatening, it was freezing cold, and the prospect of standing in trains and buses together with chancy accommodation and dreadful food hardly appealed. He countered my objections with the offensive remark that I could hardly return home from a war without being able to say that I had once roughed it, and added the only time I had been wet was on a golf course. Still, off I went for the three days we had in harbour, and I must say that the view of Durham Cathedral from the opposite side of the Wear River, with those massive towers dark with time, is one of the most exciting in the land. More recently, in a survey carried out to mark the 150th anniversary of the Royal British Institute of Architects, this Norman shrine was voted 'the best building in the world', ahead of the Taj Mahal and Parthenon. Before we sailed, Captain Fall replaced Captain Battle.

The cold of New York in winter more than matched that of Scotland, and most activity occurred at night, when the contrast with the 'morning after' was occasionally painfully sharp. Take as an example the occasion of U.S. gunnery officer Frank Di Cashio's birthday. A party of six from the ship began the evening with dinner at Billy Rose's Diamond Horseshoe where the sparkling floor show rivalled that of the Latin Quarter. When the performance was about to be repeated for the theatre crowd, we moved on, having brief refuelling stops at Jimmy Ryan's and Toots Shor's, both regular appearers on the New Yorkers' recommended lists. The remainder of the long night was celebrated at the Russian Bear which had captured the excitement of the war. Soviet tanks were rolling westward, devastating the Germans reeling back from East Prussia, and the place was packed, not only with Russian migrants who had done well, and a few officers from Russian ships, but also with many Americans. The balalaikas, high-kicking booted dancers, and of course vodka, brought it all on. Better value could not be found in town, but the Bear's fur subsequently proved to be insufficiently thick to survive the Cold War.

There was no escaping the morning after. I awoke about 11 a.m. feeling quite dreadful. Further sleep was impossible on account of a frightful din coming across the water from Pier 88 where, through my windows, I could see gangs of workmen preparing to refloat the *Normandie*. Beyond, at Pier 90, billows of steam rising from the *Queen Mary*'s stacks signified her imminent departure. Should it only be us! Looking around the cabin, partly filled glasses, a deceased bottle of White Horse, empty cigarette packs, souvenir matches and swizzle sticks, all told the story. Di Cashio's violin balanced on the edge of the other bed. The tray of tea, cold and untouched, together with the unopened New York Times, lay on the table beside my bed. A faint knock on the door was followed by my elderly steward James peering around the corner. His eyes dropped to the contents of an ash tray, scattered on the floor. I tried to recall how Bertie Wooster would have handled this situation when confronted by Jeeves. If you were good at self-deception, described as the most common of human traits, you could have blamed it on the war. Now, at a distance, the memories of the night before still made it seem worthwhile. We did our best not to allow this to happen too often.

During the period of this chapter between 4 September 1944 and 17 February 1945, the transportation of U.S. and Canadian troops continued unabated. Reinforcements were urgently required to maintain the momentum in Europe, and all the trained airmen being turned out in Canada were being fed in to Bomber Command's escalating campaign against German cities. The independently routed troopships were moving as rapidly as the port facilities could turn them around.

An unusual incident occurred off Land's End on 18 December 1944 when a U-boat, in the process of attacking a freighter, ran itself aground off Wolf Rock, Cornwall. The lighthouse keeper reported his sightings and on arrival, HMCS *Montreal* rescued forty-three of the fifty-one crew and then attempted to take the prize in tow. However, it had been holed and sank quickly on its first movement.

During January 1945, the Admiralty estimated that about sixty U-boats were at sea, with those not fitted with Schnorkels operating in Mid-Atlantic and off Halifax, where four merchantmen were sunk during that month. The *Queen Mary*'s sailing from New York, scheduled for 1 November, was delayed for two days on account of fog. The troops became agitated and additional food and water had to be loaded. Finally Captain Bisset agreed to sail, and assisted by ten tugs, the *Mary* was positioned in the middle of the Hudson when the fog suddenly lifted. The *Queen Mary* returned to New York on 19 November where she remained until 10 December after a period in dry dock for urgent maintenance. At this point in his reminiscences, Captain Bisset subsequently wrote,

> The teeming life of the thousands of troops below deck and at their emergencies drills is something that may never be repeated in nautical history for, though they were only five days at sea, every moment of their passage was lived on the alert for disaster that could come without warning, and they knew it. But always came the landfall, and the rattling of the anchor cable in the hawse-pipe at Gourock, or the fussy tugs nosing alongside off the Statue of Liberty, ready to ease her into the dock and the ring-off of the engines.

An Admiralty signal dated 24 December 1944, based on information supplied by Ultra, advised that three days earlier two U-boats were ordered to specified positions (detailed) in the Atlantic to report on the weather. The U-boat commanders were informed that 'weather reports were of the greatest importance in connection with the German offensives on the Western Front'. This was referring to the attack which had begun in the Ardennes on 16 December. The dates indicate that the enemy message had taken three days for Ultra to decrypt. It is unlikely the Allies would have attempted to attack these U-boats on account of the risk of compromising the Ultra operation.

In January 1945 only five U-boats were destroyed, followed by seven in February, with British and Canadian ships claiming the majority of the victims. The reduced success rate, in spite of the numbers of the enemy at sea, was attributed to reluctance by the U-boat commanders to attack the heavily protected convoys. Further advantages were conferred by the transference of Liberator aircraft to European land operations. By now it had become apparent that war's end could be only a matter of some weeks away. In the wardroom at tea one February afternoon, one of our learned young deck officers gave us a quote from Shakespeare's poem, 'The Rape of Lucrece' which was received in silence: 'Tis double death to drown within ken of shore.'

CHAPTER 17

The Final Weeks

Between mid-February 1945 and the formal end of the war in Europe on 8 May, the *Aquitania* completed another six crossings. Two of the return journeys unfortunately brought us back to Halifax, although in one instance we made a diversion to New York between Halifax and the Clyde. The number of U-boats spread across the Atlantic was still sufficient to require maximum vigilance, but the greatest concentration remained in British coastal waters and to a distance of about 200 miles west of Ireland. The wolf pack tactics had not been revived, and the majority of submarines were operating independently, attempting to pick off stragglers and unescorted vessels.

In January 1945, the First Sea Lord, Sir Andrew Cunningham, wrote to the effect that the Schnorkel was giving the U-boats much more protection than had been expected: 'The scientists have not yet caught up and the air are 90% out of business'. March saw eighteen U-boats destroyed at sea with three bagged by the Twenty-First Escort Group patrolling north of the entrance to the Clyde. In the three months from January through March, ninety-three new U-boats were commissioned, a record for any three months of the war. In April, Admiralty estimated Germany had seventy-two U-boats operational out of a fleet of over 300.

That 'Scarlet Pimpernel', Herbert Werner, now enters the narrative for the last time. Having been decorated with the Knight's Cross by Admiral Doenitz in January 1945, Werner sailed from Bergen on 7 February on his final patrol. His route took him west of Ireland to the English Channel from where he set out to return via the Irish Sea six weeks later. He would have been in the vicinity of the entrance to the Clyde on 2 April, the date of our second last wartime sailing from Scotland. Kapitanleutnant Werner made it safely home to become a survivor of a breed whose courage many could not help admiring.

Fate had brought Werner and the *Aquitania* the same way on seven different occasions, and if it had been possible for him to have added to that extraordinary run of luck which enabled him to survive the war, he may have been recorded in history as having made the biggest killing in any

A collection of cuttings from the German press following the sinking of the *Wilhelm Gustloff* by the Russian submarine *S13*.

war at sea. That distinction, assuming it is the right word, goes to the commander of Soviet submarine *S13*. On the morning of 30 January 1945, the 25,000-ton German liner *Wilhelm Gustloff* sailed from Gdynia, near Danzig, laden with refugees, wounded German soldiers and U-boat trainees. About 50,000 Germans had crowded the wharf area, attempting to escape the encircling Russians, and after about 6000 had been documented aboard, the ship pulled out into the stream to prevent the gangways being rushed. A further 2000 passengers consisting of women and children were then loaded from lighters. At 9 p.m. that evening the

Russian submarine fired two torpedoes at close range, and the west-bound ship sank within an hour at 55N 17E, about 23 miles from the coast. The German heavy cruiser *Admiral Hipper* charged into the area, but the captain, refusing to stop, managed to chop up swimmers with his propellers. The rescued numbered 964, leaving over 7000 drowned. Perhaps Werner would have considered himself lucky not to have had those numbers on his conscience.

A number of incidents occurred during the following weeks. Approximately six hours after sailing from Halifax for New York on 16 February, our rudder jammed whilst the ship was altering course in the zigzag pattern, and for about an hour we described a circle at a full rate of knots until the engineers rectified the fault, the only machinery break-down in all my crossings. On 23 February, sailing out of New York, a column of water, thrown up by an explosion about 250 yards astern, indicated a 'Gnat' had missed and had exploded at the end of its run. Nothing else was seen. On another occasion an escorting destroyer dropped a pattern of depth charges at the entrance to the Clyde. On 8 April, while being escorted by the Canadian destroyer *St. Laurent* about 300 miles east of Halifax, an aircraft sweeping ahead sighted a U-boat outside torpedo range on our port bow. While we turned hard away, the destroyer joined the Liberator in a depth charge attack, and that was the last we saw of our escorts. We did not learn of the outcome, but the day after we sailed on 14 April, a ship was torpedoed 100 miles from the harbour entrance, and it may well be that the same U-boat was involved.

When the *Queen Elizabeth* was westbound north of Ireland in March, two escorting destroyers gained an ASDIC contact on a U-boat ahead. After receiving a signal – 'We have contacted and are attacking', Captain Ford decided the ship was too close to turn away without presenting a target. He wrote: 'I made up my mind to go ahead ... we saw depth charges all around us but that was all'.

On 20 March, HMCS *New Glasgow* had been involved in a collision also north of Ireland. The Schnorkel of *U-1003* had been seen by a lookout about 100 yards dead ahead and the impact damaged the U-boat which dived and lay on the bottom. Three days later the submarine was forced to surface and was abandoned with thirty-one crew members being rescued. The inward-bound *Aquitania* passed through this area three days later. On our 5 March sailing from Gourock, the two escorting destroyers from the 6th Flotilla dropped depth charges as we emerged from the Clyde Estuary, sending severe shudders through the ship. Two hours passed before the destroyers returned to their escorting positions.

Halifax improved a little on acquaintance. The Lord Nelson Hotel, one of the Canadian Pacific chain, provided excellent meals, and I

Troop transport *Nieuw Amsterdam* of 36,300 tons was the fourth largest liner engaged in the 'Shuttle Service'. (Courtesy Holland America Line)

celebrated my 26th birthday there on 10 April. We managed to overcome the absence of a wine list by the surreptitious use of bottles shaped to resemble hip flasks. A pilot from an R.C.A.F. Liberator squadron in nearby Dartmouth offered to take me on an anti-submarine patrol on the day before we were due to sail. I sought the Captain's permission, but he wisely vetoed the proposition on the grounds that bad weather might force the aircraft to land elsewhere.

On the afternoon of 12 April, when walking back to the ship after a game of squash, we saw the *Halifax Daily Star* had a screamer headline – 'Roosevelt Dies' – and said the President 'died unexpectedly today from a cerebral haemorrhage'. The *Aquitania* flew British and American flags half mast, and I attended a memorial service aboard. This great man whose economic policies in the 1930s perhaps saved America from communism, had been denied the four weeks which would have enabled him to celebrate the European victory towards which he had contributed so much.

Unlike the waning efforts of their armies and air force, the enemy's Uboat resurgence did not escape the notice of the politicians. In the House of Commons in February, speaking on the Navy Estimates, the First Lord of the Admiralty, A.V. Alexander stated: 'the Germans are making great efforts to renew the U-boat war on a big scale ... the enemy still

London's *Daily Sketch* brings good news to its readers.

considers it to be his best hope of avoiding defeat'. A neutral press report from Berne on 18 April stated: 'The North American Navy Minister Forrestal ... reported in Washington that the U-boat danger in the waters around England was very serious'. The report also referred to Canadian Navy Minister McDonald who 'expressed himself in similar terms, stating that German U-boats had even risked entering the Gulf of St. Lawrence where they had shown no large scale activity since 1942'. On our last two sailing conferences at Greenock, the commander had suggested to our Captain that all gunners should be 'watch on watch' and that they and all deck officers should sleep in their clothes until we reached 10 degrees west.

This U-boat threat would have been considerably greater but for the efforts of the R.A.F. and the R.A.A.F. in attacking the enemy in their Norwegian bases. Not only U-boats were attacked and sunk, but also ships carrying supplies and U-boat crews from Kiel, Hamburg, Bremen and Vallo to the U-boat bases at Bergen and Trondheim. From early 1944, 455 Squadron R.A.A.F., operating Beaufighters out of its base at Leuchars on Scotland's north coast near Dundee, had relentlessly attacked enemy shipping in the Skagerrak, Kattegat and in the Norwegian fjords. These areas were subjected to hammerings during the latter months of the war. In one particular incident in April, a wing of Mosquitoes attacked three U-boats. The first U-boat exploded, wrecking the leading aircraft and damaging two others to the extent that they were forced to land in Sweden.

Aquitania was still loading troops to full capacity, even though it appeared the war was about to end. On the 14 April sailing we were routed north of Ireland, but a last-minute diversion to the south to approach through the Irish Sea added almost a half day to the voyage. During our previous visit, an invitation for lunch was signalled from the *Nieuw Amsterdam* which was riding nearby. The host was her U.S. senior gunnery officer, Ed Seim, and with two *Aquitania* counterparts, Frank Di Cashio and John Tofte, I crossed by launch. Welcoming us were Ed and his new bride Maureen, an attractive W.R.E.N. officer formerly attached to the *Nieuw Amsterdam* staff.

Although the U-boats were still concentrating in the Western Approaches and Home Waters, a number of Ultra-inspired Admiralty signals during April revealed the movements of U-boats towards the 30-degree west meridian. Another enemy signal revealed three others were directed to operate in the New York – Cape Hatteras area. The delays in decrypting appeared to average about three days.

The European war was now reaching its conclusion, as evidenced by the variety of front page headings of the 26 April edition of the London Daily Sketch.

> Berlin encircled – Russian forces under command of Marshals Koniev and Zhukov have linked up and completed encirclement – Allies sweep beyond River Po – R.A.F. drop 12,000 lb. blockbuster on Hitler's chalet – British over Elbe – Patton's Third Army reaches Danube.

Enough space was left on the front page to tell us that Field Marshal Sir Bernard Montgomery had sent a message to the Right Reverend Basil C. Roberts, secretary of the Society of the Propagation of the Gospel. Perhaps Montgomery was letting him know that the Gospel hadn't done much for the leaders of the Christian country who had initiated the Holocaust. Not being a cynic, I would be the last to suggest this was Montgomery's first intimation that he intended to run for Parliament. Religion hardly helps politicians in Britain.

The ship sailed for New York on 27 April, and we were escorted by destroyers through the Outer Hebrides. The night before we arrived in New York, I had dinner with Captain Fall. After hearing on the B.B.C. news that surrender by Germany was imminent, he instructed his tiger to produce a small bottle of wine which was, for him, I was told, almost unprecedented. We arrived in New York late on 4 May and were preparing for that first night ashore, when the word was passed around that a city regulation now compelled the closing of bars and nightclubs at midnight. At least it was a mercy that the authorities had not come up with that earlier. There was nothing for it but to start a party on board, which continued on and off for the next few days, as many wished to keep close to a radio.

The 9 a.m. news on Monday 7 May announced that Germany had surrendered unconditionally at 2.14 a.m. French time at Reims in a 'little red school house', the headquarters of Allied Supreme Commander General Dwight D. Eisenhower. Both the *Queen Mary* and *Queen Elizabeth* were docked nearby, and all three ships blew their sirens in unison, an incident which was reported in the B.B.C. news an hour later. This had to be an occasion for celebration with the boys, and we set out in the afternoon on a 'pub crawl'. As the day progressed we concentrated on the Cunard haunts in 46th Street between Times Square and Eighth Avenue, and with both *Queens* also in port there was plenty of action. Traffic in Times Square was periodically blocked by the crowds, and after the midnight bar closure, we finished up in plush offices on Madison Avenue, where an advertising man, who had joined us on the way, offered a first-rate cupboard. Emotionally I would have much preferred to have been in London. The bombs had dropped right there, and the people had suffered greatly, in complete contrast to New Yorkers who nevertheless had fully supported the war effort.

The next day, 8 May, was officially V.E. Day, and after Churchill had broadcast his victory speech over the B.B.C. radio, the three Cunarders again sounded off with their sirens, and 'Land of Hope and Glory' was played over our sound system. Even the sombre New York Times spread itself with four headlines all the way across page 1.

THE WAR IN EUROPE IS ENDED!
NAZIS SIGN SURRENDER TERMS:
V-E DAY WILL BE PROCLAIMED TODAY:
LAST FIGHTING IN CZECH POCKET.

On 4 May, Admiral Doenitz had signalled all U-boats, which included some seventy at sea in the North Atlantic, to surrender. His signal included these words: 'Unbeaten and unblemished, you lay down your arms after an heroic fight without parallel'. The captains were instructed to surface, to fly a black flag, and to report their positions. Orders were then broadcast announcing the port to which each U-boat should proceed, and eventually about half arrived in Britain whilst others went to Canada, the United States, Norway, France and Germany. Two turned up in

A U-boat crew surrendering to Allies at Wilhelmshaven. Their heads are bowed in spite of the signal from Doenitz - 'Unbeaten and unblemished you lay down your arms after an heroic fight without parallel'. Perhaps a machine gun was aimed at their backs. (Courtesy Imperial War Museum, London)

Forty-one surrendered U-boats line a wharf at Lislally near Londonderry in Northern Ireland. (Courtesy Imperial War Museum, London)

Argentina many weeks later, having ignored their instructions. In addition to the submarines which capitulated at sea, 156 surrendered to the Allies intact, and another 221 were scuttled by their crews. The *Queen Elizabeth* and *Queen Mary* had both remained in New York after 12 April, and did not sail again until all the U-boats at sea had been accounted for. No such luck for the *Aquitania*.

It was evident that Germany still had sufficient submarines and crews to pursue the Battle of the Atlantic, particularly with the new types of U-boats having underwater speeds of 18 knots being commissioned – but the overrunning of her land bases, combined with the defeat of her armies and air forces, made inevitable the surrender of the U-boat fleet. In the final days of the war, HMS *Victoria* sank a U-boat off the Northumbrian coast. The wreckage floating to the surface included a dinghy in which was stowed, according to the official report: 'six dozen good brandy, fortunately none of them broken'. Another singular event was the sinking of a U-boat off the Norwegian coast by HM Submarine *Toplis* – one of the rare instances of one submarine torpedoing another.

Our sailing conference took place on 8 May, when it was emphasised that a number of U-boat commanders might make a last-ditch stand by firing off their remaining torpedoes. Blackouts and zigzagging had to be maintained, and the guns and lookout posts were manned as usual. We still had two further crossings under wartime conditions ahead of us. Arriving back at the ship from the conference, I found a hand message from the British Naval Liaison Office had been delivered. Originating from British H.Q. in Washington it read: 'Pass following Admiralty general message to H.M. ships in port – 'Splice the Main Brace''. A similar message had been transmitted to all H.M. ships at sea, the wording being the traditional means advising the ship's company there would be a double issue of rum. The expression and tradition had persisted for hundreds of years, but the occasion has to be special to justify the celebration, such as the sinking of an enemy, or the King's birthday. We had the designation of 'His Majesty's Transport', and I suggested to the purser the instruction should be followed, and that Cunard could send the account to their Lordships at the Admiralty. All who happened to be aboard participated, including the merchant seamen.

One of the *Aquitania*'s youthful third officers to take part in the celebrations was Mortimer Hahir. He had joined the ship some months beforehand and became a very popular figure, but little did we guess how far he would go. In 1972 he reached the career pinnacle in the world's merchant navies by becoming Captain of the *Queen Elizabeth 2*, and he retained that appointment until his retirement in 1976.

NAVAL MESSAGE

SAKER   RBNO NY DEMS NY   BRLO NY   BNLO NY   From: BAD

Immediate   TOR 0800 May 8, 1945.   BA 1

Pass following Admiralty general message DTG 081500B to

HM ships in port:

"SPLICE THE MAIN BRACE"

This signal, for which many had been waiting for up to six years, was hand delivered to the Cipher Office.

The reported suicide of Hitler was one disappointment common to all. These seamen were far from vengeful by nature, and I cannot recall them expressing any vehement hatred of the Germans. But as for Hitler himself, we agreed he should have been forced to squirm in the dock, but he had saved the dirtiest trick of them all for the end by doing himself in. We heard Ed Murrow's radio broadcast from London, and his signature sign off – 'Goodnight and good luck' – carried the ring of fulfilment. Later that evening, we saw newsreels at a movie ashore of Hitler's ghastly death camps. It remains incredible we had known nothing of this earlier, but not all were ignorant.

In April 1945 twenty-two U-boats were sunk in the North Atlantic shipping lanes out of an estimated seventy-two at sea. British ships sank nine compared with five by the Americans, aircraft claimed seven and a mine destroyed another. In May only one U-boat was sunk in the Atlantic, after Doenitz had ordered the surrender. This happened on 6 May 1945, when *U-881*, commanded by Kapitanleutnant Frischke, was sunk by the U.S. destroyer *Farquhar*. More than thirty U-boats were sunk from the air in enemy territory by 8 May. During the period covered by this chapter, from 17 February to 8 May, forty-five U-boats were destroyed in the Atlantic. British ships accounted for twenty-two, American vessels eight, shore-based aircraft twelve, mines claimed two, whilst another ran aground. The Germans claimed they scuttled 128, many being the new XXI and XXIII types, in the ports of Wilhelmshaven, Hamburg, Travemunde, Kiel and Flensburg. With opened main vents and hatches, they simply went down.

The designated surrender ports ranged from Narvik to Portsmouth in New Hampshire, with Lislally near Londonderry receiving forty-one. The captured U-boats in German ports which remained unscuttled were sailed to British ports by supervised skeleton German crews, and subsequently over 100 were sunk in the Atlantic under 'Operation Deadlight'. A number were retained and distributed amongst the Allied Navies.

U.S. records showed the following shipments of American troops from the Eastern Seaboard:

Boston	768,898
New York	3,273,009
Hampton Roads	764,939
Charleston S.C.	36,654
Total	4,843,500

Cunard statistics show that during the war its ships carried 2,223,040 troops in all theatres, dwarfing the figures of any other shipping line. The *Queen Mary* and *Queen Elizabeth* carried 1,243,538, including the period before they entered the Atlantic Shuttle Service. Taking into account the carrying capacities of the *Queens,* their number of crossings, and after making seasonal adjustments for sleeping accommodation, it is likely that on their eastbound journeys across the Atlantic they would have carried just over 400,000 each. By making similar calculations, the *Aquitania* would have transported about 200,000 bringing the combined total to slightly above one million, or just over 20 per cent of all troops shipped from North America. Approximately three million would have crossed while I was in the *Aquitania.* Cunard lost half its fleet of eighteen passenger ships by enemy action. These included *Scythia, Laconia, Lancastria, Britannic II, Alaunia* and *Carinthia.* The *Mauretania* made a major contribution, remaining in the Atlantic throughout the war. Unfortunately we saw little of her, due to her sailing into Liverpool and docking in Downtown Manhattan. In addition to being engaged in the transportation of 'souls', a term frequently favoured by seafarers, Cunard's freighters carried 9,223,181 tons of cargo.

We sailed for Britain on 9 May. I gathered from discussions with a number of the troops that many experienced feelings of deprivation in that the European War had actually ended before they could reach the theatre. Now there were plenty of destroyer escorts to spare, and we were met several hundred miles west of Ireland. When within sight of the Irish coast, we overtook a frigate escorting two U-boats flying black flags, heading for their designated surrender port of Lislally. A number of Germans could be seen on the conning towers, and for those who understood English it was just as well they were out of earshot. The majority of U-boat crew members who survived the war were more likely to be young men aged under 23 years with limited training. Weeks on end were spent in cramped quarters, breathing foul air, and only with difficulty could the men shave, bathe or wash clothes. Without a vestige of privacy, they were continuously subjected to claustrophobia, and intermittently to the terror of attacks by aircraft and surface vessels. Above all, there was the statistical probability that after an average of three voyages, they would be no more. It was estimated that out of about 40,000 German sailors who underwent U-boat training, some 30,000 died. Many 'Hitler Youth' who proudly goose-stepped before the Fuehrer ended their brief careers in the deep. In 1981 West German film makers turned out 'Das Boot' (The Boat), the story of *U-96*. Their most expensive film ever made, it was hailed as having restored national pride in the U-boat fleet. The crews were portrayed as average men, experiencing all the range of feelings of submariners. The film was widely distributed overseas with dubbed English, and provided some uncomfortable memories for ex-sailors.

We arrived at Greenock on 15 May. I was advised that ciphers would remain in use, and that I could not expect to be discharged from the ship before at least one more round voyage. We sailed for New York on 21 May, again being escorted by two destroyers for 36 hours. At the sailing conference, we were warned that a number of U-boats, known to have been operating in the Western Approaches, had not reported to base, and we continued with the zigzag and blackout. The ship carried 8000 U.S. troops, the majority of whom had taken part in the invasion of Normandy. The precautions generated an atmosphere of some danger, and inhibited the relaxation the troops otherwise may have enjoyed.

A 'Coming Home', which would now provoke any Vietnam veteran to grind his teeth, was about to be experienced. We were the first Cunarder to return since V.E. day, and nothing was spared. As we moved into the 'narrows' where thousands of cars filled the roads on both sides, the show started. The ship, already dressed with flags, was met by an elegant Mississippi River stern wheeler complete with a W.A.C. orchestra and a bevy of girls kicking and swinging their legs, Rockette style. The band played 'When Johnny Comes Marching Home Again', 'The Sidewalks of New York', 'Turkey in the Straw', 'Dixie' and other stirring numbers. Boats from the Fire Department pumped plumes of water hundreds of feet into the air, blimps and helicopters flew overhead, and flotillas of small craft tagged along abeam and astern. Passing vessels and Staten Island ferries blew V for Victory on their sirens, cars sounded their horns, and paper wafted down from a number of skyscrapers. Cunard had

The *Queen Elizabeth*, dressed and loaded with 16,000 triumphant troops, slowly approaches a tumultuous welcome at Pier 90, New York, weeks after the *Aquitania*'s arrival. (Courtesy Frank O. Braynard)

decked out their piers with flags, and crowds gathered in 12th Avenue. In her '*Manhattan '45*' the author Jan Morris wrote,

> In the early afternoon of June 20, 1945, the grey-painted British liner *Queen Mary*, 80,774 tons, appeared out of a misty sea at the Narrows, the entrance to the harbour of New York City. She was the second largest ship in the world, and probably the most famous, and she was bringing home to the United States 14,526 of the American service men and women who had just helped to win the war against Nazi Germany – the first big contingent to return from the great victory.

Naturally I have to dispute this claim made for the *Queen Mary* – the *Aquitania*'s arrival on the morning of Monday 28 May over three weeks

earlier, combined with a welcome on a similar scale to the *Mary*'s, surely earned her the distinction of carrying the 'first big contingent'. Jan
Morris describes the *Mary*'s welcome in the next four pages of the prologue and again makes reference to her arrival in the epilogue. The
particular emphasis given to this arrival is on account of that writer con-
cluding that, 'It was the town of all towns and this was a culminating
moment of its history'. The 8000 troops of the *Aquitania* could hardly be
described as other than a 'big contingent' – she had the third largest
capacity of them all. No matter. I am confident Miss Morris would allow
the 'Old Lady' to share in what she sees as one of the great events in the
history of that 'town of all towns'. *TIME* Magazine reviewed the book at
length.

During this visit to New York I spent a weekend with friends of Sarah
at Mountain Lakes in New Jersey. Rowing and swimming in a nearby
lake and tennis made the time pass quickly in this beautiful, hospitable
part of America. Remembering there was clothing rationing in Australia
and in Britain, I set myself up with something of a wardrobe, but buying
more on 34th Street than on Fifth Avenue. The sailing conference took
place on 8 June. We learnt that nearly all U-boats believed to have been
operating in the Atlantic had been accounted for, and that the formation
of convoys had ceased as from 28 May. The U.S. gun crew had been discharged, and blacking out and zigzagging were no longer required.
Lifebelts were stowed away in cabins, and blackout screens and dead-
lights removed. The quartermaster steered in full light of the binnacle,
radio sets reappeared, red and green running lights and cigarettes glowed
on deck at night, music blared out over the water, and the Red and Blue
ensigns together with the Cunard House flag snapped in the breeze. But
the guns, the grey paint, and names carved in teak handrails including,
of course, Kilroy's, served as a direct reminder as to why we were there.
The Cunard colours were soon to be repainted when the *Aquitania*
would again sail with a black hull, white superstructure, red funnels with
black top and two black rings.

The 600 passengers were mostly British women and children who had
been evacuated to America during the Blitz. Travelling by the most direct
route, we saw many ships by day and the glow of their lights by night. On
arriving at Greenock, I learnt the next round trip should be my last. The
destination was Halifax and accordingly I made a pitch to HMS *Orlando*
at Greenock that there was nothing to keep me on board, and that I
might just as well spend the time playing golf around Scotland, particularly as the weather had picked up. They said the Admiralty seemed
baffled about me and that nothing could be authorised, so off I went
again, just for the ride. The ship had a full load of high spirited Canadian

troops, and their behaviour proved to be something of a handful for the administrative staff. Maurice Hobday and the British gunners also came along for the ride. The *Halifax Chronicle* had the entire front page filled with photographs and articles about the arrival of the *Aquitania*, and the troops received an appropriate welcome from huge crowds which packed the dock area. According to the press: 'The giant liner *Aquitania* arrived in port last evening bringing over 7000 servicemen to their homeland from war torn Europe'.

Maurice Hobday had an invitation for two to stay with a widow, one Mrs. Day, at Mahone Bay, a picturesque inlet about 50 miles south of Halifax. He understood a chaperone was seen to be required, and he told me I was just the chap for the part. This was about the only order he ever gave me. A chauffeured sedan called, and at the house everything was *comme il faut*. The lady did not put in an appearance until 11 a.m. when she arranged the flowers. At lunch she naturally wore a hat. Fingerbowls were in place, drinks were served at the appropriate times during the day, and most meals brought forth a different visitor, usually a person of local distinction.

Lt. Cdr. Hobday, then in his late thirties, was the cultured English gentleman par excellence, complete with a Mayfair accent – as expected of a Wykehamist, an 'old boy' of Winchester. A white handkerchief always protruding from the shirt cuff was a nice touch, and he went over very big in New York – not only with the girls from Delmonico's, but particularly if he met their mothers. One evening on the final voyage, after a few drinks, he told me I had not turned out to be altogether what he had expected of an Australian, and was kind enough to say I could possibly pass for an Englishman with a peculiar trans-Atlantic accent. He was a good companion and our arm's-length duty relationship with the Captain in the middle enabled us to get along well. These days at Mahone Bay had been a complete change, with a hostess of the utmost kindness. A phone call to Sarah in New York was to turn out to be an adieu.

The *Aquitania* sailed from Halifax on 3 July, and we arrived at the Clyde five days later on my last and fastest ocean crossing. Having no duties to perform, I played bridge during the day and did some drinking at night, usually in the public rooms where the bars were in full operation – 'Happy Days Are Here Again' according to the amateur orchestra. The Old Cunard Hands had their memories of the palmier days revived. I would never again be consuming Scotch Whisky at $1.20 per bottle, and looking back I am thankful the opportunity was not neglected. The peacetime routines however had hardly been restored. The five or six meals a day, menus with 70-80 items, professional orchestras, dancing, fancy dress and masked balls, Captain's cocktail parties, the swimming pool, luxury shops, the organised games and gambling, would all have to wait.

The *Aquitania* arrived at Gourock on 7 July. Hobday had orders to disembark the gunners, coders and signalmen, but nothing was forthcoming about the cipher officer. I made enquiries with the Naval Control Office at HMS *Orlando* in Greenock where I was told they would again check the position with Admiralty. After two more days nothing had arrived, the ship was now due to sail within two days, and I was facing the prospect of just another boat ride.

Now that the enemy had departed, and together with the continuing attractions of New York, the prospect was not too daunting, but the decider came when I learned the destination was Halifax and likely to remain that way for some months. I reported to the purser and signed off the ship's articles without any difficulty. That step reduced my status from 'Supernumerary Deck Officer, H.M.T. *Aquitania*' to Lieutenant (Special Branch) R.A.N.V.R., which seemed to me something of a comedown. My next move was to phone the Australian Naval Liaison Office in London where my old friend from Melbourne, Angus Calder, took some initiative and told me to report there within a few days and to forget about Greenock and the Admiralty.

During my period of service in the *Aquitania* I had never received any communication from the naval authorities in Australia. The Admiralty's failure to replace Milne and the absence of any offer or instruction regarding leave suggested that perhaps after all this appointment had become 'forgotten'. Fortunately the department of the Director of Naval Accounts at Navy Office Melbourne had notified the Australian Naval Liaison Office at Australia House in London of my expected arrival and pay rates. This information was subsequently passed on to the naval shore establishments HMS *Orlando* at Greenock and HMS *Saker* in New York, where I could present a pay book. In early 1995, I applied to the Department of Defence in Canberra for official details of my war service. In a letter dated 24 April 1995, my overseas war service was described as: 'Appointed to Kuttabul (a shore establishment) additional ciphering duties H.M.T. No 2'. In a section relating to service stars was stated: 'Served in *Queen Mary* and *Queen Elizabeth* 23-3-43 to 2-7-45'. Following a request for elaboration, a reply from the Department dated 6 November 1995 stated: 'According to our records the ship referred to as H.M.T. No 2 was the *Queen Mary*. Unfortunately we are unable to determine the exact dates that you served on the *Queen Mary* or the *Queen Elizabeth*'. It would follow that the Australian Navy had, and still has, no idea where I was, and that Admiralty had not heard of me! As the French would say: '*C'est la guerre*'.

I left the ship on 12 July, having remembered to remove my diaries from the safe which had housed the confidential books. Two years and four months had passed since I had my gear placed in State Room A10 in Sydney in March 1943, and I believe that on account of no formal leave, I was the only member of the ship's company who made the fifty crossings up to the end of May 1945 when the Atlantic was declared free of the German menace. Three crossings under peacetime conditions had followed. Beginning earlier, the *Queen Elizabeth* had made sixty-four crossings and the *Queen Mary* fifty-six. I probably could have contrived to remain in the U.K. for a couple more months, but I applied to Australia House for an early passage. Australia was greatly indebted to the United States in saving our country from Japanese occupation, and it seemed the place to be – then and at most other times for that matter.

Advice came from Angus Calder at Australia House that I would be sailing for Australia from Liverpool on 25 July in the ageing Peninsular and Orient Line vessel, *Maloja*. I set out from Gourock on 12 July, and leaving most of my stuff at Liverpool, I continued on to London, again staying at the club off Grosvenor Square. The streets teemed with servicemen from various Allied countries awaiting passage home. Many Americans expected to be transferred to the Pacific area after a period of leave, and some of the British were similarly situated, although a shortage of troop ships guaranteed delays of several months for the majority. Servicemen were hardly in the mood for 'make-work' exercises in camps and barracks, and leave passes to visit London were not difficult to obtain. My naval colleagues in Australia House were helpful as always, and I was able to negotiate sufficient pay in advance to see me through the remaining period in England, and the voyage home.

Australians had converged on London, and Mayfair was full of chance encounters. A servicemen's cricket team played a match against the English equivalent at Lord's, the traditional headquarters of this game, and here I passed a pleasant afternoon. Out of a concern that I might never again have the opportunity to visit Britain, I made an excursion by train into the West Country, and stayed at the legendary town of Bideford. It was from Bideford Bay that the privateers – the Drakes and Hawkins, the Gilberts and Raleighs, and the Grenvilles set sail for the West Indies to intercept the vessels of the conquistadors laden with their plundered treasure. To many, the North Devon coast is the most delightful part of the United Kingdom, particularly the stretch taking in Bideford, Clovelly, Westward Ho! and Ilfracombe. I also visited Cambridge.

Back in London, I happened upon a colleague from Melbourne, Graham Oakley, who was also scheduled to sail in the *Maloja*, and on 21

July we moved up to the old Roman walled city of Chester in North Wales, within twenty miles of Liverpool. Next day, a U.S. Army major staying at the same hotel – inevitably equipped with a blonde, a car, and petrol – kindly invited us to join them motoring through North Wales along the coast to Llandudno, Beaumaris and Caernarvon. We returned inland via Mt. Snowdon, and one of the most delightful villages in Britain both in appearance and by name – Betws-y-coed.

On boarding the *Maloja*, I found myself in an upper bunk of an eight-berth cabin shared with six Fleet Air Arm lieutenants who were on their way to the Pacific, expecting to catch the last days of the war against Japan. The other occupant was a lieutenant from the Royal New Zealand Navy. Originally designed as a two-berth cabin, the accommodation resembled submarine conditions. The following morning we sailed for Australia.

The Bay of Biscay, notorious for rough weather, could not have been more benign, and late the following afternoon – 'Nobly, nobly Cape St. Vincent to the North-West died away' – just as it had for Robert Browning. After we had ploughed through the Straits of Gibraltar, our route took us intermittently within sight of the coast of North Africa, and gave distant views of Algiers, Bizerta, Derna and Alexandria. The ship lay at anchor for several hours off Port Said, but shore leave was not granted, and the famed Simon Artz Emporium nearby was out of reach. The only relief from boredom and heat discomfort occurred when the Egyptian wallahs, rowing alongside to flog their wares to the troops, were drenched together with their merchandise by British soldiers wielding firehoses. However, the troops spared the gulli-gulli men who came on board and did their tricks with chickens and eggs. Then there were other Egyptians who would dive and wriggle to the bottom for silver coins. The sport for the troops here was to wrap coppers with silver paper and then enjoy the abuse when the chaps resurfaced.

It proved to be a long voyage home. The heat of the Red Sea was unbearable below, and the only alternative was to try to sleep on deck. I did not adjust easily to living in the crowded cabin, but the Royal Navy fellows who had come up through naval college – and all that goes with it – had an enthusiasm which enabled them to cope. Oakley and I had a keen bridge group operating, and it is a tribute to the game that it could be played for over twelve hours a day without boredom setting in. The ship had been victualled in Liverpool, and the food was inevitably of poor standard. I nevertheless did not believe the rumour that the Captain had been seen after dark, sitting in a lifeboat eating the emergency biscuits. Blackout restrictions were in force, there being the odd chance of an attack by a Japanese submarine.

The ship arrived in Colombo on the morning of 14 August, and about two hours later an announcement was broadcast that the war against Japan had officially ended. Again, shore leave was not granted, and one could only sit and imagine the celebrations taking place in various Allied capital cities. The ship had been dry throughout, and if a 'Splice the Mainbrace' signal were received, the passengers did not learn of it. There was nothing for it except to shuffle the cards again. Colombo harbour teemed with ships of the British Pacific Fleet, which had now changed its name from the Far Eastern Fleet. Until late 1944, the naval war against Japan had been conducted by the US Pacific Fleet, assisted by the Royal Australian Navy to the fullest extent our resources and commitments to Britain would allow.

By V-J Day the British Pacific Fleet consisted of four battleships, including the recently commissioned *Anson* and *Howe,* eleven fleet aircraft carriers, eight escort aircraft carriers, ten cruisers, forty destroyers, eighteen sloops, thirteen frigates, twenty-nine submarines and hundreds of support craft.

The *Maloja* arrived at Fremantle, the port of Perth, on 24 August, and now we were allowed ashore. Just as well, I would say, otherwise the troops might have dived over the side. Somehow, they managed to help each other back on board by the time the ship sailed next day. We reached Sydney six days later, and I was home in Melbourne the following afternoon.

CHAPTER 18

Reflections

Several countries participated against the Germans in the Battle of the Atlantic, but the part played by the British outweighed the efforts of all other countries combined. The Canadians, Australians and New Zealanders were involved from the start, and the Norwegians, Poles, Dutch and French were also among the early combatants. Australian sailors contributed to the 'Yachtsmen's Scheme', providing officers and ratings for crews of numerous British anti-submarine vessels. Warships carrying the Australian flag were engaged mainly in the Mediterranean and in convoy duties in the Indian Ocean, but after Japan's entry into the war these vessels operated principally in the Pacific.

After the United States entered the war in December 1941, her naval forces were largely committed to the Pacific theatre, while the Royal Navy continued to play the major role in the Atlantic. It should not be forgotten that the United States, whilst not actually a combatant beforehand, had materially assisted Britain in every sense of the word. In September 1940, the U.S. made available fifty reconditioned four-funnel destroyers, and in return, the British allowed the U.S. to make use of Newfoundland, Bermuda and four Caribbean bases for defence purposes.

By the spring of 1941, warships of the supposedly neutral United States were escorting British convoys as far as Iceland, and on 10 April USS *Niblack* depth-charged a U-boat which appeared to be acting in a hostile manner. On 4 September 1941, three months before the U.S. formal participation, the destroyer USS *Greer*, whilst stalking a U-boat near Iceland, had two torpedoes fired at her and retaliated with depth charges. Following this incident, Roosevelt declared that U.S. ships would attack any submarine which came within sight of her warships. A month later, the U.S. destroyer *Kearny* was torpedoed off Iceland when escorting a British convoy, and although she managed to reach harbour, a number of her crew had been killed. It follows that the U.S. was a participant in the Battle of the Atlantic on a limited scale when Germany declared war on her.

One of the most effective contributions of the U.S. was the production of four-engined Consolidated Liberator aircraft – they were crucial in turning the tide of the Atlantic Battle. Another decisive role was her operation of escort carriers such as USS *Bogue, Core* and *Santee* and supplying the British with the escort carriers to be named HMS *Archer, Attacker, Battler, Biter* and *Dasher.* The part played by British and U.S. teams in the successes of Ultra was inestimable. The fact remains that Britain bore the brunt of the German onslaught in the Atlantic war, and was responsible for approximately three quarters of the U-boats sunk.

In the Second World War, 2603 merchant ships – mostly British – were sunk in the Atlantic, as were 175 Allied naval vessels. It is a tribute to the officers and crews of the small escorts, and the organisers of the convoy system, that approximately 70 per cent of merchant ships sunk were unescorted, whilst less than 30 per cent were torpedoed when sailing in convoy. The remainder lost were mostly stragglers which had, in effect, become unescorted. The extent of the contribution of the British Merchant Service to the Allied victory in Europe is revealed by the fact that approximately 35,000 men out of about 150,000 participants lost their lives – a ratio of almost one in four. Officers and men of the R.N. under the Western Approaches Command who died totalled 6061, their names being recorded in the Liverpool Cathedral. And many of these R.N. personnel had been drowned whilst serving as D.E.M.S. volunteers in merchant ships. At war's end the Royal Navy had 14 battleships, 12 aircraft carriers, 50 cruisers, 182 destroyers and 226 frigates – a total of 484 vessels of these types.

Merchant seamen who survived Atlantic crossings in ammunition ships and in tankers carrying high octane fuel would never forget their experiences. When torpedoed, these ships went up before they went down. The number of deaths in the Second World War in the merchant service more than doubled the First World War losses, and proportionately were much higher than in any other branch of the British services. Five of the eight world's largest passenger ships, counting all nations, were lost one way or another. The *Aquitania* was the only four-stacker to survive.

In 1963 the Naval History Division of the Office of Chief of Naval Operations, Washington D.C., put out a publication entitled *United States Submarine Losses, World War II.* Included were details of German U-boat casualties, providing the date, the number of the U-boat, the location in terms of latitude and longitude to the nearest minute, the name of the last commander, and the cause of the sinking. The name or nationality of the killer warship or flight squadron was included. I extracted the U-boat sinkings in the Atlantic in the wartime North American – United

A tanker was always a high priority target and the merchant seamen who survived an attack would never forget the experience. (Courtesy U.S. Archives, Washington)

Kingdom shipping lanes. The following figures show year-by-year sinkings:

1939 (from September)	4
1940	11
1941	19
1942	42
1943	144
1944	93
1945 (to May)	52

Although Allied shipping losses were significantly reduced after mid-1943 when U-boat attacks on escorted convoys were scaled down, these figures confirmed Germany's ability to maintain her submarine strength at sea. The number of the enemy sunk in these shipping lanes after April 1943, when the *Aquitania*'s continuous service began, reached 252, against 113 beforehand.

Sailors are superstitious, and it was taboo to speculate what would have happened had the *Aquitania* been struck by a torpedo, by bombs from an aircraft, or had been shelled by a raider or had hit a mine. You simply did not talk about those eventualities. The superstition had it that if you acknowledged a disaster might happen by talking about it, then it would happen – a maritime version of Murphy's Law.

A U-boat torpedo-man makes adjustments to the settings of the deadly acoustic weapon. (Courtesy German Federal Archives, Koblenz)

The track of two torpedos, fired successively along the same path by a U-boat. Photographed from a shadowing German aircraft engaged in homing a wolf pack. An Allied freighter has been struck by the second torpedo, whilst the first is about to strike another. (Courtesy Suddeutscher Verlag Bilderdienst, Munich)

During our last voyage when nearly all the U-boats had been account-ed for and peacetime procedures were in force, some limited discussion on these subjects took place. The most intriguing aspect was the proba-ble enormity of the disaster had the ship been sunk when eastbound carrying 8000 troops plus a crew and permanent staff of over 1000. With the exception of the subsequent dropping of atomic bombs on Japan, the sinking of one of the large Cunarders would probably have been described as the greatest 'one shot' disaster of the war. In the North Atlantic, the most casualties followed the loss of Cunard's 16,000-ton *Lancastria* which was bombed and sunk off St. Nazaire on 16 June 1940, resulting in over 4000 deaths. The survivors formed an active association.

Enemy mines were something of a danger – particularly in coastal waters – and on two occasions the *Aquitania* had narrow misses. The degaussing girdle provided protection against magnetic mines, and the likelihood of striking a drifter in mid-Atlantic should have been slim, although three were sighted from the *Aquitania*. The vulnerability of merchant ships, with their thin hulls, to mines was demonstrated by the sinking in less than an hour of the 46,000-ton White Star liner *Britannic* in the First World War after striking a single mine.

The torpedo was of course the major menace, and the Germans were able to maintain their U-boat fleets at close to full strength to the end. However, evidence suggested that the morale of the young crew members of the U-boats began to wane after the invasion of Normandy, by a seeming reluctance to attack escorted convoys. The largest Cunarders, namely the *Queen Elizabeth*, *Queen Mary*, *Aquitania* and *Mauretania* all came through untouched by U-boats. Nevertheless there were occasions, as indicated by adjacent U-boat radio transmissions, sightings by aircraft, ASDIC detections by escorts, radar contacts at night, and acoustic torpedo explosions following an expended run, when disaster would have been near.

The speed of these zigzagging ships had the effect of making a successful attack by a submarine very much a matter of chance. Should a U-boat have closed within up to five miles of a liner's track, the Germans might have computed an accurate lead and struck home with at least one torpedo out of a spread pattern, and either stopped or slowed the ship sufficiently to score further hits if necessary. The *Queens* had an additional 30 per cent margin of speed over the *Aquitania* while presenting a target of only an extra 12 per cent, but considering they carried up to 15,000 troops, this additional margin of safety could be regarded as necessary to justify these vessels proceeding alone.

A single torpedo was generally sufficient to cripple if not sink a merchant ship with a thin hull and bulkheads of comparatively light construction. The entry of water into one or more compartments usually required an immediate and substantial reduction of speed to avoid further structural damage, even if the engines and boilers were intact, and the chances of a torpedoed merchantman escaping were slim. By comparison, the hull of the *Bismarck* withstood ten strikes by torpedoes before sinking.

It is impossible to speculate on the likely number of survivors had one of the *Queens* gone down. For a start, the numbers exceeding 8000 could almost be discarded, the chances of rescuing any significant proportion of the men assisted only by life jackets from an unescorted ship in the Atlantic being slight. Further, experience has shown that the chance of fully utilising all the lifesaving equipment such as life boats, carley floats, carley drums, life buoys and rafts was equally unlikely.

Sinking ships rarely go down with an even trim, particularly when torpedoed – within minutes they tend to develop a steep list creating great problems for the lowering of the boats. On the side opposite from where the torpedo strikes the lifeboats must scrape their way down the sloping hull, tipping many occupants into the water. The history of disasters at sea, both in wartime and in peacetime, highlight the difficulty of saving the lives of passengers unless assistance is nearby. And no other ocean approaches the North Atlantic in this respect.

Other survival and rescue factors include the height of the waves, the strength of the wind, air and water temperatures, beaching opportunities, the distance from harbours, the arrival of rescue ships, the period of time before the ship sinks and the degree of panic. In Atlantic convoys, with other vessels including specially-equipped rescue ships nearby, the rescue rate proved to be slightly better than 50 per cent. It would be expecting a great deal to hope to approach this percentage with thousands of men and indeed some women struggling for swimming space.

Three Cunard captains who had commanded these ships all opposed increased troop numbers on the grounds that they tended to make the ships unstable, promoting rolling of up to 30 degrees. Concern was expressed that men might sustain fractured limbs by being thrown out of the four-tiered standee bunks. The British, as we have seen, left the decision to the Americans who opted for the increased numbers in the interests of pursuing the business of winning the war as quickly as possible. The men who were not allocated to a specific boat were advised,

> As long as the ship floats, the best place is on board. Have lifejackets properly adjusted. It will support you for a very long time. There are ample ladders, scramble nets and knotted ropes to allow everyone to enter the water without jumping and go for a raft.

Commodore Bisset, Master of the *Queen Mary*, wrote in his book *Commodore*,

> I cannot imagine in any future war such huge vessels will ever again be in service as transports, or that such risks will ever again be taken to embark the equivalent of one complete army division in one ship, to cross an ocean under hazard of enemy attack. I would not admit it or show it, but I was inwardly deeply perturbed at the responsibility thrust upon me. Yet I was to become accustomed to it to some extent. The

difference between transporting 10,000 souls and 16,000 souls is a matter of mathematics rather than quality. In either case, there would be an appalling loss of life if the ship were sunk.

In reply to a comment regarding abandoning ship, Bisset said,

Not as fervently as I hope it ... The Captain must be the last to leave the sinking ship. I can't see myself having much chance at the end of a queue of 15,987 men on the boat deck.

The effect on public opinion by the loss of one of the Cunarders might have resulted in the abandonment of the unescorted trooping programme. Ten thousand or so instantly-bereaved mothers are a lot of mothers, especially American mothers. An official cover-up would have been impossible.

A brief reference has already been made to the failure of the Luftwaffe to attack the Cunarders either at sea or in the Clyde. In the Pacific battles between the U.S. and Japanese fleets, the aircraft was the principal instrument of attack. Why did Goering not make an all out attempt to use his Luftwaffe to sink the Cunarders which were bringing U.S. troops to Britain at the rate of about 45,000 per month? The Reichsmarschall had been able to spare his bombers to devastate areas populated by civilians throughout the British Isles, although this capacity decreased as the war progressed.

An air attack on a Cunarder in the Western Approaches, in the Clyde Estuary or at anchor in the Clyde itself, was always regarded as likely, but never happened. In terms of gaining the greatest benefit at an acceptable cost, surely a concentrated air attack on these ships should have been one of the higher priorities for the Germans. Enemy intelligence should have been able to determine approximate arrival times at the Clyde. New York departures would have been known to representatives of sympathetic neutral countries by simple observation from a Manhattan apartment or office. It is true that the Clyde had substantial anti-aircraft defences and fighter aircraft were based in the area, but surely some German aircraft out of an attacking force would have reached their targets. Does anyone, remembering the Japanese one-way Kamikaze operations which sank or damaged over 400 ships, question Japan's ability to have disposed of these liners had that country been in the position of the Germans? Hardly a major German or Italian warship or liner escaped the attention of the R.A.F.

The Royal Navy and Coastal Command argued continuously with the Allied Air Command over the allocation of long-range Liberators. The R.A.F., led by their Chief of Staff Sir Charles Portal, and supported by

Air Marshal 'Bomber' Harris, strenuously maintained that the bombing of Germany should receive priority over the war against the U-boats. Churchill inclined his support towards the bombing campaign, and the reduction of the Atlantic Gap was delayed by these attitudes.

Towards the end of the war, Goering concentrated on the production of jet fighters which were expected to slaughter the Allied air forces. He succeeded in producing about 1000 of these aircraft, but on account of a chronic shortage of fuel, and runways of insufficient length, bombing of factories and airfields, and particularly the lack of suitable metals, he was unable to bring them into use in worthwhile numbers. Had the invasion of Europe been delayed, or had progress been slower, the Allies may have had to deal with both these jets and the Type XXI and XXIII U-boats.

These comments would be incomplete without a further reference to the air crews of R.A.F. Coastal Command, and the Allied Air Forces who provided these troop transports with protection. Under conditions of appalling weather, discomfort and boredom, these men would fly out over the Atlantic for up to 1000 miles or further, to put down and if possible attack U-boats which may be lurking ahead for the liners. After a sweeping period they would head back to their bases with the risk of interception by enemy aircraft, and of perhaps landing in snowstorms under conditions of considerable danger. The rapid transportation of troops across the Atlantic would not have been possible without the protection the flyers of this arm of the services provided. There were no 'reluctant dragons' here.

I have only the highest praise for the coding and signalling staff in the *Aquitania*. These British lads had volunteered for the D.E.M.S. Reserve, were particularly well trained, and usually had put in sea time before this appointment. Their dependability and efficiency was a credit to the service. I also wish to pay tribute to our Chief Petty Officer Telegraphist Robertson, a permanent member of the Royal Navy. His knowledge of the working of the R.N. helped me avoid many mistakes both at sea and ashore. Coders included Beck, Jefferies, Major, Jewitt and Posner. My apologies to two or three others whose names I cannot recall. Their faces are well remembered.

Above all, my praises go to the men of the British Merchant Service. The traditional fighting services, the Navy, the Army and the Air Force have never lacked spokesmen to champion their performances, causes and welfare, which can not always be said for the service to which I did not actually belong, but with which I was proud to serve.

Epilogue

Alex Milne had settled in Canberra, and I saw him a number of times over the years. His talents took him to the position as Chairman of the Australian Public Service Board. In the 1960s he developed a heart condition which the authorities accepted as being due to war service. He died a few years later, and I was saddened by the passing of a fine wartime companion. Maurice Hobday visited our home in Melbourne in the early 1950s from where he was then living in New Zealand, and he subsequently retired to Cornwall overlooking the wild Atlantic.

In 1958 I had a chance encounter with our former Junior First Officer, Aussie Austin, in Venice. This occurred during a five-month round the world holiday by sea with my wife and three year-old daughter, Claire. Cunard's cruise ship *Caronia* called, and on making enquiries I learned that the Chief Officer was Aussie. I located him in St. Mark's Square and we arranged to meet later that month where he lived outside Southampton bordering the New Forest. He invited our former Senior Second Officer Ken Milburn to be present, and with our families, it became a memorable day.

Ken Milburn moved to Hong Kong after leaving Cunard to take up the appointment of Harbour Master before rising to the eminent position of Director of Marine, Hong Kong, and which led him to be awarded an O.B.E. He became elected Commodore of the Hong Kong Yacht Club. Ken visited us in Melbourne on two occasions with his wife whom he had met in her capacity as a hostess at Delmonico's Hotel Officers' Club in New York.

In 1991 Ed Seim, U.S. Army Captain in charge of our American gun crew, together with his wife Maureen, a former W.R.E.N. officer, visited us. After the war he rose to become a vice-president of the Westinghouse Corporation and in charge of their European operations from Brussels. As detailed elsewhere, his parents had been unstinting in their hospitality during our visits to New York and Boston. The old diaries were brought out and we relived some of the memorable occasions.

The war, perhaps surprisingly, had the opposite effect of deterring me from sea-travel. In 1965 we again set out cruising to Japan calling at various Pacific and Asian ports, and enjoying the privilege of the table of Captain Lawrence. Cunard ships had rarely visited Australia, but in 1983

An *Aquitania* reunion in 1958 in the New Forest at Cadnum, Hampshire. From left - Author, Aussie Austin (ex Senior First), Mrs Austin, Ken Milburn OBE (ex Senior Second).

Author with Captain Edwin Seim (left), senior gunnery officer in *Aquitania* April 1942 - June 1944. This meeting occurred in Melbourne in February 1991.

an opportunity arose to cruise down memory lane. My wife and I flew to New Zealand, and after two weeks touring through the magnificent scenery of the South Island, we boarded the *Q.E.2* in Auckland, and following a stopover in Wellington, we sailed across the South Pacific to Sydney. This was but two segments out of the flagship's annual thirteen-week cruise originating in New York, and taking in twenty-nine ports of call. About 1400 of the 1600 passengers were Americans, and the nightly display of jewellery suggested the majority were far into the millionaire category.

The *Q.E.2* had been refitted a short time beforehand, following her voyage to South Georgia during the Falkland Islands War of the previous May, when she had carried 3500 Scots and Welsh Guards and a Gurkha regiment. All my former Cunard shipmates had now retired, the last being the previous Captain, Mortimer Hahir. During the many 'happy hours' which extended into some very happy days, I met a number of passengers who had travelled to the European war in the Cunarders, including the *Aquitania*.

Captain Lawrence of Peninsula and Orient Line's *Himalaya* welcoming author and wife to cocktail party, May 1965.

Everything was there. Between the gourmet meals, overweight passengers queued at poolside booths for complimentary hamburgers, generously covered with salt. No matter – prominent specialist, Dr Eleanor Z. Wallace had been thoughtfully shipped along to lecture and to answer questions on hypertension. Other lecturers included Sir Edmund Hillary who spoke on 'Everest Revisited', while the subject of Brigadier Tony Wilson O.B.E., M.C. was 'The Falklands Crisis – the *Q.E.2* and the Voyage South'. A U.S. professional carefully analysed one's golf swing and he demonstrated he was right with a videotape. Albatrosses following the wake survived the clay-pigeon shooting tournaments, as far as we could tell. The shops bulged with goods supplied by Dunhill, Dior, Gucci and Burberry. The accents of the junior pursers could not be faulted.

At 10 p.m. every evening, famed British orchestra leader of yesteryear, Joe Loss, sprung the dancers to their feet when he struck up 'Tie a Yellow Riband round the Old Oak Tree' – the theme song attached to the then-recent return of the Iran hostages. The Americans had all responded, demonstrating their undoubted patriotism. The rich widows did not lack dancing partners, and rumour had it that batches of refreshed, presentable young men, were shuttled out by the company to the major ports.

At midnight, for those in need, the Columbia Room opened its doors to an exotic cold buffet, giving Joe Loss and his band, and also the

Author's wife relaxing in the 'Queen's Room' of the *Queen Elizabeth 2*, (claimed to be 'the most beautiful room afloat') following the ship's refurbishment after the Falklands War.

croupiers, a respite. One evening, at a cocktail party in the Queen's Room given by Captain Arnott, we were talking with an American couple. It eventuated the husband had sailed from New York on 10 May 1943 as a private, had received a commission in England, and was again promoted in the field at St. Lô when advancing with General Bradley's forces. After the war he returned to his home town of Durango in Colorado, gained a General Motors dealership, and this was now his second world cruise on the *Q.E.2*. He was Joe Staaff, the chap we first met in the prologue!

The *Queen Elizabeth* and the *Aquitania* have ended their days, while the *Queen Mary* survives in a fashion. She sailed from Southampton for the last time on 16 September 1967, having outlived her economic usefulness on the Atlantic run. She was granted the dubious distinction of becoming the 'World's Largest Floating Exhibit' and where else but at Long Beach, California, the nearest port to Hollywood. The ship has also been described as 'A Shore Front Amusement Centre', and now is imprisoned in concrete. She has been purchased by the City of Long Beach, and ranks as a tourist attraction somewhat astern of Disneyland, Knott's Berry Farm and the 'Tour of Universal Studios'. The dining saloon was converted into

The *Queen Elizabeth I* being consumed by flames in Hong Kong, 1972. (Courtesy United Press International, through Paul Popper)

a convention hall where the Long Beach Rotarians triumphantly displayed their plaque. In 1980 I saw her from a hotel window at Anaheim. By 1990, $57 could buy a night aboard. Captain Treasure Jones, who had sailed the *Mary* to California, subsequently wrote,

> ... down came our flag and up went the U.S. flag, and the Long Beach flag went up in place of the Cunard House Flag ... The mayor, wearing a Cunard sailor's cap on his head, came down the gangplank with me ... and I shed a couple of tears.

The *Queen Elizabeth* fared even worse, although this may be arguable. Purchased in 1968 by Philadelphia entrepreneurs, the intention was to operate her as a floating hotel off Port Everglades. The money necessary for restoration and conversion was not subscribed, and in 1970 she was resold to one C.Y. Tung, a Hong Kong millionaire with plans to convert her into a floating academy, named Seawise University. The ship eventually reached Hong Kong after a disastrous voyage around the Cape of Good Hope, the numerous breakdowns being the result of neglect of maintenance – a slow boat to China indeed! On 9 January 1972, following the expenditure of over $5 million, three separate fires broke out, and

Pleasure boats not warships, Jaguars rather than Jeeps, were evident in the Clyde Estuary thirty years later.

The 'Great Park' viewed from Hopetoun House, the residence of Marquis of Lithlithgow, Viceroy of India. A tourist attraction thirty years after my wartime visits.

she burned to the waterline. That was how the *Queen Elizabeth I* ended her career.

Merchant seamen develop a love for ships and they have their favourites, often for reasons they cannot explain. I have listened to discussions regarding the qualities and idiosyncrasies of the various Cunarders, and of the ships of other lines, and heard the views of some of the captains with whom I sailed. The favourite would have been either the *Aquitania* or the 'Old' *Mauretania* which saw service between 1908

Bergen Harbour became Germany's principal U-boat base following the Allied recapture
of the French Atlantic ports. The U-boat pens have now all disappeared.

and 1935, and not even the *Queen Mary* nor the *Queen Elizabeth* could
take the place of these older ships in the hearts of many.

Sir James Charles, then the company's commodore, made his 728th
and last voyage in the *Aquitania* before his scheduled retirement in July
1928. When homeward bound from New York, he collapsed as the ship
entered Southampton harbour and died shortly after, said to be of a 'broken heart'. Sir James Bisset movingly tells of attending the funeral at
Netley Cemetery on the shores of Southampton Water, and to which
hundreds of crew members had walked many miles to pay their last
respects to the Captain of Cunard's majestic flagship.

> When the Bishop of Winchester at the open grave had read Tennyson's
> 'Crossing the Bar', many a hardened seaman was close to tears.

The turn of the *Aquitania* had come in 1950 after four years on the
Halifax run, apart from a return to Australia in October 1945 transporting over 2000 R.A.A.F. personnel. She was sailed to the shipbreaker's
yards at Faslane in Scotland after a record 884 Atlantic crossings, having
steamed in excess of 3 million miles. A kilted Scot then piped her out of
service. To many there was an element of sadness in cutting apart a ship
with her record in two World Wars and selling the pieces to the highest
bidder in the scrap business. Some people prefer to be buried at sea, and
I am sure that if the 'Old Lady' had been offered the choice, she would
have elected to have steamed out under her own power from the country she had served so well into the deep waters of the North Atlantic, and
to have gone down to her rest with all the dignity she possessed.
However, her unique service in both World Wars assures her place in history as the most famous troopship of them all.

Bibliography

Battle of the Atlantic (Official Account) (H.M. Stationery Office, London
    1946)
Bekker, Cajus, *Hitler's Naval War* (Hamburg 1971)
Birt, Douglas Phillips, *When Luxury Went to Sea (Aquitania)*
    (Devon 1971)
Bisset, Sir James, *Commodore* (Sydney 1961)
Blair, Clay, *Hitler's U-Boat War* (London 1999)
Calder, Angus, *The People's War* (London 1969)
Charles, Roland, *Troopships of World War II* (Washington 1947)
Chisholm, Anne, *Nancy Cunard* (London 1979)
Churchill, W S, *The Second World War* (London 1950)
Coleman, Terry, *The Liners* (London 1976)
Costello, John, & Hughes, Terry, *The Battle of the Atlantic* (London
    1977)
Cremer, Peter, *U-333. The Story of U-Boat Ace Peter Cremer* (London
    1984)
Davie, Michael (ed), *The Diaries of Evelyn Waugh* (Boston 1976)
——————————, *The Titanic – Full Story of a Tragedy* (London
    1986)
Dean, Sir Maurice, *The Royal Air Force in Two World Wars* (London
    1979)
Diggle, E G, *The Romance of a Modern Liner* (London 1963)
Dobson, C, *The Cruellest Night - The Sinking of the Wilhelm Gustloff*
    (London 1979)
Doenitz, Admiral Karl, *Memoirs* (London 1959)
Falconer, John, *Sail and Steam* (London 1993)
Frotheroe, Ernest, *Sailing Boats & Liners* (London 1930)
Gill, G H, *The Royal Australian Navy* (Canberra 1957)
Hart, Liddell, *History of the Second World War* (London 1970)
Hoehling, A.A. & M, *The Last Voyage of the Lusitania* (London 1957)
Johnston, Howard, *The Cunard Story* (London 1987)
Jones, Geoffrey, *The Month of the Lost U-Boats* (London 1977)
Josephson, Mathew, *The Robber Barons* (London 1962)
Konings, Chris, *Queen Elizabeth at War* (Northampton 1985)
Lewin, Ronald, *Ultra Goes to War* (London 1970)

Longmate, Norman, *How We Lived Then* (London 1977)

Lord, Walter, *A Night to Remember* (London 1956)

Macintyre, Donald, *U-Boat Killer* (London 1956)

Maddocks, Melvin, *The Great Liners* (Amsterdam 1978)

Maxtone-Graham, John, *The North Atlantic Run* (London 1973)

Miller, Byron S, *Sail, Steam and Splendor* (New York 1977)

Miller, William H., and Hutchings, David F, *Trans-Atlantic Liners at War* (Newton Abbot 1985)

Morris, Jan, *Manhattan '45* (London 1987)

Morton, H V, *Atlantic Meeting* (London 1943)

Pitt, Barrie, *The Battle of the Atlantic World War II* (New York 1977)

Pope, Dudley, *73 North* (London 1958)

Potter, Neal, and Frost, *The Mary – The Inevitable Ship* (London 1961)

Preston, Anthony, *Submarines* (London 1979)

Robertson, Terence, *Walker, R.N.* (London 1958)

Roskill, Stephen, *Churchill and the Admirals* (London 1977)

Schaeffer, Heinz, *U-Boat 977* (London 1952)

Shaum, John H. Jnr. and Flayhart, William H. III, *Majesty at Sea* (New York 1981)

Shirer, William L, *The Rise and Fall of the Third Reich* (London 1959)

Simpson, Colin, *Lusitania* (London 1972)

Sproule, Anna, *Port Out Starboard Home* (Blanford Press 1978)

Stevenson, William, *A Man Called Intrepid* (London 1976)

Wall, Robert, *Ocean Liners* (London 1977)

Wardlow, Chester, *The U.S. Army in World War II: Movements, Training and Supply* (Washington D.C., 1956)

Werner, Herbert, *Iron Coffins* (New York 1969)

Winton, John, *Air Power at Sea* (London 1976)

——————————, *Freedom's Battle* (London 1967)

Index

Page numbers in *italic* refer to illustrations.

Abbreviations

CPO = Chief Petty Officer; HM = His/Her Majesty; HMS = His Majesty's Ship; HMAS = His Majesty's Australian Ship; HMCS = His Majesty's Canadian Ship; HRH = His Royal Highness; NSW = New South Wales; NZ = New Zealand; RAF = Royal Air Force; RAAF = Royal Australian Air Force; RANVR = Royal Australian Naval Volunteer Reserve; RN = Royal Navy; RNR = Royal Naval Reserve; RNVR = Royal Naval Volunteer Reserve; US = United States; USS = United States Ship